Acoustic Territories

Acoustic Territories

SOUND CULTURE AND EVERYDAY LIFE

**by
Brandon LaBelle**

continuum

NEW YORK • LONDON

2011

Continuum International Publishing Group
The Tower Building, 11 York Road, London SE1 7NX
80 Maiden Lane, Suite 704, New York, NY 10038

www.continuumbooks.com

ISBN 978-1-441-16136-9 (paperback)
ISBN 978-1-441-15724-9 (hardcover)

Library of Congress Cataloging-in-Publication Data
LaBelle, Brandon.
Acoustic territories : sound culture and everyday life /
by Brandon LaBelle.
    p. cm.
Includes bibliographical references and index.
ISBN-13: 978-1-4411-5724-9 (hardcover : alk. paper)
ISBN-10: 1-4411-5724-7 (hardcover : alk. paper)
ISBN-13: 978-1-4411-6136-9 (pbk. : alk. paper)
ISBN-10: 1-4411-6136-8 (pbk. : alk. paper)
1. Sound in mass media. 2. Sound--Social aspects. 3. Performance
art. I. Title.

P96.S66L33 2010
306.4--dc22

                                                    2009042864

Typeset by Newgen Imaging Systems Pvt Ltd, Chennai, India
Printed and bound in the United States of America

Contents

List of Illustrations

Acknowledgments

I would like to extend my heartfelt thanks to the colleagues and friends with whom I have had the pleasure to work and engage in many lively discussions over the recent years, and who have significantly influenced my involvement in the cultures of sound and sound thinking. Especially to the sound and radio studies group at the University of Copenhagen: Erik Granly Jensen, Tania Ørum, Marianne Ping Huang, Torben Sangild, Bente Larsen, and Jacob Kreutzfeldt, with whom I shared many thoughtful conversations and working days during my postdoctoral research fellowship. Through this fellowship, and within the generous framework of the Department of Arts and Cultural Studies, I was able to elaborate upon my doctoral research and to further expand the scope of my work. I am also indebted to Mikkel Bogh for his support, and to Professor Doris Kolesch for her invitation to participate in the Department of Theater Studies at the Free University of Berlin. Sharing in the teaching of the Acoustic Territories seminar with her lent greatly to the final organization and understanding of my project. In this regard, I am also thoroughly appreciative of the assistance given by Maxi Loehmann, whose ceaseless energy was a constant source of support and enjoyment.

In addition, I am grateful to Milos Vojtechovsky for his generous and personal help in exploring the history of the Prague Underground—visiting him in the winter of 2009 gave important insight for better understanding the Plastic People of the Universe and their music; also to Karel Cisar for offering his insightful thoughts on the underground cultures of Prague.

Of course, such a project as this evolves organically over the course of years, involving not only primary research but also many small moments of generous listening and occasional mirroring on the part of friends. With this in mind, I extend much affection to Ken Ehrlich, Octavio Camargo, Robin Wilson, Jennifer Gabrys, Barbara Penner, Maia Urstad, Tao G. Vrhovec Sambolec, Ines Schaber, Lawrence English, and James Webb—I'm happy to have shared this writing with you even if at times you did not realize I was taking notes within my quiet thoughts. I would also like to thank David Barker of Continuum Books for his editorial patience and thoughtfulness, and for making the grueling task of publishing a pleasurable undertaking.

Much of my work as a writer and researcher is inextricably tied to my practice as an artist. Through artistic projects I am given the chance to put to work various imaginings, and to weave together conceptual ideas with their performative materialization. Such a crossover is both a vital platform for finding points of involvement and interaction within culture, as well as a personal space for furthering my sense of place within these spheres of discourse and life. For this reason I am deeply grateful to those who have supported my artistic work over the recent years, in particular Georg Weckwerth, Sabine Breitsameter, Carsten Seiffarth, Enrico Fornello, Tuca Nissel and Debora Santiago, Margit Leisner, Alex Hamburger, Dorita Hannah, Christina Barton, Laura Preston, Marianne Bech, Tine Seligmann, Enrico Passetti, Rune Søchting, Carmen Cebreros Urzaiz, Chloé Fricout, Resonance FM, Kunstradio, Robert Worby, Richard Whitelaw, Micki, Marcus Gammel, General Public Berlin, Yvan Etienne, Bastien Gallet, Jørgen Larsson and Lydgalleriet Bergen, Frans Gillberg, and Mathias Holmberg.

Finally, I would like to thank Paula Crabtree and Jeremy Welsh, along with the entire community of the National Academy of the Arts in Bergen, whose support and enthusiasm for my involvement in activities there continually give a boost to my feelings for future work and collaboration.

I must also express my deep gratitude to Allen S. Weiss and Steven Connor from whom I continually gain much inspiration and support. Also, to Maria for being such a special person, and to Jan and Chuck for sharing in the ups and downs. And especially to Annette for our

mornings with oatmeal and Deutschlandfunk, walks in the neighborhood, shared travels and journeys, inside and out, and who taught me
the importance of being personal.

* * *

A number of chapters presented here, though extensively reworked,
have appeared previously in published form. Chapter 3 was included
in the anthology *Performance Design*, edited by Dorita Hannah and
Olav Harsløf, and published by Museum Tusculanum Press, Denmark.
I extend my gratitude to the editors, especially to Dorita Hannah for
her critical engagement and friendly support. Chapter 4 was included
in an issue of *The Senses and Society*, edited by Shelley Trower. I am
grateful to the journal and Berg Publishers, and especially to the
editor. Finally, Chapter 6 is included in the anthology *Re-inventing
Radio* published by Revolver. I am extremely grateful to the editors
Elisabeth Zimmermann and Heidi Grundmann for their support, and
ongoing collaboration.

INTRODUCTION: YOUR SOUND IS MY SOUND IS YOUR SOUND

Sound provides the most forceful stimulus that human beings experience, and the most evanescent.[1]

—Bruce R. Smith

The boy looks to his father and asks, "Where do sounds come from?"

My ears prick up, as I glance to the father, anticipating his response. He smiles at the boy, chuckles to himself, and then says, "From a very special place."

I smile back at the father and think quietly to myself, "That seems about right . . ."

Of course, I also want to chime in with a few extra points, as did the father from what I could tell, as he seemed to spend the next few minutes pondering the boy's question.

In that pause of silence, the boy suddenly furthers his line of questioning, jumping up with the words, "But where do they go?"

The father smiles even wider now, and brushes the boy's hair with his palm.

"They go to an even more special place than from where they came."

The boy looks a little confused, and as if to clarify, the father silently points to his chest, then raises his finger into the air, and brings it back down again onto the boy's chest, smiling.

A small group on the tram have now taken notice, and in a gesture of sympathetic agreement a number of them smile back at

the father, all of us nodding and absorbing the subtlety of this small exchange.

I have kept this memory with me for years now, and retell it here as part of introducing this work, for it brings forward the extreme simplicity at the heart of all these pages. *Where do sounds come from and where do they go . . .* This forms the core resonating query carried throughout *Acoustic Territories*. Regardless of the specificity of its varying narratives and histories, or the theoretical figures that come to circle around so many perspectives onto culture, the founding thread or impetus can be teased out by following this exchange between father and son.

In exploring this core reflection, I've been led to recognize the complexity surrounding sound and listening in deeper ways. The seemingly innocent trajectory of sound as it moves from its source and toward a listener, without forgetting all the surfaces, bodies, and other sounds it brushes against, is a story imparting a great deal of information fully charged with geographic, social, psychological, and emotional energy. My feeling is that an entire history and culture can be found within a single sound; from its source to its destination sound is generative of a diverse range of experiences, as well as remaining specifically tied to a given context, as a deeper expressive and prolonged figure of culture. In this regard, I take Bruce R. Smith's words to heart—that sound gives to us a deeply powerful stimulus that is equally evanescent, passing—which opens up to a highly suggestive horizon for my own auditory journey, and its continuation into writing: that in the combination of intensity and ephemerality, the significance of auditory experience may be located.

What I like about this story of father and son is the final movement of the hand: from one body the hand then rises to point openly into the air, finally falling back down again onto the other's body. This arc, this soft trajectory, is a beautiful rendering of sound as an itinerant movement that immediately brings two together; it suggests the intensity and grace with which sound may create a relational space, a meeting point, diffuse and yet pointed; a private space that requires something between, an outside; a geography of intimacy that also incorporates the dynamics of interference, noise, transgression. From one body to the other, a thread is made that stitches the two together in a temporal instant, while remaining loose, slack, to unfurl back into the general humdrum of place. Sound might be heard to say, *This is our moment.*

The story of the father and son is also a story of creating something—knowledge formation, a sharing, language. In the movement of sound, the making of an exchange is enacted; a place is generated by the temporality of the auditory. *This is our moment* is also immediately, *This is our place.* Auditory knowledge is a radical epistemological thrust that unfolds as a spatio-temporal event: sound opens up a field of interaction, to become a channel, a fluid, a flux of voice and urgency, of play and drama, of mutuality and sharing, to ultimately carve out a micro-geography of the moment, while always already disappearing, as a distributive and sensitive propagation.

From my perspective, this makes sound a significant model for also thinking and experiencing the contemporary condition, for as a relational spatiality global culture demands and necessitates continual reworking. It locates us within an extremely animate and energetic environment that, like auditory phenomena, often exceeds the conventional parameters and possibilities of representation. The momentary connection found in the arc of sound is equally a spatial formation whose temporary appearance requires occupation, as a continual project. *This is our place* is also potentially, *This is our community.* The dynamic of auditory knowledge provides then a key opportunity for moving through the contemporary by creating shared spaces that belong to no single public and yet which impart a feeling for intimacy: sound is always already mine and not mine—I cannot hold it for long, nor can I arrest all its itinerant energy. Sound is *promiscuous.* It exists as a network that teaches us how to belong, to find place, as well as how not to belong, to drift. To be out of place, and still to search for new connection, for proximity. Auditory knowledge is non-dualistic. It is based on empathy *and* divergence, allowing for careful understanding and deep involvement in the present while connecting to the dynamics of mediation, displacement, and virtuality.

I trace out all these sonorous movements because what is at stake for me is to explicate a position that is also already unfixed—a position that is in tune with the material and paradigmatic energy found within sound, that weave of intensity and ephemerality, of animate flexibility and charged spatiality, and importantly, within listening as a central and organizational perspective. It is my sense that an auditory paradigm is tacitly embedded within the contemporary condition and offers a compelling structure for elaborating what is already in play. The radical transformation of global experiences, in shifting the position of the subject, the operations of economic markets, and the borders of the nation-state, initiates new trajectories and struggles that cut across social reality. Questions of belonging and migration, of environmental and political conflict, swarm through everyday life and touch the smallest corners of so many places. How to participate within this mass of information, to figure oneself in relation to all the presences that come flooding through each day to carry numerous identities? How to be located within the flux of multiple geographies both proximate and remote? It strikes me that such a contemporary condition also brings forward a shift in critical focus, requiring more situational and networked understanding. In this regard, I follow the example of Les Back outlined in *The Art of Listening* in which he calls for a shift in sociological approach that might begin to engage the ways in which private lives are now more fully wed to public society. For Back, "sociological listening is needed today in order to admit the excluded, the looked past, to allow the 'out of place' a sense of belonging."[2]

Acoustic Territories seeks to further engage such concerns by examining the exchanges between environments and the people within them as registered through aural experience. Scanning the urban topography, the work offers a rendering of auditory life, and the weave of the private and the public found therein. In doing so, I aim to provide careful consideration of the performative relations inherent to urban spatiality, and also to expose sound studies as a practice poised to creatively engage these relations. Combining research on urban theory, popular culture, and auditory issues, the work opens up an expanded perspective on how sound conditions and contours subjectivity by lending a dynamic materiality for social negotiation. It gives challenge to debates surrounding noise pollution by appreciating the breadth of sound as based on conditions of disjunction, temporality, and difference. From such a base, my intention has been to chart out an "acoustic politics of space," unfolding auditory experience as locational and poignantly embedded within processes of social exchange.

Sound Studies

Sound studies continues to emerge as an expanding discipline involving many concentrations and discourses. From musicology to anthropology, histories of media and cultural practices, to performance and voice studies, the range is dynamic and also highly suggestive. I take this as no surprise and want to underscore such diversity as integral to the significance of auditory experience. In the movement from *where does sound come from* to *where does it go* figure multiple points for distraction, divergence, and interference, as well as connection and conjunction. The *associative* dynamic of sound lends greatly to triggering *associate* forms of discourse and knowledge. This is both participant within the physics and phenomenological behavior of sound, as well as forming the conceptual and psychodynamic frame for recognizing how hearing is already an associative act. For what we hear is not mostly what we see, nor can it strictly be pinned down to a given source, or brought into language. Often sound is what lends to directing our visual focus—we hear something and this tells us where to look; it eases around us in a flow of energy to which we unconsciously respond. Sounds are associated with their original source, while also becoming their own thing, separate and constantly blending with other sounds, thereby continually moving in and out of focus and clarity.

Steven Connor gives a highly lucid account of such associate behavior in his text "The Modern Auditory I." As Connor explores, the diffuse and disintegrative movements of sound open out to a multiplicity of sensorial configurations, technological networks, and shifts in spatiality. This auditory dynamic locates us within "the switchboard experience" of modern life, found initially in early telephone systems, radiophonic broadcasting, and cinematic matter, which would necessitate a new shuffling between sight and sound.[3] Accordingly, listening became more fully an act of imaginary projection and transference, often occupying a temporal zone where a visual source was suspended and reconfigured according to auditory association.

Following such divergent and imaginary productions, the construction of the self, as a modern subject, was redrawn through the particular "rapture and capture" of sound. As Connor proposes, "The self defined in terms of hearing rather than sight is a self imaged not as a point, but as a membrane; not as a picture, but as a channel through which voices, noises and musics travel."[4] Such diffuse and associate experiences have only intensified throughout this past century, allocating the switchboard experience to the entire field of everyday life, among the weave of the actual and the virtual.

Sound studies takes such ontological conditions of the sonic self and elaborates upon the particular cultures, histories, and media that expose and mobilize its making. *Acoustic Territories* aims to lend to this field of research, following the sonic self as a special figure embedded within a sphere of cultural and social habits, what Richard Cullen Rath calls "soundways," or the ways people come to express their relation to sound and its circulation.[5] In particular, *Acoustic Territories* traces the soundways of the contemporary metropolis, rendering a topography of auditory life through a spatial structure— beginning with underground territories, through to the home as a site, and then further, to streets and neighborhoods, and finally to the movements of cars and the infrastructure of transmission towers that put messages into the air. This structure follows sound as it appears in specific auditory systems, within particular locations, as it is expressed within various cultural projects, and ultimately queries how sound comes to circulate through everyday life, to act as medium for personal and social transformation. This leads to an appreciation for how sound is manifest in forms of local practices that also echo across greater historical and geographical terrain.

It is my emphasis that sound reroutes the making of identity by creating a greater and more suggestive weave between self and surrounding. As I tried to show in my earlier work, *Background Noise: Perspectives on Sound Art*, the rich undulations of auditory materiality do much to unfix delineations between the private and the public. Sound operates by forming links, groupings, and conjunctions that accentuate individual identity as a relational project. The flows of surrounding sonority can be heard to weave an individual into a larger social fabric, filling relations with local sound, sonic culture, auditory memories, and the noises that move between, contributing to the making of shared spaces. This associative and connective process of sound comes to reconfigure the spatial distinctions of inside and outside, to foster confrontations between one and another, and to infuse language with degrees of immediacy. In this regard, sound studies and auditory knowledge contribute greatly to understandings of the "geographic" and the modern legacy of spatial production with a view toward engaging the influential energies and ideological processes that lie in and around what we see and touch.

Acoustic Space

The specifics of an auditory ontology, as Connor further details, can be appreciated according to the ways in which sound performs to "disintegrate and reconfigure space."[6] The temporal and evanescent nature of sound imparts great flexibility, and uncertainty, to the stability of space. Sound disregards the particular visual and material delineations of spatial arrangements, displacing and replacing the lines between inside and out, above from below.

As Edmund Carpenter and Marshall McLuhan propose, acoustic space creates itself in time, for "auditory space has no point of favored focus. It's a sphere without fixed boundaries, space made by the thing itself, not space containing a thing. It is not a pictorial space, boxed in, but dynamic, always in flux, creating its own dimensions moment by moment."[7] Thus a sound is generally in more than one place, leading to what Jean-François Augoyard has named "the ubiquity effect," which "expresses the difficulty or impossibility of locating a sound source."[8] Sound, in its distributive and dislocating permeability appears as if from everywhere; it flows as an environmental flux, leaving objects and bodies behind to collect others in its movement. Curiously, he further links this effect to the urban milieu: "because of their particular conditions of propagation favoring the delocalization of sound sources, urban milieus and architectural spaces are the most obvious locations for the emergence of a ubiquity effect."[9] The city, as a particular sonic geography, highlights sound's inherent dynamic to "disintegrate and reconfigure," bringing forward its spatial and temporal particularities.

Policies in urban noise abatement interestingly reveal the degree to which acoustic space, and its ubiquitous impingement, is also difficult to control. Though allowing for flexible participation, for a temporal contour, acoustic space is often a disruptive spatiality. It sparks annoyance and outrage, while also affording important opportunities for dynamic sharing—*to know the other*.

The demands to introduce increasingly defined acoustic guidelines for future building and planning initiated across the European Union since 1998[10] (which includes major noise mapping of all industrialized and metropolitan areas) is a growing indication of governmental consciousness on the issues of noise pollution, as well as a more general concern for acoustic space.[11] As an example, London's Ambient Noise Strategy (ANS), initially developed by Mayor Ken Livingstone, may provide a glimpse onto the issues surrounding acoustic space and its status in relation to the modern metropolis. Developed since 1999, the ANS is part of a larger governmental proposal to respond to the current noise problem in cities like London, and is structured around three key areas: securing noise-reducing surfaces related to road construction and traffic, securing a night aircraft ban across

London, and reducing noise through improved planning and design strategies related to new housing. Notably, transport and traffic stand as essential noises to be dealt with and can generally be seen as key elements to consider in most other developed cities.[12] The unbounded nature of sound though leads to difficulties in designing spaces and related infrastructures, such as roadways, forcing the ANS to consider a more overall approach: "However, tackling one noise on its own may not always solve the problem. It can make another, also annoying, noise more audible. So, better ways of co-ordinating action on noise will be needed. This includes new partnerships at the strategic level, and more resources for action in local areas."[13]

Acoustic Territories

By interlacing the pragmatic concerns of ambient noise strategies, and the challenges of noise in general, with Carpenter and McLuhan's more positive and poetical acoustic space, we arrive at a crucial auditory tension. For on one hand there is no denial as to the intensities with which noise interferes with personal health and environmental well being, while on the other hand noise may be heard as registering a particular vitality within the cultural and social sphere: noise brings with it the expressiveness of freedom, particularly when located on the street, in plain view, and within public space; it may feature as a communicational link by supporting the passing of often difficult or challenging messages; and in its unboundedness it both fulfills and problematizes the sociality of architectural spaces by granting it dynamic movement and temporal energy. Noise can partially be heard to give form to the radically formless, creating space for the intensities of diversity, strangeness, and the unfamiliar. "Noise, then, can be heard not merely as a symptom of symbolic vulnerability or theoretical disorder, but as the evidence and the occasional catalyst of dynamic cultural change operative across the urban topos."[14]

Acoustic space thus brings forward a process of acoustic *territorialization*, in which the disintegration and reconfiguration of space

Connor maps becomes a political process. Accordingly, I've sought to impart meaning to the ambiguity inherent to acoustic space, as a productive form of tension. The divergent, associative networking of sound comes to provide not only points of contact and appropriation, but also meaningful challenge; it allows for participation—importantly, as Back suggests, for the excluded—that is also already unsteady or demanding. In this sense, I've been more interested to push the question of noise away from an analysis of sound pressure levels and toward a general inquiry into the meanings noise may have within specific contexts, for particular communities. Thus my work begins with sound and at times arrives well past its physical trajectory, for in traveling away from itself, sound is picked up elsewhere, overheard, carried forward, or brought back, through memories and recordings, to enliven the making of social space. Acoustic territories are then specific while being multiple, cut with flows and rhythms, vibrations and echoes, all of which form a sonic discourse that is equally fever-ish, energetic, and participatory. Sound is shared property onto which many claims are made, over time, and which demand associative and relational understanding.

To develop an analysis of acoustic territories, I have chosen to focus on specific locations and sites within the everyday. From the underground to the sky, these sites act to knot together multiple forces and trajectories found within daily conditions. In this way, the everyday is an open geography shaped and contoured by specific forces and relations. To engage these territories through the mode of listening, and according to auditory behavior, I'm interested to define such geography as generative, full of dynamic resonance, as an orchestration of sharing and its arrest; that is, to recognize the already existing relational movements of the contemporary situation which mark the globe. I can say that sound has brought me closer to these relational movements by insisting on more than a representational semiotic, giving way to a sense or need for actual meeting. *Sound explicitly brings bodies together*. It forces us to come out, in lyrical, antagonistic, and beautiful ways, creating connective moments and deepening the sense for both the present and the distant, the real and the mediated. If, as the contemporary situation seems to pronounce, we continue to meet the other, in the flows and intensities of so much connectivity, then sound and audition readily provide a paradigmatic means to understand and engage such dynamic.

To map out the features of this auditory paradigm, I have sought to explore in greater detail the particular behavior or figures of sound. It is my view that sonic materiality operates as "micro-epistemologies," with the echo, the vibration, the rhythmic, for instance, opening up to specific ways of knowing the world. Accordingly, I have traced each chapter by following a particular sonic figure. For instance, in exploring the underground I tune in to the specific ways in which subterranean spaces are conditioned and bring forward the echoic: the space of the underground generates experiences of the echo to locate the listening subject within its disorienting and transformative verve. Exploring the underground in this way, the echo then suggests a discourse for engaging the cultural significance found in being below ground.

In this sense, the presentation of specific acoustic territories should not be exclusively read as places or sites but more as *itineraries*, as points of departure as well as arrival. As territories, I define them as movements between and among differing forces, full of multiplicity. Exposing them to listening I also map them onto an auditory paradigm, exploring them through a particular discourse, while allowing them to deepen my own listening, to influence and infect what I have so far imagined sound providing—*intimacy*, in provocative and complex scale. Sound creates a relational geography that is most often emotional, contentious, fluid, and which stimulates a form of knowledge that moves in *and* out of the body.

Detailing the micro-epistemologies and everyday terrains of auditory experience, I've come to hear sound as a movement that gives us each other, as both gift and threat, as generosity and agitation, as laughter and tears, marking listening as a highly provocative and relational sense. In response, I've attempted to push my own work so as to follow the precarious, temporal, and detouring behavior of sonority. Subsequently, it is my proposal that in the promiscuity of sound, its reproducibility, in its anxious and restless transfiguration, we might identify a means for occupying and exploring the multiple perspectives of the present.

1

UNDERGROUND: BUSKING, ACOUSMATICS, AND THE ECHO

And the public wants what the public gets
But I don't get what this society wants
I'm going underground, (going underground)
Well the brass bands play and feet start to pound
Going underground, (going underground)
[so] let the boys all sing and the boys all shout for tomorrow
—The Jam

It was also noticed that the experience of living underground encouraged an anti-authoritarian and egalitarian spirit, as if the conditions above ground could be reversed . . . So those under the ground instilled an element of fear in those who remained above it . . . it is the fear of the depths.[1]
—Peter Ackroyd

Where buskers, giant alligators, and resistance fighters lurk, and the acoustical thrust of the echo manifests in unseen voices and musical glory, to disorient and confuse.

To enter this topography of auditory life, I start below, within the underground, which is also immediately a set of images: underground passages, caves and tunnels, the subway, subterranean creatures or nocturnal monsters, covert operations and secret clubs, the underground as hold-out against political reality, or the site of resistance, and a vessel for the manufacturing of science fiction fantasies. To go underground is to bump against a plethora of signifiers, all of which resonate with so many impressions and presences that no less contain significant historical and cultural narratives and meanings. The underground acts as a reverberant space; cavernous and dim, it echoes with sounds and voices to unfold in uncertain yet urgent messages.

> And consequently the echo flourished, raging up and down like a nerve in the faculty of hearing, and the noise in the cave, so unimportant intellectually, was prolonged over the surface of her life.[2]

The haunting cave scene occurring in *A Passage to India* is defined through its echo, as an unstable, penetrating and violating sound that follows Miss Quested, threatening her and the community of British colonists living in the city of Chandrapore during the British Raj. "The sound had spouted after her when she escaped, and was going on still like a river that gradually floods the plain." This acoustical trauma gains intensity by unfolding from within the darkness of the cave—caught in the murky shadows of the cavern, the defining lines that hold this volatile community in place are subject to traumatic upheaval. Against such echoes sparked in the cave, the stability of forms, of origins and relations, are brought into question.

The underground is a space of such hyperbolic sounding—an acoustics that brings together the inherent potentiality of sound to echo, expand, and disorient while being interwoven with forces of struggle, hope, and resistance. The underground is where sound carries as physical matter, a mass of energy billowing out along passageways and tunnels, caverns and tombs, to pinpoint the intensities of secrets and anger, terror and criminality. The dynamism of the echo threads through the underground to bend and shape its topographic image. Through this acoustical conditioning the underground provides a key geographic coordinate for acousmatic experience (which I will return to).

As a space, the underground is also full of all the submerged and hidden materiality of the urban topography—an extensive network of tunneling, cabling, and piping that carries the flows and movements of energy distribution, data networking, and the like, as a humming, vibrating strata. A patchwork hidden from the common eye, the underground is replete with electromagnetic waves, surges of temperature, and pulses of infrastructural systems, as a vibratory crust of earth that in turn comes to rise up in countless narratives of ghouls and zombies often brought back to life through unseen forms of energy flashes. Revitalizing the dead body turns the underground into a ghost town, a haunted soil populated by the undead always readying itself to surface in terrifying shapes.

The underground then is a space of creaks and murmurs, a slow shifting of acoustical particles that hover on the threshold of perception, and which carry the possibility of threat, danger, and inversion, suggesting that what lies underneath surreptitiously mirrors what lies above in full view. We might think of that resounding heartbeat found in Edgar Allan Poe's "The Tell-Tale Heart," which sounds from below the floorboards, leading the protagonist to admit his guilt as a murderer and reveal the buried body to the unsuspecting detectives. The underground is thus a space of repressed guilt, a zone full of secrets. Poe's haunting narrative draws forward the shadowy darkness that surrounds every space, every room or home, and which radically shapes the urban topography.

Countless films harness the spirit of the urban underground to supply the imagination with an array of images of terror: from giant rats flooding the streets of New York City to ancient reptiles breeding in the city sewers, and to more psycho-dramatic depictions, as for instance, found in the Vienna underground in *The Third Man*. This shadowy, labyrinthine underground comes to life in the dizzying sequence of the final chase, where Harry Lime (played by Orson Welles) attempts to outwit the police by hiding in the dark, scurrying through the sewer tunnels as a shadow among shadows. The visual fragmentation of the sequence utilizes to great effect the space of the tunnels, and is furthered by the push and pull of the related audio—the scraping and shuffling of footsteps echoing through the tunnels, which fall in and out of sync with a visual image, supplements the disorienting narrative, heightening by fragmenting single perspective the sensation of suspense. As in *A Passage to India*, the underground acts as a dizzying and dangerous acoustics, articulating criminality or assault and supplying the topographic chase with an active reservoir of haunting outcomes. Such multiplicity forms a key to my own investigation, itself a chase of the senses that tries to capture the gradations of an acoustical strata while releasing the resonances that might add to that particular experience we call *listening*. Within the underground listening is unmistakably charged by the echoic.

Underground Sonics

Michel Chion's audio-visual theories greatly expand understandings on the cinematic while importantly detailing sound's potency in contouring perceptual experience. For Chion, sound imparts temporality to the experience of looking, underscoring how "the ear isolates a detail of its auditory field and follows this point or line in time."[3] Hearing positions us within the unfolding of time that in the space of cinema "*vectorizes* or dramatizes [film] shots, orienting them toward a future, a goal . . ."[4] The temporality of sound thus opens a horizon toward which narrative and the movements of looking are directed. Yet Chion also suggests that sound operates through a general act of rupture according to its behavioral nature, which "necessarily implies a displacement or agitation, however minimal."[5] Sound, as the result of a series of material frictions or vibrations, arises from a given object or body to propagate and leave behind the original source—*it brings the original source from there to here*. This movement grants the feeling of a progression; the temporality of sound, in vectorizing the image, does so by always leaving behind its origin to enliven sense of place with continual animation.

This temporal dynamic is given further expression in the event of the echo. If sound generally occurs through displacement, moving from a point in time to another, the echo renders this to such degree as to make concrete the vectorizing, temporality of sound—*the echo exaggerates the passing of sound, staging it as a performance.* The echo literally continues the vector of sound, staggers it, and supplements it with a further set of sound events that ultimately fill a given space. The echo brings back the original event, though, reshaped or refigured, thereby returning sound and rendering it a spatial object: the echo turns sound into sculpture, making material and dimensional its reverberating presence. In this regard, the echo contradicts sound's temporal behavior. Making sound into an object, the echo displaces the linear relation of origin and horizon, past and future, by prolonging the sound event to a point where it takes over; it overwhelms by turning the time of sound into a spatial dimension—the echo moves into space to replace it with its own compounded and repeating energy.

The ruptures performed by the echo thus unfix the temporality of sound to further the integral displacement sound comes to impart onto the senses. In doing so, the echo disorients and distracts; it wanders and returns in the same moment to confuse where we are and where we are going. The horizon of the echo is folded back to support the making of another spatial dimension—a loop verging on feedback and repeating sound's initial acoustical force.

In the underground, the echo comes to life. As in the scene from *A Passage to India*, the entire rupture of community relations that follows is made possible by the confusing movement of the echo: the cave reverberating with an uncertain action not only confuses Miss Quested, but imparts an entire disorienting spin on the seemingly stable relationship found between the colonists and their local counterparts. The echo might be heard to uncover and bring forward what has otherwise remained repressed. The vector of time, in this case the conditions of history found in British India, is broken to bring forward transformation and potential revolt. It is to the echo then that our underground experience is partnered to form an inexplicable mix of fear and hope.

To unfold the echoic dynamic of sound in the underground, I want to journey down into the subway. The interwoven intensity of the underground mapped out thus far can be additionally heard in the movements of underground trains and their related maze of tunneling. Existing as underground spaces, the subway comes to shadow the above urban experience: as a zone of transience, it teases out the fleeting, mesmerizing condition of the urban by adding an intensity of sensorial input. From the dank atmosphere to the often noxious smells, the shadowy or overly lit tunnels to the bustling closeness of bodies on the go—the subway heightens all the density of that experience known as *the urban*. It further exposes such experience by locating us within a heightened functionality: in the depths of the urban system we circulate as rather mechanical figures, funneled through an infrastructural circuit that fills the senses with a demanding array of influence. With the subway train crashing through the tunnels, service announcements indecipherably flooding the platforms, alongside all the signaling and acoustical thrusts of mechanical systems at work, the subway comes to epitomize the urban condition as a system always on the verge of breakdown, rupture, and concealment.

The subway might be said to supplement the urban imaginary with subterranean events and visions, materializing in a mixture of social confrontation, shadowy reveries, sensory experience, and aggression. The subway's cartographic overlay and fragmentation— *where are we in the midst of all these tunnels and passageways, all these fleeting and speedy trajectories?*—produces a set of highly unique social transpositions and coordinates, generating innumerable intersections of social difference that realign demographic delineations or markings. For the subway is for everyone (even those who can not pay, for instance, seem to find a way in), and yet it's mysteriously without individual character: as an urban space it is largely systematic, mechanical, with each station linked into a greater, uniform identity, while supporting the unique movements of individual itinerary. As Marc Augé tellingly observes:

> Transgressed or not, the law of the metro inscribes the individual itinerary into the comfort of collective morality,

and in that way it is exemplary of what might be called the ritual paradox: it is always lived individually and subjectively; only individual itineraries give it a reality, and yet it is eminently social, the same for everyone, conferring on each person this minimum of collective identity through which a community is defined.[6]

The uniqueness of the subway is acquired precisely through this social paradox. It brings together by enabling separate journeys; it structures individual desire and yet in doing so it remains strangely impersonal, resistant to intervention. (Even the occasional graffiti seems to fade into the infrastructural character of the subway, becoming absorbed into the many signs and markings existing down there, as an expected visual object.) Yet performances do take place that might harness or generate subjective tracings, sudden interactions, making more concrete the minimum of qualities Augé notes as defining community. These performative instances come to supplement the rather isolated movements of the journey, suddenly crossing the lines separating bodies, bringing smiles or grimaces to the faces of passengers, or requiring more outspoken responses in the form of yelling or scolding. (On a recent journey on the Berlin subway an elderly woman broke the social barrier by scolding a young man who was playing music too loud through his mobile phone. Her outspokenness seemed to even surprise the young man, who obviously relied upon the assumed fact that his disturbance would go unheeded by the general atmosphere of tolerant quietude, or social trepidation, usually occupying the subway train.)

Piercing the isolation of the individual journey, such performances and their responses contour the underground with degrees of hesitant and sudden interaction. The many spaces on and off the train offer a stage for the more dedicated performer who utilizes the forced collectivity the subway produces. In particular, musical performance finds conducive space in the underground, drawing upon the acoustical and social architectures found down there. The subway becomes the site for innumerable musical acts. From accordion players from Russia found in the Berlin subway to glam rockers in the London Tube, music and the subway intersect in the form of busking. The subway forms a literal platform for a musical culture wed to the acoustics of an underground public space. Extending a larger history of street entertainment, from the figure of the minstrel to the troubadour, the busker is an itinerant acoustical actor, panhandling for spare change through the offering of a song or musical interlude. An informal interweaving takes place, where sound and its reverberations supplement the social choreographies found on the subway. The busker is an underground sound incarnate through whose idiosyncratic, bold or shy actions come to also represent fantasies of the authentic voice or musical artist. The subway busker functions quite literally as an "underground artist," harnessing the term and its signifying echo: the underground is the designated site where radicality, marginalization, and authenticity are often to be found and heard.

IMAGE 1   Busker in the Berlin subway, 2009. Photo: the author.

Musicians have gone on to make professional recordings in the subway, utilizing the acoustical quality of the space while also seeking to incorporate the particular social and emotional feeling the subway seems to generate. For instance, the work of Peter Mulvey, a busker turned professional musician, recorded his *Ten Thousand Mornings* CD in the Boston subway in 2001. As he states, "Phillip Glass called music a sublime currency between people. Here, that exchange happens utterly openly."[7] Such an approach places the musical gesture within the underground, seeking to capture not only an interlacing of different sonic material, from the instrument and voice to the random sounds of the space, but importantly the atmospheric contour of being down under. Might the underground in this case form an inspirational envelope that acts as an effective texture in forming the final work? Within the echoing acoustics, the busking musician couples together a mix of mystical spiritualism and urban pain, figuring the musical expression as a shimmering voice arising from the depths of the city.

The image of the street musician comes to accentuate certain mythological tracings, lending to the notion of an authentic sound that might hark back to folk traditions, of acoustical instrumentation and singing from the heart, aimed at countering established and professionalized productions. Mulvey's return to the Boston subway is underscored in this fashion, drawing upon his roots as a busker. "It comes down to the relationship between performer and audience, and there are few places where that relationship is closer, or more honest, than in a subway tunnel."[8] The lone musician occupying the down below of the subway fulfills the expectant mythology of the underground while prolonging its reverberant energy. Listening to Mulvey singing Marvin Gaye's "Inner City Blues," recounting the frustrations of everyday life, of high taxes and crime, Mulvey locates the song onto its lyrical site, and further: the subway acts as a register for those inner city blues, and busking itself an absolute expression of being down and out.

The musician Susan Cagle finds similar resonance for her work in the subway. Rising to fame through her CD *The Subway Recordings*, in 2006, and her subsequent performance on the Oprah Winfrey Show, Cagle spent years performing as a busker in various subway stations in New York City. Performing alongside her brother and sister, her lyrical reflections on life seem directed at the subway traveler and stem from the general situational conditions of urban life. As she sings in "Stay": "Feels like living in the city / Is getting harder every day / And people keep on getting in your way / Seems like everybody's talking / About the mess that we have made / And everybody wants to get away / But I think I'll stay around a little while / See if I can turn some tears into a smile."[9]

Her lyrics carry all the resonating tensions of urban life, suggesting insight gained from her own city experiences; the city seems to congeal for Cagle *within* the subway, where the particular dreariness of urban life often appears in the exhaustion and annoyance of train riders. Deciding to record her album in the NY subway reflects her involvement and belief in this underground condition, as site for revelation or artistic insight, looping her work back to the very location where inspiration is found, and where the meaning of the work finds its ultimate audience. In listening to the CD, the acoustics of the subway dramatically conditions the sound, punctuated with the passing of trains and the cheering of passersby. With her words ringing out through the tunnels, blending lyrical content with locational energy, the journey of the artist resonates to infuse this underground experience with empathy.

Cagle's *The Subway Recordings* was released on Columbia Records after record executives discovered her performing in Herald Square station, leading to her second CD recorded in the studio and released in 2007. In looking at her MySpace web page, photographs of the singer depict her somewhat glamorously sitting in a wooden chair in an orange dress holding an electric guitar against what appears as an authentically urban backdrop.[10] These representational features come to signal "musical authenticity" by specifically aligning the artist with the urban, extending the city as a mythical texture necessary for conditioning genuine artistic expression, with the subway being one of its essential spatialities and sites of experience. Locating music there, from an artistic perspective, is a heartfelt attempt to ingrain the musical work with this texturing print.

As a site, the underground offers other acoustical opportunities, beyond the realm of the urban subway. Exiting the specifics of the subway or metro space, musicians have found sonic beauty in other subterranean locations. For instance, Stuart Dempster's recordings made in the cistern at Fort Worden, Port Townsend just north of Seattle are startling soundings of the 186-foot diameter water tank with its 45-second reverberation time. Working mainly with trombone, his *Underground Overlays from the Cistern Chapel* CD collects a series of live recordings made with a group of students that, as Dempster proposes, "bring about a uniqueness that renders the result exceptionally meditative—indeed, spiritual."[11] Organized through various compositional and performative strategies, many of the tracks are based on setting up relations among an ensemble of players. With Dempster located at a central point in the cistern, the other players spread out through the space and respond to Dempster's lead. Given the extreme reverberation time, the process of playing demands an elongated duration to the point where each player is in effect performing in relation to the space as it echoes back, in the form of these trailing notes, their own playing. A series of sustained pitches arise and then fade out to be transposed with the arrival of the following notes, accentuating the cistern's special quality as surmised in Dempster's poetical and suggestive observation that "This is where you have been forever and will always be forever."[12] For Dempster, time seems to stand still down in the cistern, and the meditatively slow circulation of these voluptuously haunting tonalities enrapture the listener in a web of transcendent waves. It's here, in the underground that all references seem to dissipate, where earthly nature is suspended and time fragments into an altogether diffuse presence. The cistern becomes an enlarged instrumental envelope, giving the players its deep resonating chamber for the production of this other world, a pure sonorous energy to which each contributes and through which each communes with the other.

What Dempster, and by extension Mulvey and Cagle, captures is the reverberant dynamic of the underground. As I've suggested, the echoic relation of sound in the underground imparts degrees of disorientation, agitation, and rupture to the vector of sound and its temporal unfolding. With the return of the sound event in the form of echoes, origin and horizon fold back on each other to create feelings of timelessness. As Dempster points out, down below it is as if all things stand still. Yet, things stand still by also coming back; the echo, in bringing sound back, breaks the sense of progression. This animating dimensional object of the echo also suggests a voice: the dynamic of the echo, in becoming a space-time object, seems to return as if *speaking back*. To recall the original myth, the mountain nymph Echo was punished by Hera the wife of Zeus by having her voice taken away. Echo was left solely with the ability to repeat what others say, that is, to echo back only what she hears. The echo is an auditory mirror returning to the original sound event its own sounding image; the echo *speaks back* and in doing so seems to replace the original with a doubling whose animating presence takes on a life of its own. The echo comes to stand in space, as a figure whose shape and dimension remains unsteady but whose meaning suggests an ambiguous field of signification: every echo seems to *come alive*.

The movements of the underground echo, as I'm exploring here, follow according to theories of the "acousmatic." As detailed by Pierre Schaeffer (and Michel Chion) within the field of electroacoustic music, the acousmatic is a sound heard whose origin we do not see. The acousmatic forms the beginning of electroacoustic composition by allowing a sound to be removed from its contextual and indexical source to acquire other meaning. In particularly, the acousmatic sound is split from its visual source and brought into an auditory field to participate in the making of a more concentrated listening experience.

Mladen Dolar, in *A Voice and Nothing More*, details the acousmatic by returning to a greater history found in the Pythagorian philosophical tradition.[13] To recount, the Acousmatics were disciples of Pythagoras who listened to the teachings of their Master as he remained hidden from view behind a curtain. Dolar pinpoints such a move as forming the heart of philosophy by specifically raising the authority of the voice that in turn leaves behind the body, not only as a visual image but as a terrestrial figure bound to the earth. The "spirit" of the meaningful voice thus appears from nowhere, as a seemingly omniscient source.

The acousmatic carries forward the tracings of a voice that leaves behind the material world, to appear as is from the shadows. From this perspective, the underground echo is an acousmatic sound; it makes every sound a voice that breaks from its source to become something greater, more powerful and suggestive, a sound no longer bound to the earth. That is to say, the echo is a sound that comes back to haunt, returning as transformed through its diffusion and ultimate regrouping into an altogether different expression. *The echo delivers our own alter-ego*.

To return to the underground, the meanings of this acousmatic echo might be heard in Dempter's appreciation for the "uniqueness" forged from the magic of a 45-second reverberation, and in addition from Mulvey and Cagle's subway mythology. Being down under might extend the artistic voice beyond human proportions, to gather up all the intensities of a language seeking another body, another figuring. The artist underground finds a double, as an echo that in bringing back an individual reverberation also delivers the energy of a social and supernatural message. Dempster's understanding of the "spiritual" can be folded back onto the subway recordings of Mulvey and Cagle, suggesting that the truth and authenticity sought through sound and music finds support or generative relation through an acoustical sitedness full of reverb, texture, and shadow. Might the underground then feature as an explicit zone for transformation, whether as site for the dead or in the transporting sonics of an acousmatic sounding?

In following the dynamics of underground sonics I'd like to take a further historical detour onto the London streets, and in particular by focusing on the noises occurring there in the eighteenth century. The London streets at this time were radically marked by a conflict of the senses, where the intense growth and emerging density of the urban center brought forward a powerful mix of sounds, smells, and sights, often forcing confrontations between the upper classes and those relying on street trade. The urban street literally became a site for new intersections of difference, and in terms of sound, the intensification of noise. Street musicians in particular lent to the intensity of noise levels and were progressively haunted by the establishment of legislation aimed at providing local residents with means to counter the intrusion of street music. "The types of noise that attracted most complaint among the literate and vociferous citizens were those sounds made by the poorest citizens—especially the sounds made by popular entertainers and low-profit traders."[14] As a letter from a professor of music reveals, the noise of the street came to interrupt the professional classes:

> I am a professor of music; my work is very often seriously inter-
> rupted by the street-organ nuisance. Indeed, I am frequently
> compelled to relinquish altogether my professional avocations,
> and lay them aside until the noise is over. I beg to forward
> you a memorial, signed by the leading musical professors in
> London, and also by the pianoforte-tuners—a class whose
> work is entirely stopped when street music is going on.[15]

Such complaints were increasingly common in the nineteenth century, and eventually led to the Metropolitan Police Act of 1839, which enabled residents to request street musicians to move on from a given location. The Act provoked numerous oppositions, underscoring the degree to which street music and the related players heightened certain class tensions: arguments were made by the professional class to outlaw street music altogether while others rallied behind it as providing entertainment for the "common people." These tensions reveal a fundamental base for the ongoing debates around street noise even today, where the urban topography embodies an oscillation of opinion, and where quiet is often gained by those who can afford it.

Given that the street musician brought forward such wrath, it is not surprising that with the opening of the London Underground in the nineteenth century it quickly became a site for busking. The Underground allowed the busking musician new-found opportunities to play outside the particular tensions walking the London streets had; and one could reach an extensive public without having to roam the streets through the rather unpredictable weather. Yet occupying the Underground also further marked the busker as an itinerant, panhandling beggar by contrasting to the more professional classes that the Underground trains mostly served, a characterization which fed many arguments for the banning of busking altogether—street music was perceived as a form of vagrancy or filth lending to a general degradation of the city and its public thoroughfares.

Following this history, busking comes to signal a set of artistic qualities, which find notable expression in the 1960s with the popularization of folk music. An interesting case can be found with the London street musicians Alan Young and Don Partridge who were catapulted into the spotlight as they started to perform on the London streets. Being hailed as a new generation of musicians resurrecting the dying tradition of street entertainment, their circulation through the city eventually landed Partridge onto the music TV program *Top of the Pops* in 1967, turning the busker into an instant celebrity with his song "Rosie." This success led to ongoing gigs, and a radical shift in lifestyle, finally resulting, as a kind of exultation of street music, in a concert of street musicians held at the Royal Albert Hall on January 29, 1969. Organized by Partridge and his manager, the concert was an all-star lineup of street music, featuring figures such as the Road Stars, Banjo and Spoons, the Earl of Mustard, the Happy Wanderers' leader George Franks, Dave Brock (later of Hawkwind), and many others. Though presented in support of the street musician, the event seemed to cast street music as a form of musical expression worthy of more cultural appreciation and attention. Once removed from the street, the musician garners cultural validation. Yet it also comes to mark a turning point that further echoes the earlier championing of the street musician as a valuable cultural figure—that culture requires and is constituted by voices found on the margins of society. We might follow the long history of the street musician, moving between the dire conditions of the itinerant life to the comforts of the king's palace—that is, between the margin and the center—as an articulation of cultural history in general. The Royal Albert Hall event from 1969 only further stages this movement, validating while at the same time curiously shifting the cultural significance of the street musician. As David Cohen and Ben Greenwood suggest in their illuminating history of busking, "The event may have been a statement about the regeneration of a tradition, but it also meant that busking had been commercialized. A long-playing record of the highlights of the concert was made, but most of the tracks were either mixed or over-dubbed in a studio, and some were actually re-recorded there." Such a process for Cohen and Greenwood suggests a turn-away from the authentic gesture of street music: "The essence of street music is not its technical perfection or its tonal quality, so much as its spontaneity and freedom, and to falsify the sound in a studio seems to be a contradiction of all its values."[16]

As with much of the folk tradition, and its presence within the 1960s, from Joan Baez to the more complicated and telling example of Bob Dylan,[17] the question of authenticity often came down to a relation to commercial structures, systems of representation, and the notion of the true acoustic sound. Any form of technological intervention, or electronic supplement, would radically undermine claims toward folk authenticity. The busker's social and cultural value are based on his or her ability to locate sound on the street, deep in the city, and to carry forward, through song, all the intensities found there.[18]

An interesting further example can be found with the on-line database www.buskerdu.com.[19] Started in 2006, buskerdu.com is a database housing recordings made of street musicians in subways and other locations from around the world, though most of the recordings seem to come from Seattle, Boston, and New York. Using dial-up, the recordings are sent in by anyone picking up a public telephone, dialing in, and using the phone as a recording device. The database automatically posts the recording, to provide a free archive of street music. Though having little sonic quality, the project nonetheless captures the pedestrian movements of sound, music, and people as they intersect in the subway, on the street corner, and elsewhere. The project gives sonic appreciation for the public situation of the street musician, as a personality circulating through the urban environment. And further, to inaugurating the underground as a space for the rogue movements of an aural history.

Underground Lives

The underground comes to supply space for an array of sonic and musical expressions, in whose acoustics a cacophony of both pleasures and pains are driven. Such oscillation can be appreciated by returning to the subway ride, this time in Mexico City, where the busker appears in other forms. Riding the subway in Mexico City a passenger is susceptible to another kind of performance, where urban hawkers pass through the train selling CDs, amplifying various tracks at an incredible volume. Adorning backpacks or modified bags fitted with portable CD or playback systems, loudspeakers and amplifiers, the sellers cruise the subway, timing their movements to the rhythm of the stations: they each take one car at a time, entering at one end and making their way through until they reach the end generally at the same time the train is pulling into the next station. Upon leaving the car, at the other end another seller enters, this time presenting an altogether different musical genre. From romantic ballads to hip-hop to country music, the CDs are pirated CDR compilations with photocopied covers offering the latest survey of a genre. Blasting into the subway, the music cuts into the general quiet of the train, bombarding the ear with their offerings. Here busking is unabashedly an economic endeavor, affording no particular sense of artistic gratification or pleasure; it might be said to abuse the forced immobility of the individual traveler, using the subway as an impromptu space for informal economics.

IMAGE 2 CD seller in the subway, with speaker-backpack, Mexico City, 2009. Photo: Berenice Pardo.

The busker, by brandishing particular musical gestures, adding to and utilizing the acoustical fabric and flows of the underground, brings forward often-difficult economic relations—of those with against those without. The busker should be heard not only as a musical carrier, an artistic voice reverberating through the tunnels of the subway, but also as a sound that marks space with an economic tension. As on the eighteenth century streets of London, busking continues to draw out the differences of class, contouring sound with a definite economic and social intensity. The sudden appearance of community observed by Augé on the Paris Metro can be glimpsed as well in the confrontation with difference as it reaches across the mysterious dividing lines of the subway. The music of busking is a sort of acousti-cal reach contoured by an ethical demand to give. To listen (willingly or not) then is to enter into this field of exchange, where acoustics wraps the listener within a space of masked begging. The subway, as a prominent space of busking—where the individual is caught and can thus be highlighted or initiated as an involuntary audience—comes to resound with multiple acoustics: the echoic reach of the music gives the busker an extended opportunity, to draw in as many individual ears as possible, and to thus situate these singularities into a sudden community. I hear the music of an accordion player and am drawn into a circle that places my recognition on a social scale between giving and taking, offering and buying, recognition and response.

The subway is replete with such performances and economic frictions, found not only in the form of the busker, but also in the presence and display of the homeless body. As a space, the under-ground is a site for numerous occupations and usages that often cater to the homeless, the itinerant, and the social outcast. The subway functions as a home for such drifting, and related distresses. From the homeless woman who sits on a bench down under for an entire day finding warmth to the more elaborate communities that occupy various tunnels of the NY subway, the underground is literally an extensive marginal space for marginal occupations.

Occupying these marginal spaces of the NY subway, homeless individuals come to appropriate underused or derelict tunnels for living quarters. The Mole People, as they've come to be known, form an underground community that turns the subway system into a space of homelessness, insanity, and death. "The train tunnels under Grand Central Station contain perhaps the largest collection of squatters. There, in a mere three-quarters of a square mile, thirty-four miles of track stretch out along seven distinct levels before funnelling into twenty-six main rail arteries going north, east, and west. Police have cleared out as many as two hundred people living in a single community . . ."[20]

Jennifer Toth's account of the Mole People offers a deeply moving, troubling, and absorbing series of underground stories. Having spent a year getting to know the homeless who occupy the tunnels, and discovering the rituals, communities, expressions and concerns that circulate below ground, Toth attempts to shed light on the problematic condition of the homeless, and in particular, what it means to live in the tunnels. The tunnels become the very last stop of the homeless, a space from which there is seldom return to society, a horrid territory which in turn surprises Toth during her visits and interactions with many instances of unsettling beauty, intimacy, and brutal survival. Her notes from the underground emerge as a chronicle that, while a written text, is also a journey through voices and the acoustical resonances that pass between her and the others. "With hundreds or thousands living underground, many die there, either in accidents or from disease, perish because they lose their way . . ."[21] in the shapeless, infectious, and mesmerizing qualities of the tunnels.

Moving below ground, the appearance of things changes, the references to social reality, to the cultural framework, to the visibility of things, vanishes; the darkness, the dilapidation, the extremity all come to replace the temporal and spatial movements that happen aboveground. Miss Quested's troubling echo from the cave in India, as a suggestive flooding of the earth, is brought to a deeper and more profound reality down in the NY tunnels, as an absolute space of echoic and rank darkness. Toth's narratives are shaped by such shifting perspectives and are brutally marked by the conditions of what lies below and the voices that resound therein.

"I can't hurt you, lost angel."

The words come out of the tunnel's blackness without warning when I stumble into a cavelike recess.

"But I can hurt those you care about," he says silkily. In the dusty tunnel light, I feel eyes to my left and turn to find him facing me, hands on his hips in a bold and graceful stance. He is barely four feet from me.

I stare, stunned.

"Some of me is within you," he says, shielding his eyes with his left forearm as though there is a flood of light that I don't see. "Not enough for me to hurt you. But enough for me to hurt others close to you. You have a fascination with the darkness of my tunnels. The evil within it. And it is evil," he says with cool force, a fine layer from fury. "Everything down here is pure evil."[22]

The confrontations that occur between Toth and the tunnel dwellers resound with such blending of terror and sudden poetry, an inter-mixing of pain and friendship, of threat, danger and companionship, which comes to disorient the forms of social exchange and the fixity of right from wrong. Dempster's Cistern recordings, which for him open up to a rich enveloping acoustics, a spiritual timelessness, seem uncannily close to Toth's confrontation with the Dark Angel. Each contains recognition of the perturbing dynamic of the underground, to break time and space, and nurture radical transfigurations of human relations and experience. Such echoic disorientation might be said to define the underground, as a cultural image, forming a space upon which fantasies and nightmares of otherness are projected, and which ultimately come to find shelter.

Through Toth's account, this intersection of fantasy and reality, of the notion of the underground and the actuality of its occupants, unfold through the voice, forming an oral history captured on the page. Toth essentially goes underground to interview, to research, to speak directly to the figures and bodies that duck below manholes, sneak through hidden conduits, and walk the tracks deep into the darkness. "He lives under Grand Central, like many other tunnel people, but he is entirely unlike any other. None have set up camps anywhere near his. He hisses, spits, and screams. He is unforgetta-ble, in part, because of his words and his forceful delivery."[23] The Dark Angel, as he is called, comes to embody the sheer potent darkness of the underground. Referring to himself as the Devil, the other tunnel dwellers are deeply afraid of him, and the police in turn recognize his menacing and threatening potential, with one officer remarking that "under there anything is possible, you know what I'm saying?"[24] This image of the underground shadows the situation of the busker, riding like an uncertain particle upon the songs reverberating down there. In addition, Toth's account further outlines the echoic dynamics of the underground. The interactions with the Dark Angel, as one example, must be remembered to occur within the absolutely shadowy and uncertain spaces of the tunnels. The voice and the entire soundscape are dramatically determined by this darkness, which locates all bodies within its vague territory.

The acousmatic condition of the underground echo supports the overall terror of Toth's experiences. The Dark Angel remains out of complete view, a voice "hissing" in the dark. His features are seemingly defined according to the horror of the underground. Yet this horror might lend to suggesting that the acousmatic itself, as sounds that appear beyond reach of a visual source, carry with them an inherent grain of terror. "The voice, separated from its body, evokes the voice of the dead"[25] and thereby infuses listening with a haunting uncertainty. Chion furthers such a view when he writes, "A sound or voice that remains acousmatic creates a mystery of the nature of its source, its properties and its powers . . ."[26] Such mystery is at the heart of the echo. The disorienting propagation of the echo brings us into a space without perspective, for the echo diminishes orientation and spatial clarity; it locates us on the threshold of the dead, as a voice without a body. As Dolar finally queries, "The real problem with the acousmatic voice is: can we actually ever pin it down to a source?"[27]

These underground narratives find curious inversion in the London Underground in the twentieth century. In response to the impending threat of Zeppelin bombers at the beginning of the First World War, London Underground officials prompted the population to take refuge below ground, referring to the Underground as a place of safety.[28] As one advertisement ran in 1914:

> Never mind the dark and dangerous streets
> Underground
> It is warm and bright
> Be comfortable in well-lit trains and read the latest war news.[29]

The protection afforded by the Underground instilled within the population a deep fear of being caught aboveground during an attack, leading to continual and expanded occupation of the Underground for shelter, which included whole families riding around on trains for days, camping out with pets, and even setting up make-shift stoves. This extended beyond concern for the safety of the population, leading the British government to relocate parts of the National Gallery collections, and other prominent Museum works and archives, to parts of the Underground for safekeeping.

IMAGE 3 Henry Moore, Tube Shelter Perspective: The Liverpool Street Extension, 1941. Reproduced by permission of The Henry Moore Foundation.

The use of the London Underground as shelter was further expanded during the Second World War, with all 79 stations being used, and an entire infrastructure of sanitation, first aid, and food supplies being installed. With 6 feet of station platform given to six people, three in bunks and three side by side on the floor, the stations quickly became an organizational challenge, leading to an elaborate system of crowd control. For instance, "Meals on Wheels" organized by the Salvation Army or the Women's Voluntary Service catered to the hunger of the Underground dwellers, which could amount to 7 tons of food and 2,400 gallons of tea, coffee, and cocoa being served in a single night. In addition, some 300 doctors and 200 nurses were on watch for dysentery and other ailments, such as lice, and the spread of disease by mosquitoes, leading to continual visits to the many shelters and constant examination of the population of dwellers.[30] At many stations entertainment facilities were also installed, such as film projectors, as well as libraries, in order to distract occupants, or utilize the hours spent below ground for educational purposes, for many could not sleep during the long hours, and instead spent their time "chatting, watching any entertainments that might be organized, or listening to records on the wireless."[31]

The occupation of the Underground ironically counters original fears of subterranean construction. With the developments of underground travel, in London and in Paris, in the early part of the nineteenth century, numerous fears were sparked. Partly based on greater cultural understanding of the earth as the ground of the dead to more recent fears of contagion, disease, and filth, underground travel and the building of subways ignited countless images of epidemics spreading by the unleashing of noxious vapors lurking just under the ground. As one opponent wrote, "What mephitic exhalations will not be released? Who can foresee what consequences may lie in mucking about in this putrefying earth?"[32] Living underground thus carried forward a complex weave of safety and fear, drawing together the lingering trepidations of the metro ride—as a confrontation with "a succession of unnameable odors, unbreathable emanations, a mixture of sweat, coal-tar, carbonic acid, metallic dust, etc."[33]—and the total fear of bombs dropping.

The acoustical life of the Underground in such instances shifts from the haunted imagination to that of the possibility of safety. From the nefarious movements of uncertain creatures and acousmatic shadows to the surprising laughter and music resounding against the looming threat of bombers, the geography of the subterranean oscillates.

William Strange's journalistic text, "The Brave and Happy Shelterers," reveals the conditions of the Underground, highlighting the site as an acoustical dynamic. Visiting a shelter at Piccadilly Circus Tube station during an air-raid siren, Strange makes the compelling observation—"That's one thing about this underground railway business: no one had even heard the sirens!"[34] The depths of the Underground not only lent safety to the population, but afforded much-needed quiet. As Strange continues: "Then I spoke to a young and weary-looking mother. 'It's chiefly on account of the kids we come down here,' she told me, with an odd half-cultured accent. 'It's far enough below the ground that you don't hear too much noise. After all, the kids have got to get their sleep, even if we have learnt to do without' . . . And so, the roaring of the trains leaves them completely undisturbed, and they neither feel the draughts nor heed the waiting passengers. Compared, indeed, to London's anti-aircraft barrage and the thunder of the bombs, these small sounds are as nothing."[35]

The underground then, as a space of darkness and threat, pivots to function also as potential haven, sanctuary, or site for resistance, itself often tied to the reality of war. With the terror on land and in the sky comes the refuge sought below ground, minimizing the fear and challenge of the experience of war-noise. Though the London Underground was not without its dangers. With crowds fleeing to the stations during air-raid signals, and bombs dropping just above, a number of disasters did occur, for instance at Bounds Green Tube in 1942, which made the dark and cramped station a scene of terrible occurrence. As one account by a volunteer ambulance driver reveals:

Here was a scene of almost indescribable chaos. To the left of us the narrow platform was crowded with people; railway officials, police, stretcher and rescue parties and civilians. Over the heads of this crowd I could see a mountain of clay, reaching up and vanishing into a great hole in the roof, extending the whole width of the tunnel (which was completely blocked), and from that direction came an appalling mixture of screams and shouting, and the sound of clinking tools. These sounds were intensified in an eerie manner, echoing from the concave walls, and down the tunnel at the other end.[36]

The echoic, disorienting space of the Underground comes to intensify the chaotic and troubling blend of fear and horror. Unable to make a direct link between a single sound and its source, the situation becomes "eerily" indeterminate, bringing back the echoic uncertainty and the figure of acousmatic death.

Even against such disastrous possibility, the underground offers a place for hiding, especially against the real or perceived threat of invasion and death. Such movements find bold articulation in the 1960s in the US with the "Fall-Out Shelters Mania." As documented by Arthur Waskow and Stanley Newman in their detailed chronicle *America in Hiding*, America's sense of the looming red scare catapulted the entire nation into an underground frenzy. Initiated by the developments both in Berlin and Cuba in 1961, President John Kennedy issued a statement to the nation in July of that year, stating:

Tomorrow, I am requesting of the Congress new funds for the following immediate objectives: to identify and mark space in existing structures—public and private—that could be used for fallout shelters in case of attack; to stock those shelters with food, water, first-aid kits, tools, sanitation facilities, and other minimum essentials for survival; to increase their capacity; to improve our air-raid warning and fallout detection systems, including a new household warning system now under development; and to take other measures which will be effective at an early date to save millions of lives if needed. In addition, new Federal buildings will include space suitable for fallout shelters, as well as normal use.[37]

Following this statement, numerous initiatives within the Congress led to an amazing increase in defense spending, fuelling within the population a pervasive sense of paranoia about an inevitable nuclear attack. As a result, America went underground, building fallout shelters in backyards across the country and spawning an entire market for a variety of camping goods, and supporting a rather dubious culture of newly founded construction and manufacturing companies specializing in fallout structures. Suddenly, "the swimming pool contractor has become an authority on bomb shelters. The hardware merchant has relabeled his line of camping gear—now it is survival equipment. Trade associations for cement, clay, steel, and wood are vying for the opportunity to provide shields against the gamma ray. Makers of everything from air fresheners to waterless soap are rephrasing sales literature to argue that ownership of their goods is deterrence against 'the bomb'."[38] Curiously, the shelter was also promoted through a lens of the spiritual, claimed by Dr. Frank Caprio as a "haven for the spirit, a sanctuary to take stock of ourselves and our course in life."[39] Being underground then might serve the population, allowing America to reflect upon its spiritual well-being, bringing forward an echo of monastic life, where seclusion, silence, and a set of meagre rations lend to hours of soul-searching. Yet the acoustic of this underground situation cannot go unmarked by the absolute threat of annihilation that hovered in the form of the Bomb. Might the underground be heard additionally as a condition of anticipation? A space that already awaits the appearance of the echo, the specter of the acousmatic voice, to announce a break in the vector of time and meaning?

IMAGE 4 Exposed layout of a bomb shelter, USA, 1963.

Resistance

I've been exploring the underground as a concrete space as well as a geographic coordinate that comes to generate particular fantasies and social exchanges; tuning in to the acoustics of the underground reveals a larger set of ambiguities, myths of marginality, and the force of an echoic listening. In addition, fear and instability gain momentum through the reverberant, cavernous acoustics of the down under, fuelling notions of a lurking threat previewed or announced by noises in the dark.

This unsteady space of the underground, with its troubling echoes, can be situated alongside Michel Foucault's well-known theory of heterotopia. By acting as a space distinct from others, the underground comes to reflect back to those spaces their own condition, performing as an inversion to the terrestrial. Thus heterotopia is the very spatial coordinate of otherness, a differentiating geography that has "the curious property of being connected to all the other emplacements, but in such a way that they suspend, neutralize, or reverse the set of relations that are designated, reflected, or represented by them."[40]

Heterotopia of the underground is brought forward by performing a certain *mirroring* of what is above: whether in the echoes of the cave or in the busking musician that reflects back the city above, the underground opens up to reveal what is already hidden within terrestrial light. Yet, following Foucault, heterotopia also provides an understanding on how such spatial experiences or sites are perpetually negotiated, unfixed, or shifted. The process of marginality and subsequent co-optation by established culture, bemoaned by earlier proponents of the avant-garde as the struggle between center and periphery, is unsettled and rethought through the notion of heterotopia. For what Foucault suggests is that spaces, in being processes of relations, are perpetually charged by the ideological and cultural forces that play out across their topography. As I've tried to show, the spatial acoustics of the underground shifts through a register of meaning. From the busker whose music relies upon the underground as an architecture to draw out his or her project to the gathering of the population in the London Underground during the Wars, marking the tunnel with hope and protection, the secrets or echoes that haunt the subterranean world can radically shift. Yet by following the movements that lie below, I might also suggest that going underground remains the passage through which to imagine transgressing the constraints of the visible, the established, the norm. To seek the underground, even in the rather ordinary subway ride, might be to take pleasure in exposing oneself to a dizzying uncertainty or to releasing the desire for otherness and the differentiating vagueness of the echo. Underground heterotopia imparts forceful matter into the economy of the social. Like the zombies in *Dawn of Dead*, that rise up from the grave to haunt the American suburb, the subterranean offers the aboveground the challenge of always having to negotiate its own hidden dreams or desires in moments of uprising, fantasy, or struggle, which shift the relation between form and formlessness, temporarily unmarking any strict notion of above from below, inside from outside.

These oscillations are further glimpsed in understanding the underground as a significant location for forms of resistance—itself the very mark of existing outside or below the established system. Literally, "going underground" is paramount to forging tactics of resistance, terrorism, and other forms of political agitation or escape. The space or image of the underground functions as site for clandestine movements, and in particular operates as a networking systemization for radical organization and expression. Whether in the establishment of the Underground Railroad throughout the nineteenth century, aiding slaves in their plight for freedom to the Northern sates of America, or the Weather Underground, a small community arising from the student movement in the late 1960s aimed at bringing the terror of the Vietnam War home to American streets, underground movements haunt or reflect often embedded realities of a nation. They bring into pressing relief moral and political injustices while remaining out of bounds, or outside the law. In doing so, they provide an image of the very possibility of reshaping the present by always tipping the established equilibrium.

The fact of going underground provides a deeper image of what lies above, and in terms of an acoustical movement finds embodiment in the underground club—that space whereby musical cultures form into shifting communities and often interlock with specific political struggle. In mirroring terrestrial, aboveground culture, the underground club and its related bands or music can be heard as a *counter-sonic*, finding resonance in subterranean spaces, basements or abandoned barns on the outskirts of town. For example, the history of the Czech band The Plastic People of the Universe (PPU) brings forward this counter-sonic through a blending of avant-garde rock and counter-cultural politics of the late 1960s and early 1970s. Their story is interwoven with the particulars of Communist Czechoslovakia and reveals the degree to which State policy and underground cultures interlock.

The Plastic People of the Universe

Formed in Prague in 1968 immediately following the crackdown by the Soviet Union in August, the PPU developed into an active circle of musicians, poets, art historians, and cultural critics. Taking their name from a Frank Zappa song, and playing cover songs of the Velvet Underground and the Fugs, along with their own compositions, the band found guidance and inspiration from the music of the West, enlisting Paul Wilson, a Canadian living in Prague, as their singer and translator in 1970. At this time, through an intensification of their musical presence and their avant-garde, Western aesthetic, the government revoked their music license, essentially banning them from playing live or making records, forcing the band underground.

During this initial period of censorship the band only furthered their musical project, incorporating lyrics from the work of the banned poet Egon Bondy. In addition, their manager, the art historian Ivan Jirous brought a self-consciously Warholian flair to the group, infusing it with a larger sense of cultural activity and relevance. Jirous' influential ideas, summed up in his theory of "Second Culture," were to become a general ideological platform for counter-cultural agitation and expression within the community that gravitated around the band, leading to the organization of the First Music Festival of the Second Culture in 1974. The idea of Second Culture was quite literally premised on carving out an autonomous space within the First Culture of Soviet totalitarianism, defining a zone completely outside dominating policy. As Jirous states in his "Report on the Third Czech Musical Revival" written in 1975:

> The goal of the underground in the West is the outright destruction of the establishment. In contrast, the goal of our underground is to create a second culture, a culture completely independent from all official communication media and the conventional hierarchy of value judgements put out by the establishment. It is to be a culture that does

not have as its goal the destruction of the establishment . . .
The real aim is to overcome the hopeless feeling that it
is of no use to try anything and show that it is possible to do
a lot . . .[41]

Following this first music festival, a second gathering was planned
and attempted in 1976, which the secret police interrupted, leading to
the arrest of 27 musicians, including the PPU. In defiance to the
government, the band's various recordings had come to filter out
of the country and into the American and British music scenes,
leading to sudden attention onto the subsequent Prague trial of
the band, and the government's attempts to further undermine the
related underground cultures. Subsequently, a number of the band
members were jailed for over a year, and Paul Wilson was deported
(even though he had officially stopped performing with the band
years earlier).

Following the trial, a cultural and political protest was mounted
through the amalgamation of various threads of resistance that had
been taking place in the country since 1968. Spearheaded by Vaclav
Havel, a letter and petition was written and signed by members of the
literary underground (of which Havel was a part) and a faction of
Catholic opponents and intellectuals, along with the artistic and musical underground groups that had circulated around the PPU. Known
as Charter 77, the letter openly opposed the mistreatment of citizens,
and demanded heightened recognition of human rights. The letter
was officially deemed "anti-State" and its signers were subsequently
persecuted, losing their jobs, being jailed, and often being forced to
assist the secret police. Remarkably, Charter 77 remained a loose
organization throughout the following years, and led many of its
signers into political and government positions following the Velvet
Revolution of 1989 (including Havel). It is worth emphasizing the
degree to which the PPU, and the culture of music, had come to
act as a central force or energy within the underground. As one
hypothesis runs, the "Velvet Revolution" of 1989 was named by its

instigators after the band The Velvet Underground whose music the PPU had helped introduce. Thus the PPU were instrumental in an ongoing struggle to reclaim forms of human rights, interlacing their musical output with a radical social presence.

IMAGE 5 Legendary pub Klamovka, meeting point of the Czech underground scene of the 1970s and 1980s, Prague 2009. Photo: the author.

The story of the PPU underscores the underground as a generative site, and conceptual project, highlighting the degree to which music, and its resonance amongst a cultural group, seeks and amplifies cracks in the established system. The energetic, countersonic of an underground music might be appreciated as an extensive resonance, circulating through a network of contacts, secret gatherings, and clandestine listening. Following Jirous' Second Culture, "the underground is perceived here as mythological, as a world of a distinct mentality, different from the mentality of people of the establishment."[42] Yet the PPU were but a single articulation of a larger historical movement defined by numerous contributors. Other bands, such as Žabí hlen, Umělá hmota, and DG307 actively participated in this underground culture, blending performance happenings, visual work, with music and text.

Musically, the PPU sound is a weave of disjointed and repetitive rhythms with dissonant improvisations, punctuated with vocals and saxophone reminiscent of the music of Captain Beefheart. Their song "Jsem absolutní vule" ("I Am The Absolute Will") is a prime example. From their live record *Jak bude po smrti* ("What happens after death") recorded in 1979, the song throbs with a brooding, clattering rhythm, layered with vocals that seem to talk over the music, harshly flailing along with a saxophone that breaks in with cacophonous tonalities. Drawing upon the writings of Czech author Ladislav Klíma,[43] the lyrics criss-cross through a medley of abject and liberatory imagery:

> Have you cast off your shackles, the heavy shackles, but not the heaviest? Have you broken out of life's bondage at all? Have you become Free, a God: Free of all? I say but three words to you: I am the Absolute Will / It alone pacifies suffering all is valueless, insignificant and for me futile all is beneficial, good, holy, splendid, blissful all, for me, is insignificant and futile all is beneath me all is beneficial, good for me everything is only my noble destiny dictated by the eternal Will I am the Absolute Will I am the Absolute Will / And to be a manic dance and the only sudden turn and the most profound madness and foolishness and sterility and stench and to be nothing—and subsequently to be unyield-ing composure and somber reason and an illuminating idea and the creator of new worlds from the charmed singing blossoms manure and from manure the blossoms grow like its small daughter nature makes Everything from Nothing, Nothing from Everything I am the Absolute Will I am the Absolute Will / Everything from Nothing, Nothing from Everything the building and singing stench and illuminating

manure the sudden manure-like turn cast in iron and the
eternal silent truth that the cheetah painted Montezuma's
Aeneid I am the Absolute Will I am the Absolute Will[44]

A blending of mythological abstraction, pantheistic cosmology, and
avant-garde counter-cultural sentiment emblazons their musical
project, giving force to the demarcating verve of an underground
mentality. In following this project, might the music of resistance find
support in the echoic acoustics of an underground culture, lending to
the mythological narrative of a band that everyone hears about more
than they actually see? The acousmatic voice from the dark, echoing
from within secret passages or abandoned buildings, might be heard
to give sonic energy to the project of a second mentality. The underground then, as echoing chamber and space of rupture, affords the
making of a new body, a new constellation of meaningful relations
based on a shift in sensorial perspective. Harnessing the charge of
the echo, of the acousmatic rupture, underground culture searches
through the dark to forge or renew imaginary societies.

* * *

The underground then is a secret, a fold, a crack, and an echo
beating out from unknown cavities, which might suddenly fill up
with bodies, forces, or cultures, to refigure terrestrial relations. Going
down, further, into the darkness, the murmur rises, increasing in
volume to become reverberating noise; energies that collect into a
mass of sudden physicality, and then collapse or dissipate. What
lies behind the door, below the surface, or inside the wall? The infrastructures of the urban metropolis, winding under foot in systems
of tunneling and cabling, piping and wiring, become the site for so
many potential uprisings. As with the NY subway system, such infrastructures might come to serve a surprising community, to foster new
meetings or confrontations, and to breed the potential of clandestine
meetings. Or in the city of Prague, from the basements of bookshops

to the overlooked tunnels lurking behind trapdoors, the desire to make music signals a larger set of imaginings—the entire image of freedom can lurk upon a cacophonous and hidden collection of notes and lyrics, to thread their way through history.

The underground is an attraction: it serves the imagination with the promise of other forms of sharing, *transfiguration*. Acting as repository of the abject, numerous films portray the subterranean world as breeding ground for corruption, and for mutant beings, accentuating particular transformative energy in the sewer. Site of contagion, the sewer system, like the cemetery, is a space where strange creatures breed, to finally rise to take up residence in an unsuspecting metropolis. As in the film *Alligator* (1980), the sewer is site for alien species, where giant alligators living in the sewers of Chicago devour its citizens undercover. The slippery and dank tunnels of the sewer transform the waste of a metropolis, transfigured to bite back its citizens with its dark energy.

Such fantasies instigate other more romantic urban undergrounds, to function as passageways for nocturnal rambling. As with the expansive network of graves that lie below the city of Paris and that come to act as meeting ground for "cataphiles"—individuals who explore the underground network of stone mines, tunnels, and graves winding throughout the city. One such group, known as the Mexican Perforation was found to have used an underground chamber below Paris for film screenings. Discovered by the police in 2004, the chamber contained film projectors, a library of various films from the 1950s as well as a collection of horror films, a kitchen, and other appliances powered through appropriated electricity lines. As Lazar Kunstmann, spokesman for the group, stated, "The Mexican Perforation is a group of urban explorers whose members have more than 20 years experience. Transforming places is what they do everyday, so making a cinema was an easy thing to do."[45]

The Mexican Perforation exists as part of the larger umbrella group les UX. Specifically organized around the appropriation and use of underground chambers in the city, the group maps the city from below, adopting the subterranean as a generative context for cultural and political organization. Located directly underneath the Cinématheque Française in Paris, the underground cinema (known as Les Arenes de Chaillot) sought to operate as a counter-space and symbol to the official, aboveground cinema, itself the leading house of the film establishment. Such a contrast was self-consciously enacted, elaborated even in their programming, which was organized in relation to the films being shown in the Cinématheque:

> For example, LMDP [Mexican Perforation] showed the inversion of personality [which] going into the underground can provoke. In the Korean film, Joint Security Area, two border guards—North and South—face each other with guns in the day, but meet as friends at night. Then in Blind Shaft, a Chinese film, it's the opposite: people act like family above ground, but when they go into a mine, they kill each other. Both of these films aren't even set in urban scenes, they're in the country, but they show one of the underground points of view.[46]

The underground cinema thus acted as a mirroring of the culture aboveground; it sought to reflect upon established culture, carving out a space for alternative viewing.

Echoic Listening

Exploring an acoustical perspective of the below, my attention has been drawn to the particular movements and expressions that align the underground and aboveground in a relational mirroring. In following these relations, the lines that separate the two might be said to demand deeper recognition of how they come to cross-fertilize, extending into tensions that carry cultural and political stakes. This cross-fertilization, interlocking below with above, can be understood according to what les UX calls "biodiversity." As a tactic, biodiversity seeks to proliferate multiple strands of life, drawing out plurality from the seeming opposition that often keeps center and margin polarized. In contrast, les UX cultivates the clandestine as a productive force within established culture; to encircle the above with the below.

The echo, as a sound that expands according to the acoustical dynamics of a given space, can be heard as a proliferating multiplication—a splintering of the vector of sound into multiple events, turning a single sound into a mise-en-scène of audible figures. It disorients the origin, supplanting the sound source with an array of projections and propagations. It mirrors back while also fragmenting any possibility of return.

This ontology of the echo, as I'm suggesting, partially makes unintelligible the original sound. In this way, it operates as an acousmatic event that has the particular effect of "decentering" focus. This effect of decentering as I'm drawing out here is also found in Chion's examination of film sound. As a sound effect, decentering shifts the focus away from the text, the dialogue, and toward the mise-en-scène. In doing so, it creates something "decidedly polyphonic," to ultimately give "the feeling that the world is not reduced to the function of embodying dialogue."[47] Decentering fragments the commanding energy of the text, as a galvanizing and determining focus, to bring forward an entire scene. Such an effect begins to describe the resounding splintering enacted by the echo. Decentering, origin and horizon enfolded, a bifurcation leading to biodiversity, the echoic recasts the single voice into haunting duplication.

The echo, as an underground sonic figure, gives way to enlarging the possibility of imaginative transformation; shifting our cognitive focus away from the text and toward an acoustical dynamic ultimately makes unsteady, through a mesmerizing shift in clarity, the movements of meaning. In doing so, the echo is a strategy for resistance and rebellion—a sonic mirroring to the point of defusing the reign of established culture. The echo performs as an acoustic bomb, exploding the vector of time, of relations, and of origins, for other perspectives.

Thinking through the echoic underground, I am led to recall the particular historical situation of the Second World War, where resistance fighters in Warsaw gathered and organized actions using the sewer tunnels of the city. Occupying these tunnels, the resistance came to partially withstand German troops not only by relying on local knowledge and the inherent darkness of the tunnels, but also through an acoustical sensitivity. Following the movements of German troops aboveground, the resistance was able to organize actions, countering the above territorial occupation with a set of underground attacks. In the sewers, the Polish fighters came to occupy the mesmerizing conditions of the echoic—*to inhabit the multiplication of perspectives so as to multiply their chances for survival*. In turn, German troops attempted to track the resistance below ground by also tuning into the echoes and reverberations that passed through the tunnels, and which might come to reveal the movements of underground organization.[48] Thus, an acousmatic sonority passed from above to below, and back again, to aid in spying and counter-spying, tracking and attacking, defining the city as a vertical territory and the ground a line broken by the echoic. To catch a sound, to concentrate the ear, there within or against the dark tunnel below, brings forward unsteady anticipation—sound in this regard might be the prescient announcement of what shall eventually come forward, into plain view, to spawn fear of the unknown or hope for the future.

2

HOME: ETHICAL VOLUMES OF SILENCE AND NOISE

Let me go home
I've had my run
Baby, I'm done
I gotta go home
Let me go home
It will all be all right
I'll be home tonight
I'm coming back home

—Michael Bublé

The house, even more than the landscape, is a "psychic state," and even when reproduced as it appears from the outside, it bespeaks intimacy.[1]

—Gaston Bachelard

In which silence and noise meet to open up a larger history related to prisons, interiority, and home life, and eventually reveal the relational antagonisms that keep them together.

Racing through the wet streets, bags slung over my shoulders and shoelaces untied, trying not to trip as I make my way through the crowd, past numerous faces and other shoes that also, in a frenzied movement, shuffle their way to other destinations; and finally, arriving, out of breath, a little sweaty, with a chocolate bar stuffed into my coat pocket for later, to finally slump back into the chair, with the other passengers, as the doors close and the train pulls out of the station. I am on the Heathrow Express bound for the airport, late for the flight but soon there, with everyone else, to

45

enter into the dull chaos of airport life, but first, a small rest staring out the window . . . When at this moment, my mobile phone rings out, and I scurry, past the chocolate bar and the bags, to get the phone, and upon answering it, I hear my father's voice, just checking in and seeing how the trip went, how the days are going . . . And there, on the Express on this rainy day, chatting away to my father and telling the story of this and that, when suddenly the man next to me, well, not next to me, but sort of at an angle and on the other side, is gesturing to me, at least at first I doubt it, but then increasingly I realize as he seems to grow more agitated, more determined. He is holding his finger up into the air pointing to a sign and insisting that I take notice, and then I understand, I am sitting in the Quiet Carriage of the Express, the one allocated for non-mobile phone use, and without radio or TV announcements, a carriage designated free of excess noise or information, a carriage for the quiet humdrum of the train tracks and the daydreaming of passing landscapes and tiny thoughts. And there I am chatting away on the phone, unaware of my annoyance to others, especially this man, with the finger in the air and the pained and insistent facial expression.

I want to start here, with this narrative, and more so, with this finger: the finger comes to impart in its unmistakable movement so much meaning—it makes a command which brings forward and knots together questions of bodies, space, and what I refer to as the *ethical volumes of silence and noise*. I start with the finger, also, because it is so clear and insistent—a single gesture carrying all the intensity and urgency of a body on the verge of violence (the finger is the first in a series of movements that can easily result in a fist). But I like this finger, because in its pointing, it also points to what I want to explore, that is, the difficult movements of noise, the longing for home, and the forces that place emphasis on quiet.

In its sudden appearance, the finger performs a demand that I hang up the phone and respect the auditory lines as they are placed here, in this carriage, between these bodies. I start with the finger then as a gesture on the way to and around silence. The finger conjures in its movement, its insistence, through a form of sign language, an entire set of meanings that places noise on the side of disturbance and that constructs, in the moment of its appearance, a radical relational play. Against the finger I am immediately out of line. Soon the other passengers take notice, witnessing the wagging finger as a shared signal against the unabashed display of thoughtless behavior I'm unknowingly performing.

It is my sense that silencing comes to perform a sort of *domesticating* arrest onto the dynamics of the social, and the subsequent movements, expressions, and idiosyncrasies at the heart of being among others: to tame, to relegate, and to constrain through a notion of social respect and consideration the forces always already within the social. While noise rises up as an index of movements and bodies, as a register of unlicensed behavior, silencing may form an index for the limits of particular social climates. An auditory geography exists then within the very meeting or interweaving of noise and silence, forming a continual articulation of what is permissible.

Following this contentious weave, I would propose that in our exposure to noise and silence we in turn confront questions of place and placelessness, of domestic rootedness and urban transience. As the finger reveals, my noisy articulations are only challenged according to the place in which they occur—the finger points to the sign and not to me directly, implicating my noise within the demarcated zone of the Quiet Carriage. Therefore, I am subject to arrest through the logic of *place*, and what appears *out of place*. From this perspective, noise by definition is that sound which occurs *where* it should not. It finds its way in, to disrupt the particular setting. The commands of silence and silencing then are place-based concepts, applied to situational events and architectural spaces: though a certain sound may always disturb wherever it occurs, it gains in specificity when located and brought into relational play. Such instances can be found within histories of noise abatement policy, and related governmental research on the question of noise pollution. Within this sphere the question of noise is immediately followed by issues pertaining to urban planning, housing, and environmental health, firmly locating noise within the geographic. It is just such a weave of issues that leads my ear to hear in noise and silence the spaces of the home, and the lingering reverberations of community life.

Interiors

I want to follow the tensions of silence and silencing, incorporating this into an auditory study of everyday life, and in this case, to use the weave of silence and noise as a lens to address the conditions of home. In addition, to extend the home across the spatial imagination overall, as an architectural heart for understanding other dwellings and situations. Might the finger already signal a form of domesticating authority, that brings forward memories of reprimand to ultimately condition how one locates oneself within, and also listens to, the world around?

Coming up from underground, surfacing from the depths, my attention turns to the home — exposed to the challenges of city life, to the tensions of so many underground experiences, of the disorienting echo, the home can be appreciated as a counter-balance to the dynamics of exposure. The experience of coming home gives us comfort and reprieve from the demands of the exterior world. To pull off the shoes, make a tea, and sit back on the sofa defines the home as a soft space for quiet moments and relaxing comfort. It is where we sleep, falling into the softness of bed and the tiny sounds of the night outside. This image of home of course has many versions, yet it lingers as the very place for the cultivation of privacy, and the related interiority of individual and family caring. It operates as a space of physical safety, an image of comfort, to extend the security and stability found in notions of homeland. To be home is to belong; to reside within the greater fold of nationhood. One tries to make home, to feel at home, seeking the domestic as fulfillment of that particular longing *to come home*. Home weaves together the idea of place with belonging: to return home is to retrieve the locus of one's first experiences.

In contrast to these projected ideals, mobility, transience, and homelessness become signs of transgression against the stability of the ordered home. To leave home is to break the bonds of family and community while also fulfilling a vision of progress, of familial extension. Further, the homeless body ruptures the lines between domestic interior and public exterior by placing acts of dwelling onto spaces of social gathering and public experience. To live in a city park is to dislocate the deep social and psychic mechanism of home life. By extension, migration, asylum seeking, and the refugee unsettle governing borders of a nation, lending to the illegal status of the alien far from home. "To the very extent that the nation has been made to seem more 'homely' to its inhabitants in the recent historical period, those such as refugees who are nationless are made to seem all the more homeless."[2] Even against the contemporary movements and complex mobility of globalized society, home figures as an unshakable core of stable living and an expression of shared values: the home might be glimpsed as a syntax for commonality, placed in contrast to the verve of urban life and all its differentiating fragments. To come home then is to go inside.

Feeling at home, making home, arriving home, homeward bound . . . The sphere of domestic space is a key geographic point within the movements and energies of everyday life. For most it is the singularly fixed space from which everything else circulates; a base from which one proceeds into the world, and to which one regularly returns. The home might be said to "regulate" the ebb and flow of one's activities, providing a key spatial reference from which all other perspectives on worldly contact might draw. As Gaston Bachelard notes, the home is a fixed yet potent concept against which all other spaces are balanced and experienced, an archetypal image generating an array of psychic projections.[3] It is understandable that the home then comes to harness the very idea and construction of interiority, helping to shape the less material forms of a private life. The home as a projected stable site, as a coordination and organization of the flows and ruptures inherent to everyday life, to the destabilized core of the self, expresses interiority by becoming an intimate reflection of life and its private rituals. The home is an emotional space balanced on orderly refinement, from the chair one sits in every evening to the favorite cup. It promises that all things find their place, and relations stabilize around a set of shared values, rituals, and performances— that one can in fact always *go home*. Such dynamic carries in it a set of complex and contradictory realities, marking the home as an extension of homeland, as the site of a social morality, as a boundary by which citizenship, ownership, and social acceptance are located. The "broken home" then becomes a tragedy of great complexity.

Interior life and the development of the private within Western society run parallel to the evolution of domestic space, as a refined sphere of the immediate family. The production of the home is intimately linked to the bourgeois conception of privacy, interweaving middle-class affluence with a steady withdrawal from the full complexity and intermixing of everyday experiences. Charles Rice, in his engaging study of domesticity, proposes that "For the bourgeoisie, dwelling became divided from work, and in this division, the conditions for the emergence of the domestic interior were made possible [in the 19th century]."[4] The making of home came to counter-balance the increased functionality of the work sphere and the intensified abstractedness to modern labor. As Bachelard suggests, the home as a "psychic state" resonates with the deep fullness of an intimacy born from quiet enjoyment and the pleasures of daydreaming. The aura of this intimacy surrounding Bachelard's home is just such a reservoir set off from the growing densities and social weave that was to shift the dynamics of emotional life. Against the growing metropolis, and the intensities of modern labor, the home became a place for alternative productions, outside or against the modern commodity—a place for re-establishing a psychic center. Domestic space became a haven, refined through object collecting, interior design, furnishing, and a general spatial ordering that might renew a feeling for the material world. As Rice suggests, "Objects as commodities could be wrenched from circulation, freed from the drudgery of being 'useful,' becoming embedded in the interior to produce a conscious, 'new nature' of domesticity . . ."[5]

The transforming effect of the home extended beyond the role of objects to that of family relations: might the home as a space for the perpetuation of patriarchal structures be seen as a further counter-balance to the work place, as site where masculinity was often put under duress by the strict hierarchy of bourgeois production? To return home from work was then to play out a renewed form of male ordering, further articulating the patriarchal regulation of worldly trade and manufacturing. Such counter-balancing finds continual expression throughout the twentieth century, with the experience of family life increasingly relocated to the peripheries of urban indus-try and the spaces of economic production. Suburban life is the completion of a long evolution of the home, and the concept of interiority, with the modern tract home acting as a logical sanctuary to the urban milieu with all its simultaneous relations, experiences, and demands.

In these domestic constructions, the maintenance of a clear set of values is expressed in the ordering of landscape, homely artifice, and the rhythms of coordinated organization. Family life is a ritualized production whose scheduling of fixed meals, agreed upon distractions and entertainments, and weave of shared experiences might be said to *make home*. This of course is not without its challenges as well as frustrations. The home is an activity in continual development that brings many important pleasures and comforts as well as difficult labors. What it aims for is regulated by the notion or image of the individual or family unit, and the expression of values contained therein. In this way, the home gains identity by reflecting back to those who occupy its spaces a set of meaningful expressions. Designing the home then is immediately reflective of needs that are physical as well as psychological and emotional. Such perspective carries within it a sense for auditory clarity, where order is equated with quiet, and the maintenance of domestic life with audible regulation. To come home is to seek refuge, however consciously, from the uncontrollable flows of noise and the harangue of the exterior. Following the move-ments of this domestic imaginary, the home is heard as a set of signals whose disruption suggests breakdown, neglect, or invasion.

In the weave of self and sound the home might be said to function as an elaborated "sonorous envelope" keeping safe, or functioning to replicate, an imaginary or primary aural warmth.[6] The home literalizes the physical and emotional needs of individual or family life, extending the wants and needs of an interior self to domestic space—*home is where the heart is* needs to be taken quite literally. Yet the home is also where the ear is, and where the tensions between comfort and disruption are put in the balance. Domestic life, as an activity or labor projecting a sort of private syntax, forms an elaborate emotional geography—even within a single room all things conspire as a unifying gesture to give shape to the ebb and flow of everything just behind the skin. The home is then an extremely sensitive construction, which is revealed in the nuanced control of the domestic soundscape and its ultimate disruption.

Karin Bijsterveld's engaging account of modern noise, *Mechanical Sound*, reveals the degree to which the home featured as a dramatic stage for auditory conflicts. In a chapter on domesticity in particular, Bijsterveld charts the intensification of noise found within the modern home, and how, in literally extending the borders of domestic space, the sounds of home became a legislative issue. With the introduction of modern appliances at the beginning of the twentieth century, such as vacuum cleaners and sewing machines, along with newly installed heating and plumbing infrastructures, domestic spaces were suddenly rippling with new sonorities that brought neighbors into unexpected contact. Suddenly, the neighbor taking a shower created new intrusion onto one's space, giving way to new forms of connectivity. Yet it was the introduction of electronic entertainment devices, in particular gramophones, radio, and finally television, which were to play a crucial and defining role in not only refiguring home life, but in stimulating an array of noise abatement acts and policies. As Bijsterveld documents, one such instance occurred in Rotterdam as early as 1913, leading the city council to approve legislation allowing local government to "interfere in situations in which people caused nuisances by using loud gramophones."[7] Interestingly, the debate led to further challenges, as gramophone noise, and its related nuisance, turned into a discussion on class and family life. With its popularity and affordability, the gramophone was understood as an object of the working class, leading to the claim that such legislation was "an elitist form of noise abatement" and that workers should have the right to their own "sound culture."

The act of disturbing the neighbors developed into an elaborate network of legislative and social challenges. By bringing questions of domestic space and sound together, early noise abatement cases were met with the challenge of how to quantify and qualify sound— how to judge and define which sounds were bothersome and why. Such questions still resound within current debates and research being conducted throughout Europe on the question of noise control. For example, the UK study on "Quiet Homes for London" from 2004 was commissioned by the Greater London Authority as part of a general appraisal of noise in the city as well as "to investigate the feasibility of developing a Quiet Homes for London initiative." Drawing upon research done in the last 20 years, the study clearly indicates that domestic noise and "noisy neighbors" feature as one of the top two areas of complaint by the population. Material published in 2003 "suggested that neighbor noise annoyed 29% of the population sampled nationally, particularly in high density housing, in social and private rented housing, in deprived areas, and in more urban areas."[8] Such a cross section notably highlights the domestic as an auditory challenge, clearly aligning the density of urban living with the experience of noise disturbances. This is furthered by an earlier 1991 national study, which demonstrated that "of all the categories of environmental noise, noise from neighbors attracts the greatest proportion of objections relative to all the people who can hear it."[9] Though on one level obvious, this alignment makes for a complex issue when placed within the area of urban planning and noise abatement. How then to regulate the movements of urban noise without seeming to undermine the core condition the urban comes to offer as a social experience or community? If sound, as I would stress, provides a key relational means for registering social contact and feelings for place, how then to silence without arresting the coming of future community?

Suburb

Following these tensions surrounding noise abatement, and specifically, how home as a space comes to signify the possibility of peace and quiet, issues pertaining to silence surface in provocative ways. Though noise abatement is not necessarily aimed at establishing absolute silence, it nonetheless locates sound upon a scale that places value on quieter volume. Such a move stages the conditions, or the promise of silence as an acoustic horizon from which all sounds may gain greater depth and clarity. This also appears within the cultural practice of experimental music, and related philosophies of sound and listening. For instance, John Cage notably brought forward silence within his musical philosophy, figuring it as a vital space for expanded listening. Silence for Cage was "non-intentional" sound drawn out so as to let in what usually lies outside musical experience or expression. Silence appears then as a generative matrix for exposing the abundant materiality of sound. Such a perspective sets the stage for giving value to quiet environments, in which silence might be heard as the very basis for individual freedom.

If silence matters so greatly, then it is within the home that it gains intensity. I want to follow this weave, of domestic space and the movements of silence and noise, with the aim of shifting the acoustic horizon to include the very possibility that noise might in the end be extremely useful. To make such a claim I immediately admit a sort of personal trepidation, not so much in my feelings of urgency around the need to hear noise differently, but more in mixing disciplinary and discursive registers. Instantly, a confrontation occurs between pragmatic solutions to the environmental problem of noise and the philosophical stage by which noise comes to signify. Currently, my treatment of the issue stems mainly from questions of representation, or more, from an engagement with the imagination in *thinking noise*. From such a perspective though, I would still venture a claim onto the pragmatic territories of urban planning, housing development, and environmental policy. In investigating how houses and cities become dynamic soundscapes, I hope to give narrative to more positive versions of community noise that might in turn inspire other possibilities for building social and spatial relations.

The history of suburban development throughout the twentieth century (particularly in the US) grants further understanding onto these complexities, carrying in its progress an engrained understanding of silence and noise as conditioning agents to domestic and neighborhood life. As indicated in the "Quiet Homes for London" report, the noisy neighbor is a key player in debates pertaining to noise abatement, and a future policy for housing in the city. In response, participants in the 2003 survey made a provocative statement, "suggesting that housing estates be structured so those 'like' groups (e.g. families) live together, rather than in all age-mix."[10] While understandable in terms of searching for practical solutions to the noisy neighbor, such a view radically lends to a general social poverty, echoing the very core of suburban planning in seeking "like groups" in the formation of "community." Silence, in acting as a social ordering principle through which domestic life finds balance, comes to perform a homogenizing effect. Functioning as an imagined base for harmonious living, a quieter environment necessarily reshapes the possibilities for social interaction, characterizing "the other" as a noise always already breaking commonality. In this way, silence is a slippery ideal as it gathers within the imagination a set of seemingly positive values that when overlaid onto social behavior and community lends to understandings of place and placement a contentious intolerance.

Suburban housing developed rapidly in the 1950s in postwar America, and is identified by its tract homes and strip malls, all of which create an environment of separation—individualized, compartmentalized, self-contained. Suburban planning originally allowed distancing from the urban working environment, giving small families the chance for more "neighborly" atmospheres. In doing so, they also eliminated the complex experiences of social difference the city quickly provides. In this sense, the suburb could be glimpsed as a reactionary attempt at controlling or limiting the forceful dynamics of urbanism.

"With each crossing of the street, with the tempo and multiplicity of economic, occupational, and social life, the city sets up a deep contrast with small town and rural life with reference to the sensory foundations of psychic life."[11] Georg Simmel's observation that the urban is defined by an intensity of input, on numerous levels, is suggestive of the counter-balancing the domestic comes to perform: to filter out through a refinement of interior elements the ongoing dynamics of the metropolis. The city offers continual experiences of negotiation by supplying a steady flow of interference. Such interference fills the urban horizon with unexpected audition by enveloping the ear in an array of stimulating and complex sounds. In contrast, the suburb attempts to secure against the unexpected, audibly defining the boundaries of privacy in decibels:

> The Dayton Daily News reports that the Huber Heights (Ohio) City Council passed an amendment to the city's noise ordinance last week that restricts noise from car stereos, effective immediately. According to the article, the noise ordinance amendment stipulates that sound amplification devices cannot be "plainly audible" within 25 feet or more from a vehicle. The council believed the amendment will help police enforce the noise ordinance with respect to car stereos. Police had said that it was difficult to enforce noise limits on car stereos because the ordinance had defined a violation as any noise in excess of 80 decibels. City Councillor Jan Vargo said, "Summer's here, the windows are down, and this gives our police a perfect opportunity to enforce the new ordinance."[12]

Begun in 1956 by Charles H. Huber, Huber Heights is a collection of housing developments often called "America's largest community of brick homes" and may function as a model for the extensive development of suburbs in the US at this time. Key to suburban planning is the establishment of community life, which is understood as the free expression of common values. To maintain this, the suburb requires a set of design strategies, notably within street layout, for securing and controlling access. For example, developers over time revised the grid-layout of streets, as found in many North American cities, in favor of interrupted parallels (as in Huber Heights) and ultimately, loops and "lollipops" in which main boulevards are complemented by sets of residential streets ending in cul-de-sacs. The lollipop layout specifically dissuades free access by limiting the movements of the random passer-by. "These street patterns thwarted easy automobile access and created successively more self-contained, self-focused, and unconnected subdivisions that made it easier for residents to control their own space."[13] Separation, division, and clarity form the spatial expressions found within the suburb. This can be dramatically witnessed in the suburban development of Valencia, California.

Located north of Los Angeles, Valencia was started in the 1960s by the Newhall Land and Farm Company, and has grown considerably since, now with a population of more than 50,000 people. As a community, it is divided into distinct "Villages" or tracts each designating particular "lifestyles" catering to particular demographics. For instance, the Belcaro Village is designed for single-family homes for the elderly whereas Cheyenne Village is made up entirely of small condominiums. Through such design strategy, each Village is formed around a set of common attributes—"lifestyle" is taken literally so as to eliminate the chance for confrontation or disruption. Commonality found in the suburb operates as means for creating "neighborhood," as a controlled and safe environment.

Within such conditions, city noise ordinances are generally aimed at limiting volume levels at certain times of day according to zoning attributes. For example, noise levels in Valencia must not reach over 65 decibels during daytime and 55 decibels during nighttime within residential zones. Recently this has been supplemented to respond specifically to "loud party calls." In response to the 20 to 45 calls the police department receives during an average weekend period, two patrol cars (four deputies) are put on duty specifically to monitor and, if necessary, shut down loud parties. An amendment to the city ordinance from June of 2009 addresses this ongoing situation by giving police enforcement officers the right to cite the home-owner rather than the offending person. Such an amendment clearly indicates that most loud parties are thrown by teenagers specifically when parents are away. Previously, the teenager would be fined $200 for the disturbance without parents ever having to be informed. With the recent amendment, the fine is now directed to the actual homeowner, which no doubt alerts parents to their kids activities.[14]

The "loud party" clearly stages a confrontation between neighbors, leading to complaints, police involvement, and penalty. In this regard, the teenager in the suburb can be appreciated as a performative figure: while the suburb caters to a particular vision of adult community life, the teenager is left to occupy a left-over zone where boredom is often rife. In the "Village" teenage life often challenges the established and controlled codes of commonality by breaking the rules. (How often the suburban teenager seeks more challenging and stimulating experiences in the city.) In doing so, teenagers bring into relief the embedded structures that come to organize social life in the neighborhood. In Valencia, the 20 to 45 loud parties turn fun into a municipal issue, bringing noise into a neighborhood that, located in the quiet zone of the lollipop, partially neglects the emergence of their own future citizens. By emphasizing this tale of teenage angst found in the suburb, noise not only expresses a challenge to maintaining decibel levels, but importantly, to community life as an imagined stable signifier.

Dolores Hayden documents, in her *Building Suburbia*, how the intense surge of suburban development revealed a deep ideological divide in the early to mid-part of the twentieth century. As Hayden points out, "The postwar suburbs were constructed at great speed, but they were planned to maximize consumption of mass-produced goods and minimize the responsibility of the developers to create public space and public services" which radically reshaped the definitions of private and public.[15] The legacy of government policies surrounding housing in the US point towards a struggle between public loan programs and private developers, often pushing the issue onto the political spectrum as part of a general Cold War ideology. Public housing projects in the US have traditionally forced to the fore a contentious divide between those in favor of the private developer and those demanding equal housing for citizens through subsidized government projects. The suburbs dramatically embody these disparate views, bringing forward questions of community life, urban planning, and further, issues of race and gender by often strengthening existing social barriers and discriminatory practices. More often than not, the private developer won out, leading to a general neglect for poorer communities and significantly influencing what has become the American suburb.

As I have tried to suggest, noise is inexplicably connected to place, bound to the particular details of given situations. In this way, we might hear place and its related community life in the agitations and annoyances that noise inadvertently brings forward. Located within the suburb, noise registers the overall social environment, which as Hayden proposes, is also about the arguments surrounding public housing and private development. Often controlled by private developers, for instance, the Newhall Land and Farm Company in Valencia, suburban development carries forward understandings of "community" as "private" enclaves limited to specific people. In doing so, the suburb performs an unsteady demarcation onto forms of "public" expression, which in the case of auditory experience coalesces around the noisy neighbor.

To further understanding on how noise might elaborate a more productive version of community life, I want to turn to the work of Richard Sennett, and in particular his book *The Uses of Disorder*. According to Sennett, the suburb acts as a physical and psychological gatekeeper, seeking to withstand or resist all that might infringe upon the establishment of common good. It further lends support to a deep psychological shield that attempts to ward off the challenges posed by the intensities of social contact. In this sense, the suburb subscribes to a notion of community according to an appreciation or need for "sameness" or similarity. As Sennett elaborates, "A fear of the richness of urban society prevails in [. . .] the post-industrial suburbs of the middle class, and the family becomes a place of refuge in which the parents try to shield their children, and themselves, from the city."[16] Sennett suggests that such a condition marks the suburb as a problematic model of community life; by eliminating the experience of intense difference, the suburban model removes opportunities for widening appreciation for other ways of life. Sennett further explores such questions in his *The Conscience of the Eye*.[17] Examining modern urbanism, he offers a compelling historical analysis of the home as a site for the negotiated meeting of internal psychologies and the external world. In Western cultures, the home has come to replace the church as a sanctuary from the diversity and intensities of street life; it is in the home that the modern individual seeks refuge, clarity, and moral conscience. As earlier stated, the space of domestic life flows as an ordered functionality through which interior states are further organized and duplicated. Yet such spatial divisions, according to Sennett, removes one from the important discoveries that come with public inter-actions and social negotiations. The retreat to the home historically initiates a spatial emphasis on interiority, which turned one's glance inward, creating a general psychological unease at exterior distur-bance resulting in greater forms of social division. If one progressively finds definition according to an increasingly reduced home experi-ence, the ability to find fluid exchange within the dramatic flux of social space inevitably leads to anxiety over *going outside*. What Sennett pulls from this is a contrasting vision for what constitutes community life. Accordingly, "communities" are only born from the experience of confronting one and another, as bodies already *out of place*. Communities that otherwise place limits, or that wipe away such opportunities, solidify into empty forms of commonality. As a counter-measure, Sennett finds productive value in *disorder*—rather than seek commonality in the form of sameness, the disordering impingement of social differences may grant neighbors fruitful contact in shaping and continually modeling relations.

The version of community life mapped out by Sennett begins to expose a number of possibilities for shifting the acoustic horizon, and modulating the ethical volumes of silence and noise. Rather than remove opportunities to interact with and experience difference and deviation, to enter the naturally destabilizing milieu of the social, Sennett proposes "to permit the freedom of deviation would be to care about the unknown, the other, in social contacts."[18] Might noise, as a deviating sonority, grant opportunity for meeting the other, to afford a productive instant of exchange in the making of community life?

Initially, I want to follow this up by suggesting equilibrium between the concepts of *noise* and *difference*, as elements that, according to Michel Serres, appear as the coming of change:

All of a sudden, without warning, the noise, a noise coming from the sky, a sound like that of the wind when it blows hard. It is produced locally, in a single direction and soon it fills the space, the whole space. In an unforeseeable fashion, it passes from the local to the global. It was a noise, a sound. It was an event in a corner of the system; it penetrates, invades, and occupies the whole house. It was heard; it is seen. They saw it appear. The noise is a chance occurrence, a disorder, and the wind is a flow.[19]

Following Serres, noise is a disordering bolt, the rending of a system, and at the same time, a beginning—"It is the beginning and the transformation; and it is in such a way that systems change order so easily." *Beginning and transformation*, noise fills space with so many instances of contact that blow in from all corners—it gives continual input into the making and ongoing modulation of a common language.

Noise in this sense is also the beginning, rather than the end, of communication, staging, as Alphonso Lingis suggests, "that last moment when all we have to say to one another ends in the silence and death of the one to whom it has to be said and in the speechlessness and sobs of the one who has come to say something."[20] The ethical volume passing across what needs to be said, what can no longer be said, and what inevitably leaves one in the noisy breaking of sobs, delivers an experience whose pain is also the beginning of care. Against the speechlessness found in approaching that which is outside (of the known, of language, of the common), to make a noise—*to sob, to laugh, to say, "I am . . ."*—is to initiate a beginning, to mark a point. I want to retain this point as the social contract noise might be understood to instigate: in disturbing you, I also create a space for knowing each other in the extreme. Noise might be said to truly make us visible.

To return to the suburb, it can be seen how the suburb attempts to harmonize by creating stable frames, countering the verve and unsteady dynamic of which social life consists. "Now, people refuse to grant worth to that which is shifting, insecure, or treacherous, and yet this is exactly what the diversity in society is built of."[21] From that screaming drunk outside my window at night to the ceaseless background music of numerous shops, noise performs as a stranger to which I must always face. In this regard, noise may offer productive input into community life by specifically disrupting it. Causing disorder, noise grants opportunity to fully experience the other, as someone completely outside my experiences, which in Valencia might be the teenager next door.

As the Huber Heights ordinance reveals, noise occupies the divide between pain and pleasure, placing a demand on the regulation of public space. It stands out, and in doing so it puts into play various devices of measurement. Noise suddenly makes sensitive the distance between you and I, which in this regard calls forward the discernment of the listening cop. The 25-feet rule in Huber Heights marks a territory against which quiet and common good *and* noise and unlawful behavior interact. Tuning the ear to the sound source, noise may cause trouble by bringing forward a challenge to the permissible, drawing a hard line between sameness and difference.

Sennett's ongoing dedication to reversing the suburban trend, both as an architectural project as well as a mental image of a good life, forges a productive link between spatial experience and the experiences of social life. Recognizing the home as site for the production and reproduction of understandings of sharing—the divisions enacted within the home function as microcosms for what one expects from social life—opens up a critical gap in the acoustical seal: how does silence and noise intersect across the material plane of social life and the philosophical terrain of acoustical thinking? And how might these intersections generate another vocabulary for engaging the shortcomings of urban planning as well as those of acoustical practices?

Prying open the enclosed sphere of the suburban home, Vito Acconci's project *Talking House* (1996) relocates the private onto the street. Placing a series of microphones throughout a home located in Santa Barbara, California (for the "Home Show II" exhibition organized by the Santa Barbara Contemporary Arts Forum), *Talking House* provides a sudden glimpse onto the average conditions of home life found in this idyllic neighborhood. Walking past the house one could hear conversations taking place in the kitchen, or residents brushing their teeth preparing for bed, or the still quiet of an empty home. Amplified through speakers set in the front yard, Acconci makes the home come to life, letting all that usually remains within to spill out: "Talk within the privacy of one's own home goes, now, away from home. The walls don't have to have ears: it's as if the walls burst open, as if the house bursts with talk, as if the house blows up and talk blows out of the house."[22] Bursting out, *Talking House* is a splayed interior, laying its content on the front lawn for all the neighbors to hear. In this way, the work provides a key transgression and alteration of the very notion of home: if the domestic is predominantly governed by an image of interiority, a cultivation of the private individual or family, *Talking House* literally gives voice to the desire to hear what shouldn't be heard—and in doing so, to undo the domestic image. Turning it up, bursting the seams with amplification, home media comes to not only bring the outside in, through televisual and medial input, but to also force the inside out. Acconci queries the domestic by inserting microphones deep into its spaces, asking: "What does a house want, what does a house want to say?"[23] What eventually does spill out might be heard to give answer, as a form of *talking back*, making Acconci's version of domesticity a fugitive sound.

Debates surrounding noise pollution, and related legalities pertaining to health standards, in seeking to achieve a quieter environment generally come to mirror particular moral regimes that locate deviant behavior as inherently *out of place*; the designing of quieter neighborhoods, as a civic project, partly positions noise on the side of violation, linking outspokenness, objection, and social difference to forms of audible excess and annoyance. Therefore, to minimize, cut off, and define limits, in volume, vibration, and leakage, orders the home and related neighborhood as insulation from the other, thereby locating notions of quiet within the maintenance of domestic stability. Though lending to the thoughtful quest for more humane audible environments, silence paradoxically supplies the mechanics of social values with a vocabulary of control and constraint. From fear of contamination, deviant behavior, and physical damage to a desire for communicational clarity, peace and quiet, in playing out within, around and against domestic life, exposes the acoustic horizon of the home as a play of conflicting emotional, psychological, and social registers. The poetical plenitude of Bachelard's domestic visions, that house of daydreaming, must be heard to also carry within them repressed struggles that make the home a site for teenage angst, domestic violence, and sleepless nights. Acconci's *Talking House* supplies the domestic imagination with an audible break, performing that noise Serres so cherishes as *beginning and transformation*.

IMAGE 6 Acconci Studio, *Talking House*, Home Show II, Santa Barbara, CA, 1996.

IMAGE 7 Acconci Studio, *Talking House*, Home Show II, Santa Barbara, CA, 1996.

Prison

In following silence and noise as spatial and ethical volumes, it can be heard how they put into play an economy of power, placing notions of community, law, and nuisance upon an audible register. In doing so, they also bring forward the question of dwelling. Sited against home life, silence and noise contour the exchanges that come to pass between inside and outside, lending input into social balance and the emergence of community. To extend this constellation—*this territorial antagonism*—I want to expand upon silence as it influences or directs other instances of dwelling. From here I hope to enlarge the critical debate surrounding noise.

As seen in the suburb, silence circulates as a projected constraint so as to support the development of a "positive community": to ensure not only quiet but also to counter the degrading influence noise might effectively enact. *To separate out, to ward off, to contain* . . . Such operations can in turn be glimpsed in the institution of the prison.

The history of prisons carries forward a set of political, social, and philosophical values. These values find embodiment in the technological regulation of the incarcerated body and its related spatial situation: the prison is an elaborate apparatus for treating, monitoring, punishing, and rehabilitating the criminal body; it comes to make concrete, through such mechanics, the forms by which law and crime meet to interweave in an elaborate choreography of controlled and timed movements.

Michel Foucault's invaluable study of the prison details this disciplinary functionality, recognizing it as deeper elaboration of a larger system. "The prison has always formed part of an active field in which projects, improvements, experiments, theoretical statements, personal evidence and investigations have proliferated."[24] Such continual working and reworking underscores the prison as a project aligned with a history of mechanistic rationality intrinsic to incarceration and the very question of social ordering. The prison, in anticipation of criminality and social rupture, expresses the ingredients of a deep cultural will, legislated through the courts and articulated spatially. The prison brings forward the full intensity of an ideological mechanics operating through an "omni-disciplinary" subjection.

The development of the American prison system, as an example, is replete with reforms designed to care for the criminal body, through structures that attempt to turn time into productive labor. In doing so, prison reform is an endless scenario aimed against making life behind bars a breeding ground for crime, as a space that paradoxically comes to nurture the criminal community. To do so, the prison functions to precisely measure and control the degree to which prisoners not only transform into socially ordered individuals but also, and importantly, come to interact, share information, and cultivate criminal bonds. As spaces of incarceration, the prison thus separates on a number of levels: to separate criminals out from society as a whole, to separate criminals within the prison itself according to the rank of the crime, and finally, to separate prisoners from each other on a cellular and individual level. This perspective ultimately resulted in the establishment of the single cell system, which was first developed in the 1770s in the US, and which is based on the belief that crime can be dramatically controlled by isolating prisoners from each other.

Initiated at the newly constructed Auburn prison in upstate New York in 1817, the project of segregating prisoners from each other in individual cells was instituted specifically as a means for controlling the circulation of criminal culture. Whereas prior models of prison architecture, notably at Newgate in New York City, were designed around communal spaces, usually with levels of criminality determining the location of prisoners, the Auburn style completely restricted opportunities for interaction to working hours, when prisoners would undertake small manufacturing or labor projects. Even these larger rooms were surveyed by officers who stood behind walls with slits cut into them so as to monitor the prisoners at all times. "The Auburn reformers appear to have been motivated by practicality and a passion to construct a veritable machine to subdue and make self-supporting the occupants of the prison."[25]

Yet physical isolation was not the sole means of containing and controlling interactions. Taking one step further, Auburn instituted its "silent system" in 1821 whereby silence was to be maintained at all times: there was to be absolutely no talking among prisoners. As the board of inspectors of the prison stated with great zeal:

> Let the most obdurate and guilty felons be immured in solitary cells and dungeons; let them have pure air, wholesome food, comfortable clothing, and medical aid when necessary; cut them off from all intercourse with men; let not the voice or face of a friend ever cheer them; let them walk their gloomy abodes, and commune with their corrupt hearts and guilty consciences in silence, and brood over the horrors of their solitude and the enormity of their crimes, without hope of executive pardon.[26]

Silence in this regard functioned as an absolute form of surveillance, control, and isolation, to confine the criminal body not only behind walls but also within an entirely restrained environment. At night, sock-wearing guards would walk through the prison, listening for any clandestine whisper, hushed murmur, or subtle noise among the prisoners—even the smallest of sounds could be overheard by officers inside the completely quiet environment of the prison.

The functional mechanics of the Auburn prison expressed a larger moral ordering based on instituting personal reflection (within the isolated cells) while creating confined interaction in the form of strict productive forms of labor. The disciplined body of the prisoner was thus under continual surveillance, monitored not only according to the limits of the body and its actions, but also and importantly by their audible extension—voice, noise, shouts, ticks and taps, and other audible occurrence were violations leading to punishment.

IMAGE 8 Auburn State Prison, cell block, 1940s. Courtesy of Federal Bureau of Prisons.

An extended passage from Jack Henry Abbott's account of prison life, while occurring at a different prison and years after Auburn had been well-established, gives descriptive indication of such conditions, and also points toward the larger sweep of the Auburn system as it proliferated throughout the US prison system:

We enter a passageway between rows of heavy steel doors. The passage is narrow; it is only four or five feet wide and is dimly lighted. As soon as we enter, I can smell nervous sweat and feel body warmth in the air. We stop at one of the doors. He unlocks it. I enter. Nothing is said. He closes and locks the door, and I can hear his steps as he walks down the dark passageway. In the cell, there is a barred window with an ancient, heavy mesh-steel screen. It is level with the ground outside. The existing windowpanes are caked with decades of soil, and the screen prevents cleaning them. Through the broken ones I peer, running free again in my mind across the fields. A sheet of thick plywood, on iron legs bolted to the floor, is my bed. An old-fashioned toilet bowl is in the corner, beside a sink with cold running water. A dim light burns in a dull yellow glow behind the thick iron screening attached to the wall. The walls are covered with names and dates—some of the dates go back twenty years. They were scratched into the wall. There are ragged hearts pierced with arrows and the words mom or love or god—the walls sweat and are clammy and cold. Because I am allowed only my undershorts I move about to keep warm. When my light is turned out at night I would weep uncontrollably. Sixty days in solitary was a long, long time in those days for me. When the guard's key would hit the lock on my door to signal the serving of a meal, if I were not standing at attention in the far corner of the cell, facing it, the guard would attack me with a ring of keys on a heavy chain. Locked in our cells, we could not see one another, and if we were caught shouting cell to cell, we were beaten. We tapped

out messages, but if they heard our taps, we were beaten—
the entire row of cells, one child at a time.[27]

The silent system is a disciplinary silence designed to bear down on the body as the final mark of the law and to force the criminal into a state of deep solitude while quite often leading to insanity: the debates and ultimate design of the Eastern Penitentiary in Philadelphia in the 1820s pointed at Auburn's initial project of solitary confinement *without* labor (which results in absolutely no interaction) as an ultimate failure. This initial design of the Auburn prison was finally retracted in favor of solitary confinement *with* labor after prisoners underwent extreme psychological distress caused by the absolute separation and silence in which they were confined. Even the then governor of New York, Joseph C. Yates, was so appalled upon visiting the initial Auburn solitary confinement cells in 1823 the he pardoned all the confined prisoners and ordered the abandonment of the system.[28]

The extreme disciplining found in Auburn though ultimately was championed in spearheading prison reform in the nineteenth century, and came to act as a model for future design.[29] The possibility of insanity though lurked as an ever-present risk, as the silent system stripped the prisoners of any real social relation. From insanity one arrives in the padded cell, which is silence made complete by the removal of even the slightest of reverberation—the padded cell is an acoustically dead space, where even the movements of one's own body is void of echo. A silent space that aims to protect the body, with the straitjacket that further separates the individual from his or her own corporeality, the padded cell confines the body even from itself.

The mechanism at play within silencing initiates a challenging sonority for the ear, contorting and controlling the play of sound and voice as means for law and order, truth and accountability, to perform. It furthers the ever-trembling balance between violence and generosity by supplying the signifying gesture of silence with ideological weight, finding deeper expression in forms of torture. Blindfolding, depriving one of sleep, and beating, all operate across the spectrum of silence and silencing. This occurs not only through enforced silence, but also fundamentally through pain. "Physical pain is not only itself resistant to language but also actively destroys language, deconstructing it into the pre-language of cries and groans."[30] Whether to silence the body or to demand the body break its silence, forms of torture align sound and silence upon a difficult balance, eclipsing the right to silence and the right to speech with terrible force.

Power

Silence runs both ways: it functions as power in the arsenal of law and order to pin the body down while also providing means to speak without saying a word—to remain silent, to take the oath of silence, to refuse to utter, all perform within a repertoire of resistance and criminality. To respond to the silencing of interrogation, of arrest, with their own form of silence, that of refusal, the prisoner seeks to withstand the pressure—*to keep one's lips sealed*. By extension, the 5th amendment of the US Constitution allows individuals the right to refuse answering questions for fear of self-incrimination, and specifically dates back to earlier times in England where torture and coercion were regularly used to extract information. To withhold information appears as an instance within a lineage of silence and silencing aimed at the greater movements of legal and societal power dynamics, further underscored in the Miranda Law's "right to remain silent."[31] In this sense, silence actively performs within the dictates of law and order, aligned as part of constitutional rights and thwarted in times of violation in which the individual is forced to speak. Silence then operates throughout the system of law and order, crime and punishment, as a vital and complicated medium.

Adam Jaworski's detailed study of silence reveals the degree to which it participates in social behavior, lending to the dynamics of communication a notable and highly flexible signifying material. As Jaworski states, "It is my strong conviction that silence can sometimes signal that the channel of communication remains open, or that one has no intention of closing it, while speech would precisely have the effect of overtly terminating the possibility of further communication between participants."[32] Silence is then a productive material lever for allowing certain information or expressions to pass between oneself and another—it articulates while at the same time operating as a covert mechanism in the choreography of social exchange. We might also think of the *silent treatment*, as a tool in conveying strong emotional responses by explicitly holding the tongue. In other words, silence can forcefully communicate. Linguistically then it is not simply empty space between or around words, or pauses during conversation. Rather, it operates as a vehicle for modulating, contouring, and performing communicative gestures.

Extending the communicative power of silence, and the power in silencing, Althusser's theory of "interpellation" describes the relation of the individual and ideology through a narrative of voice. To unfold this relation, he uses the example of that moment when a voice calls out from behind, shouting "Hey, You There!" This call for Althusser stands out as the moment of becoming a subject; the instant of recognizing oneself as the receiver of this voice, without having seen the speaker, acts as an extensive mechanism within the function of ideology. The moment of recognition presupposes that one is already part of a social structure—"interpellating" that it is I being addressed, one follows an assumed script through which subjectivity is called forth. The "Ideological State Apparatus" Althusser names is thus always already incorporated into the psychic construction of the subject, so much so that "the individual *is interpellated as a (free) subject in order that he shall submit freely to the commandments of the Subject* [God, Law, etc.], *i.e. in order that he shall (freely) accept his subjection*, i.e. in order that he shall make the gestures and actions of his subjection 'all by himself'."[33]

Althusser's moment of interpellation—of "Hey, You There!"—calls us forward precisely by triggering an incorporated sense that one is always already beholden to the inscription of law and order. This voice on the street, the one that hails, carries the authority of Althusser's "Subject" with the big "S," subjecting the smaller "s" to the unconscious understanding that one is ready to be taken, before the voice ever calls out. I recognize myself, without ever having been unlawful in the strict sense, as already caught—the hailing voice provokes my stopping precisely because I am already waiting to be called. This moment fulfills an internal recognition of being not so much guilty, but ideologically already determined. The presumed authority found in this voice also functions within the movements of silencing, preceding and initiating the moment when we freeze, caught by the presence of an authority, which we, startled, have trouble answering and yet have already answered.

Silencing and silence intertwine in an unsteady and dynamic weave, where the positive effects of quieting down slip into the force-ful grip of arresting volume. In one and the same move it discloses the possibility of mutual sharing while foreclosing such sharing; I hang up the phone there on the train, and give space to the movements of this public environment, and yet how do such forms of behavior impart an elemental control onto the promise of individual presence? Silence seems to sculpt the social with an intrinsically moral hand even while aiming to give space to the promise of being together. In this way, to instigate calls for quieter environments might benefit from recognizing the full breadth of the acoustical field opened up by silence and noise; the imagined potential found in being quiet inadvertently carries forward projects not so far from silent systems, inculcating discrete mechanisms that automatically perform to call one into line.

Gated

Though the prison is certainly an extreme acoustical example, where silence performs against the incarcerated subject, it nonetheless offers insight onto the dynamics of sound as a *value system*. Might silence, as a figure of sonority, be understood to stake out a claim on the listening body—*to territorialize* by locating one's own noise within a language of disruption or annoyance?

To return to the suburbs, and the spaces of home, I want to map out an intersection between the architectures of prisons and those of domestic life. Though the suburb is in itself a seemingly innocuous phenomenon, offering opportunities for secure housing, community life, and family experience, it stitches together a complicated relation between "inside" and "outside." This can be notably glimpsed in the development of gated communities prevalent within the US and parts of Europe. Based on enclosing a given neighborhood or tract development within guarded boundaries to which one enters through security gates, gated communities represent a number of complicated ideas and relations. As Edward J. Blakely and Mary Gail Snyder map out in their informative *Fortress America*,

> Gated communities manifest a number of tensions: between exclusionary aspirations rooted in fear and protection of privilege and the values of civic responsibility; between the trend toward privatization of public services and the ideals of the public good and general welfare; and between the need for personal and community control of the environment and the dangers of making outsiders of fellow citizens.[34]

The gated community conflates the dynamics of security and the image of neighborhood life, aiming to clearly delineate, through an elaborate physical and psychological apparatus, inside from outside. They might be understood to bring home elements of prison architecture, fixing them to the structures of a given neighborhood. In doing so, gated communities inadvertently reverse the operations of security: by keeping some out, the gated community partially confines those who seek the imagined freedom found on the inside. In the gated community, "security is viewed as freedom, not just from crime but also from such annoyances as solicitors and canvassers, mischievous teenagers, and strangers of any kind, malicious or not."[35]

On the other side of prison, law and order come to rest upon the home, as a formal structure equipped with its own systems of control. Upon the home, and behind the gates, criminality and intrusion are anticipated, giving way to elaborate fortifications, fencing, and surveillance, from automated lights and video cameras to burglar alarms. Initially developed as a series of varying bell systems triggered by the breaking of door contact, which would alert the residents of intrusion, burglar alarms have evolved into digital systems controlled and monitored by specific security companies. As an audible trigger, the alarm signal serves to both scare-off those breaking and entering as well as alert neighbors that crime is in play. The silent alarm though leaves the burglar unaware, allowing law enforcement officers the chance to capture the crook "red handed." From the clattering and clanging of bells to digital pulses and rhythmic swoops of sound, the alarm is part of an arsenal of acoustic devices that signal alert, conveying warnings of impending threat and infusing the neighborhood with degrees of paranoia.

Alarm systems serve a multitude of purposes of which alerting to acts of burglary is but one. Throughout the early Industrial era the threat of large-scale fire spawned numerous systems for surveying cities and alerting local officials and fire brigades. Most of these early systems relied upon large cast iron bells suspended in watchtowers used to sound the alarm. Historically, bell signals were then not only used to communicate messages to local communities as to the functions of the Church and religious dates, but were also taken up within urban infrastructures of emergency signaling. For example, throughout the 1800s alarm signaling operated within the city of New York through the employment of a regiment of watchmen who walked specific districts in search of signs of fire, or were seated in built watchtowers to scan the city and ultimately ring the bell when a fire was observed. Often communication was difficult and fire fighters wasted precious minutes attempting to locate the fire, trying to follow the ringing of the bell and the various shouts from local residents. The Great Fire of 1835 in New York City was partially the result of such communicational inaccuracy. Though the fire was detected early on, the relaying of signals led to confusion: from alerting local watchmen, who then alerted the nearby bell tower resulting in the actual sounding of the alarm, which was but one signal in a chain of signals—the single bell would then be used to alert the main bell located at City Hall, and which would then be used to announce the fire to the fire brigades. Subsequently, fire fighters grew to discern each district's bell, being able to locate the fire through this subtle tonal difference. Many errors occurred through this system though, and "with multiple fires, the fire brigades could not help but resemble the Keystone Kops, racing in one direction then another, unable to locate any of the fires from the clamor of bells."[36]

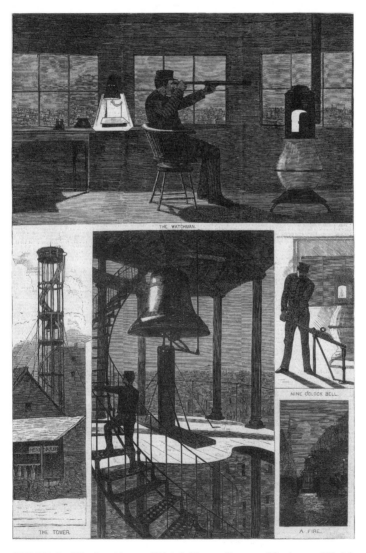

IMAGE 9 Winslow Homer, "Watch-Tower, Corner of Spring and Varick Streets, New York," from *Harper's Weekly*, New York, February 28, 1874. Reproduced courtesy of The Philadelphia Print Shop, Ltd., Philadelphia.

Against the threat of fire (which in the case of the 1835 fire destroyed seventeen blocks of Manhattan taking with it numerous residences), bell systems would progressively find their way onto the individual home in an array of warning systems and alarms. Electrical fire alarm systems, which were to replace the clamor of bells throughout the US and Europe in the 1840s and 1850s, greatly improved home alarms, employing electrical wiring and magnets to alert inhabitants, for instance, of a break-in. Placed upon the home, alarm systems weave together public alert with the security of private life. In this case, the home is perforated by the circulation of various signals and media, networking the domestic into a larger infrastructure of communication, entertainment, and security that cut into the home while monitoring such perforations.

The small audible moment of the doorbell further performs within a greater domestic history, where private life is seen to remain behind closed doors while being available, through the soft chiming, to the outside. The doorbell is triggered by the touch of a neighbor or stranger, as a request for direct interaction—*is anyone home?*—while also featuring as device for youthful tricks—*ding-dong-ditch* played by neighborhood kids who ring doorbells and run away, snickering at the appearance of a bewildered resident. The soft chime of the doorbell finds complement with the twin-bell alarm clock, which was located on numerous bedside tables (beginning in the late nineteenth century) to aid in the movements of a working day. Setting the alarm gives definite shape to the time of home life, sounding out to intentionally disturb one from sleep and announce the beginning of morning rituals. This audible ringing literally becomes a fixture in domestic life, accentuated further with the introduction of the telephone, whose bell ringing punctuates home life with a commanding signal. The phone calls out to be answered—*is someone going to get that?!* All such ringing no doubt plays out in the dreamtime of residents who start to imagine ringing in the head, in anticipation of the phone, the alarm clock, or the burglar alarm—*was that the doorbell?* The ringing bell alarm is thus a device that triggers one's attention, operating as a sounding fixture incorporated into domestic life and its functioning privacy.

The burglar alarm in particular (not to mention window bars and fences) functions within this perspective of the private home, in which domestic safety and security keeps some out while locking others in. (How often home security systems provide a way to restrict teenagers from sneaking out at night . . .) It creates an uncanny scenario by overlaying forms of security, and the physical attributes of prison systems, onto the soft space of the home, turning crime into a family issue. The sought after quiet of home life is thus ensured not only by physical and architectural material, but also by security systems attending windows and doors. Interiority is guaranteed through the implied presence of additional circuits that monitor the cracks and breaks of the home, those hinges that make the home a porous and vulnerable site. To sleep well then is based on a quiet interior that at any moment could burst forth in a chorus of haranguing bells and sirens, to jar one from dream. Such devices find completion in the gated community, in which security is embedded into the very foundations of a neighborhood.

Acoustic Community

Silence and noise circulate as sonorous material as well as conceptual structures; they operate as extreme points on the sonic spectrum, filling the imagination with powerful imagery as to the dynamics of auditory experience. To experience pure silence or to endure the magnitude of an absolute noise would be to reach the edges of perception. Within this range there are of course a multiplicity of ways to understand and appreciate silence and noise, and while I have chosen to locate them within an "acoustic politics" I recognize this as one of many possible perspectives. Ultimately, in underscoring silence and noise in this way I hope to supplement discussions on noise as environmental nuisance, which for my ear calls out for more complex and nuanced consideration.

For instance, the notion of "acoustic violence" mapped out by Federico Miyara, and others, comes to circulate through many discussions on noise pollution and noise abatement. Miyara, a researcher from Argentina and organizer of many conferences on the subject of acoustics and environmental noise, puts forth "acoustic violence" to describe how sound comes to threaten by imposing an abusive volume onto the everyday. As he states, "Acoustic violence is just violence exercised by means of sound. Often, such sound will be loud noise, but it might also be the neighbor's music going through the party wall or the constant hum of a busy city late in the night while one is trying to sleep."[37] Drawing parallels between sound and violence is not far from my own project here, and while Miyara aims to lend critical insight onto this relation he does so by locating acoustic violence within a hard moral frame. This of course is important, for violence and related suffering demands clear response. Yet, on the level of language and related discussion, it strikes me that to counter acoustic violence one must in turn think through politically all that is at stake. Miyara makes the rather simple formulation that "noise is a form of acoustic violence" without ever considering how silence might also perform violently. Further, noise, as he proposes, signals a form of abusive power on the part of audio companies, who support louder and more harmful noise levels. Yet his general call for countering "the endless din of a modern and acoustically sick society"[38] falls drastically short in reflecting upon how a legislative policy against noise itself wields a form of power that may neglect the specificity of a given noise.

To follow this further, I want to detour through the ideas of Emmanuel Levinas. His extremely sensitive examination of "responsibility" and "justice" may provide input onto the issues by shifting from the moral to the ethical.[39] Levinas' ethical philosophy begins with the simple understanding that the human begins in the responsibility *for* the other. In this regard, the opening up of the self occurs only in relation to a meeting with another: I am constituted as a subject in the relational instant of standing *face-to-face* with the one who is apart from me. This primary moment though, as a beginning, also incites a form of violence or rupture onto the scene: to confront the other is to also be called into responsibility from which one cannot turn away. This narrative of the beginning of the subject is then an act that initiates the possibility for finding commonality yet only in the rending operations of difference or otherness. I must face up to the other as a forceful demand—the presence of the other subjects this body to a form of inscription through which I in turn discover myself, as a subject. In this sense, we are *hostage* to the other. As Dr. Michael Smith elaborates, "The other is always greater than I, and my responsibility cannot be transferred to anyone else." Thus, I am bound to the other so much so that "this responsibility extends to and includes responsibility for the evil perpetrated against me!"[40]

Interestingly, for Levinas the ethical encounter, as the impossibility of turning away, is considered as an attempt to also deal with violence. Inside the rupturing *face-to-face* encounter lies the possibility for overcoming any form of totality (as in totalitarian rule) so as to leave open the infinite. It is through responsibility that we remain perpetually open and beholden to the other, as a process that also runs both ways: the *face-to-face* is a dialogical passing by which responsibility is held between, within, and against one and another.

Levinas' thinking gives much to suggesting a shift to understanding where responsibility forms, and how justice might appear. Rather than lay responsibility on the other, in moments of seeking justice, Levinas' thinking explores a relational interaction, relocating responsibility and justice within a complex ethical weave by which understanding and change are continually set in motion, as a shared project.

To return to the question of "acoustic violence," I want to open up and multiply possibilities for hearing noise. What I detect in Miyara's ideas is a shutting down of the political, which ultimately highlights the need to further discover a language for truly investigating the (acoustical) problems of society. That is, in performing his own recommendations for how to counter the growing trend of modern environmental noise, Miyara comes to cast a sort of "universal" net across the issue of noise—*is acoustic violence so easily identified and fixed?* As I have tried to show, noise is not *only* environmental disturbance. Rather, it remarkably provides a key experience for the establishment of an acoustic community *in the making*. "Acoustic" here should be emphasized as not only sounds that come to circulate through a particular situation, but importantly, a relational exchange where sound is also voice, dialogue, sharing, *and* confrontation. Following Levinas, the ethical encounter is what makes possible acts of responsibility—*to become a subject*. Though noise in the environment might be heard as an act of irresponsibility on the part of others, it also supplies a rich encounter for the making of responsibility; noise creates a forceful chance for understanding the flows of power as they move in and out of the home, as part of the intensities of listening. As Chantal Mouffe suggests, the ability to think politically today might be found not in a presumed notion of resolve, in consensus, but in recognition of the political as a process that always involves or requires the tensions of confrontation, the prolongation of an uncertain language, and the ongoing dislocation of the assumptions of a liberal perspective. For Mouffe, liberalism falls short of truly investing in thinking politically by adhering to a "rationalist belief in the availability of a universal consensus based on reason."[41] Rather than support the enhancement of pluralism, which would retain at its core an appreciation for what she terms the "agonistic dimension," liberalism turns away from the political. That is, to continue to engage politically requires an ongoing responsibility for the demands of the other, which may actually make noise a dramatically important platform for renewing political subjectivity and community today.

The equalization and reduction of loud volumes, while aiding in improving health conditions for populations (and in this regard, I hold out much respect for Miyara), runs the risk of subscribing to a model of relations defined by the idea of *keeping it down*. As I've tried to show, silence and silencing are in themselves acoustically violent, and the threat of noise often a vehicle for mobilizing extreme ordering that seeks or maps onto the social a powerful mechanism of control. Might the intensities of listening be used to promote not only the awareness of noise to harm, but also the vitality by which we may come to relate?

As a point of reference, the work of the Positive Soundscapes Project offers a valuable alternative to the question of environmental noise.[42] Established as a research project among artists, academics, and scientists in the UK, the Project is based on trying to encourage more positive understanding of how sound participates and complements experiences of public life. It tries to counter the often-negative understanding and language of acoustic engineers and city departments when discussing noise. In its place, the Project aims to create a more "holistic" understanding of how sound participates as a vibrant ingredient within community life. Through multiple strands of research, practical and theoretical, along with artistic and scientific manifestations, environmental sound and experiences of listening are detailed to reveal the highly subjective appreciation for sound's inherent diversity—how it stimulates the imagination, and supplies constant input to individual experience. From such a project we might begin to learn how to *prolong* the issue of noise so as to create opportunities to confront differences beyond prescriptive assumptions—to extend the issue as an opportunity for dialogue through which another language may also surface in getting at the political.

It seems that to think acoustic politics the frame placed around silence and noise must begin to incorporate such dynamic flexibility. To recall Sennett's statement—"to permit the freedom of deviation would be to care about the unknown, the other, in social contacts"—my intention is to stage noise as an ethical encounter from which to generate *care* for the unknown, for the other. A "critical acoustics" would lend to finding points of contact as well as difference hovering between the practical needs of quiet sleep and the social needs of feeling involved.

To echo Sennett and his proposal for the productive uses of disorder, noise might act as a form of deviation that, in circulating through neighborhoods, can fully aid in the *emergence* of community. A fugitive sound, noise may push forth as a sort of itinerant figure to spin wildly within the social and, as Michel Serres proposes, rend the system open. For my ear, such fugitive sounds may only stimulate further versions of the domestic by bringing the stranger home.

3

SIDEWALK: STEPS, GAIT, AND RHYTHMIC JOURNEY-FORMS

Well, you can tell by the way I use my walk
I'm a woman's man, no time to talk
Music loud and women warm
I've been kicked around since I was born
And now it's all right, it's O.K.

—Bee Gees

It is possible to be on excellent sidewalk terms with people who are very different from oneself, and even, as time passes, on familiar public terms with them. Such relationships can, and do, endure for many years, for decades; they could never have formed without that line, much less endured.[1]

—Jane Jacobs

How pedestrian life acts as an encounter of differing urban signals to forge an acoustic space as well as a set of operative rhythms, to narrate a step-by-step drama.

Leaving the home and coming outside, the dynamics of sound and auditory experience open up toward a realm of greater public interaction conditioned by rhythms and the mobility of being on the go. What rises up from the underground, through the floorboards of the home, and then out, through the front door and into the open, can be characterized as a rhythmical flexibility bringing one into contact. On the sidewalk, we meet the coming and going of others. In this sense, the sidewalk is a volatile stage where the individual body takes a step, and then another, to ultimately negotiate the movements of others as they shuttle pass: I push along, maybe holding a bag under

87

my arm or close to my chest, shifting left and then right, trying to thread my way through a group of kids gathered there, lingering along the steps, laughing and pushing each other. As the site of pedestrian movement, the sidewalk functions as a rhythmic intensity weaving together the fleeting occurrences defining an essential aspect of public life.

The sidewalk is a threshold between an interior and an exterior, between different sets of rhythms that come to orchestrate the dynamic passing of exchange each individual body instigates and remains susceptible to. It is in turn a structuring space or topography that positions the body between an inside and an outside; within the urban milieu, the sidewalk is the site for the potentiality and related problematics of social expression. Whether in the form of individual itineraries, or in the collective articulations forged by groups, the sidewalk is a primary site of modern public life—*of stepping out and into*—and the notion of public gathering. In its banality, the sidewalk shadows the public square, supplementing the image of democratic gathering with smaller forms of sociality. A fragmentary and mundane democracy might be said to flourish on the sidewalk, as a field of local movement and sharing, what Jane Jacobs refers to as "informal public life." The sidewalk for Jacobs acts as an important site for making contact, between neighbors, between office workers, and between children, providing space for "mediating between [public organizations] and the privacy of the people . . ."[2]

As a motif of the subject in the midst of public space, walking has featured in cultural literature as an emblem of the everyday practices of urban space. Embedded in such literature is an optimism that places great promise on the act of walking as it threads together nodes of urban intensity while also fraying the strict formulations of the urban grid. The walker from this perspective is a force of potentiality bringing forward an unlimited horizon.

Jean-François Augoyard's empirical research conducted in the 1970s at l'Arlequin, a town on the outskirts of Grenoble, underscores pedestrian experience as an interaction between the meeting of individuality and the structuring architectures of the built environment.

As he elaborates, "Every walking, every inhabiting gives itself out not only as structures, figures, but also *configuration, structuration*, that is to say, deformation of the built world such as it was conceived and re-creation of space through feeling and motor function."[3] Hence, walking forms an "articulatory process" that writes and rewrites across the existing syntax of the built through motoric action, sensation, and emotional life. For Augoyard, the primary gesture of the *step* initiates a supple and frictional topography of contacts, giving meaning to the here and now.

Through a series of detailed interviews with inhabitants from l'Arlequin, Augoyard establishes an evocative geography defined by the place of the body within a given space. For instance, the "daily stroll" is underscored as forming an "intermediate practice" by connecting different places in an individual's life. Importantly, the stroll defies "functional classifications" by occupying a fragment of the day as well as the spaces between the "main" points of living and working. The daily stroll in this regard exemplifies a spatial practice that resonates with a "highly polymorphic" expressivity worthy of detailed consideration.[4]

What unfolds, as in Michel de Certeau's later *The Practice of Everyday Life*, is a demand that understandings of the built environment incorporate a radical appreciation for the *step* as a signifying gesture. Importantly, for de Certeau such walking-writing, this *step-by-step* articulation, confronts or frays the inscriptions marked on the body as part of an administrative, socializing process enacted through the built environment. "What is at stake is the relation between the law and the body—a body is itself defined, delimited, and articulated by what writes it."[5] The major formulations of individual identity—as a legible "text" on the skin—may slacken within the minor act of the walk.

As an essential site for contact, the sidewalk resounds with acoustical expressions aimed at or initiated by the walking body. The interlocking of steps and forces of inscription, as the dynamism aligning the body and location, opens up to rhythmical expressions. As Tia DeNora elaborates, early on rhythms feature as devices for *entrainment*, defined as "the alignment or integration of bodily features with some recurrent features in the environment."[6] From children's games, such as jumping rope or hop-scotch, which are often accompanied by singing rhymes or clapping hands, to more informal gestures, like skipping down the street while singing, whistling, or humming, bodily expression or behavior is wedded to an auditory and gestural partner, fusing self and surrounding to "orient and organize themselves in relation to environmental properties . . . In this way, environmental patterns come to afford patterns of embodiment and behavior through the ways they are responded to as entrainment devices."[7] Entrainment aids in locating features in the environment to provide security and safety, through an unconscious alignment, as well as enabling self-expression by which one may find place, or escape it.

Claiming an informal space within the everyday, the walker might be said to push against "official" scripts through the force of crossing the street, or side-stepping the crosswalk for an alternative path. The daily stroll, as an intermediate practice, imparts an elemental rhythmic flux to the more fixed structures of daily routine. The individual body in this regard is not so much a resisting agent, but a movement in continual negotiation within surrounding patterns. From this perspective, the small space of the sidewalk offers a generative stage for narratives that unfold this process while bringing into relief new configurations, sudden excitement, arguments, an entire promiscuous and difficult economy at the heart of public life.

This gesture of walking, of threading through city sidewalks and streets, or out in the open, finds vibrant expression within artistic practice. Walking, as a performative act that sets into relief a dialogue between subjective consciousness and the dynamics of place, uncovers the *textual* scripting and unscripting de Certeau describes. Francis Alÿs' work in particular often incorporates or draws upon walking as a ritual tracing of material and social contact. "Walking is one of our last remaining intimate spaces," Alÿs proposes.[8] In this way, the walking body carves out within the environment a sort of refuge for making contact or for cultivating an explicit orchestration. Might walking then formulate, through its syntactical interruptions, an invitation to the other? Though Alÿs often walks alone, he leaves us clues or traces to follow; from spilt paint as a thread trailing through the city to the smear of moisture left by a block of ice the artist pushes down the sidewalk in Mexico City, all such traces and residues mount a poetical script as part of the urban texture. A process of continual departure, Alÿs writes in streaks and scrawls, in actions, as an itinerant body drumming out a set of perforations onto the city.

The promise of this pedestrian writing is located within or against the perceived systematic planning of the modern metropolis and its shortcomings. Jacobs' *The Death and Life of Great American Cities*, in laying out a detailed account of the life of cities and their spaces, aims to counter much of city planning's lack of understanding onto the nuanced and complex social interactions and configurations thriving in the metropolis. Jacobs' understanding of the sidewalk to act as mediating space between formal structures of urban systems and informal movements of private life suggests a deeper appreciation for street life in general. Not only as a heightened drama of individual bodies on the move, but more as the meeting of such bodies and the greater organizational weave of urban space. Walking might be seen to enact a *mediating action* in whose configurations the meandering flow of private life and the geometries of public institutions meet. In this way, walking as practice is not a bold step out from the greater forms of alienation, but rather a teasing or a "ruse" as de Certeau points out; it puts to use the urban system, and in doing so supplies continual energy for possible rupture or joy.

Claiming the pedestrian as a wilful user, unfolding potent trajectories within everyday life, walking amplifies quotidian experience to fill the city with social energy and imagination. Such perspectives must also include the rather mundane and at times brutal experience walking comes to express: the walker is also a body without, as in the itinerant worker, the crazy bum, or the lost teenager. From this perspective, to walk is to not only forge possible forms of urban use and everyday practice, but to signal defeat in the face of greater flows, reminding, as de Certeau further suggests, that "To walk is to lack a place. It is the indefinite process of being absent and in search of a proper."[9]

As a mediating space, the sidewalk draws out an acoustical flux of so many occurrences and events. It teems with energy, frictions, and noises to form a sonorous fabric signaling the ongoing flow of life. Opening the window of my apartment on a warm summer day, the acoustical shape of the room is flooded with overall input, remixed by the passing of cars, the humdrum of voices, birds in the trees, and the breezes that modulate this propagating jumble. Leaving the apartment, I jump into this mass of sonority, like tumbleweed tossing here and there, to find my way through its flux of energy. In the city, the sidewalk seems to overwhelm or disregard the dichotomy of silence and noise with a general hubbub rising and falling through the day and night. Pockets of intensity, zones of volume, shifting gradations of acoustical flow that makes the sidewalk a sort of sound membrane contoured by the noise of the street on one side and the buildings on the other.

Following Jacobs' notion of the sidewalk as mediating space, and de Certeau's appreciation for the walking-semantic, I want to highlight instances of pedestrian movements that actualize a meeting between the public and the private—situations that bring the individual walker into public systems of the urban. In addition, by orienting a view on walking through an auditory, rhythmic perspective, I also want to extend the visual and textual emphasis de Certeau enacts. Understandings of the walker, as a counter-narrative whose script cuts across the system of urban space, operate as a readable or signifying gesture to which de Certeau, and Augoyard, impart great textual function. In tuning in to the rhythmical beat of the step, and the acoustical envelope surrounding the sidewalk, I want to amplify the noises walking at times produces. Such instances recompose notions of private and public as fixed, to reorient the senses to the forceful mixing the city comes to enact. Within this relation, rhythm is an operative texturing, drawn into or aiding to carve out a geographic supplement to the built—it is spacing, timing, and energy flow all in one, giving a read out of the relational mix occurring on site. The sidewalk throbs with life, and the walker I suggest *beats back*. With the step, a walker imprints onto surroundings so as to draw out his or her own time signature. Walking then is a beat oscillating between the more structured or regimented time of the body and the more spontaneous or improvisatory movements that seek flexibility.

The urban soundscape is itself a material contoured, disrupted, or appropriated through a meeting of individual bodies and larger administrative systems. From crosswalk signals, warning alarms, and electronic voices, the urban streets structure and audibly shape on a mass scale the trajectories of people on the move. In contrast, individuals supplement or reshape these structures through practices that, like de Certeau's walker, form a modulating break or interference. From iPod and mobile phone use to musical instruments and live sensing devices, such signals can be heard to form a mediating dialogue between the individual body and greater structuring sounds performed by the city. In this sense, the auditory topography of the urban milieu is heard as the mingling of differing flows and rhythms that shift through gradations of freedom and arrest—an experience oscillating between feeling overwhelmed *and* supported, and beating within the scriptual economy elaborated by Augoyard and de Certeau.

Following these intensities, and the movements between formal scripts and informal pedestrian rewriting, the sidewalk provides a line to the flows and counterflows, the signals and beats, which lay claim onto the urban system. In pursuing the sidewalk as an acoustic territory, I want to draw out such dynamic instances so as to indicate the potentiality found in pedestrian life and the way in which sonority participates.

Pedestrian Sounds

The experience of the city sidewalk, as zone of pedestrian life, is partly shaped by a continual flood and movement of sonic activity.

We enter an acoustic space in continual evolution with so many perspectives. Construction noise in the distance, laughter passing here and there, the skirting and skidding of shoes on the pavement, bicycles shooting past to circulate a wind of energy by the ear, all bumping and whirling in a flood of warmth and monotony. One might draw up an inventory of the urban soundscape heard from the sidewalk throughout the course of a single day and arrive at a sonorous picture containing a mixture of manmade, machine, and natural sound pushing and pulling at each other. A superimposition of sound events that flow into a steady undulation of intensity: background becoming foreground, and back again, in a fluctuating mass of stoppages and starts that move in and out of communicational attention to puncture the air.

The sidewalk can be heard as an acoustic space that gives indication of the balance between the private and the public Jacobs finds as a key feature of urban life. Through its blend of voices, traffic, signals, and all the small audible traces of so many actions and bodies, sidewalk acoustics tosses with these intersecting flows between private address and public dialogue. On the sidewalk, I drift along on my way to work, humming to myself, and at the same time I am continually bumping into sounds around me that draw me in, repel me, and force negotiation. This sonic choreography acts as a contouring energy locating my senses within an ongoing, mediating flow that softens the borders between unconscious and conscious thought. The siren from an ambulance grabs my attention and forces reaction while my mobile phone rings and announces a sudden connection away from the immediate scene. A sort of feverish vapor, sidewalk acoustics is a connective reverberation, breaking the seal of private life while in turn countering the ongoing rush of public presence. Alongside taking steps then is the ever-present mesh of acoustical events tickling perception to resonate with or disrupt the private self.

This medley of acoustical movement finds further expression with electronic signaling, in particular crosswalk signals, which define a set of patterned movements and thereby give orchestration to side-walk acoustics. As an urban detail, the crosswalk signal (which I will concentrate on in terms of their audible aspect) may be placed within the larger spectrum of warning and distress signals. While occupying a more pedestrian application, crosswalk signals nonetheless aim to address the walker by warning of possible danger, signaling when it is appropriate to walk or not, and contouring the urban landscape with an ordered pattern. This patterning brings forward elaborate research, including statistical analysis on traffic flow, handicap access, and crowd control. For instance, *The Manual on Uniform Traffic Control Devices* (MUTCD) requires high pedestrian crossing volumes for extended periods of time, with a volume of 100 or more pedestrians over the course of four hours or 190 per single hour needed to warrant the installation of a crosswalk in the US. In contrast, the Ottawa-Carleton Department of Transportation recommends a minimum of 200 pedestrians crossing in an eight-hour period for flashing crosswalks.[10] The transportation and environmental concern imported onto the site of the crosswalk emphasizes how crosswalks provide a key structuring device for not only public safety, but also for the flows of traffic by creating breaks in traffic volume and pedestrian movement.

The crosswalk signals throughout Denmark and Sweden, mostly designed and monitored by Prisma Teknik, a company based in Sweden, function as one specific example of crosswalk signal design. Designed to be sensitive to existing noise levels in the city, Prisma Teknik's Digital Acoustic Pedestrian Signal (DAPS) is based on the delivery of up to 16 types of audible signals set to clearly define and convey traffic information according to three stages (red, green, and flashing green modes) while also being sensitive to the given environment. Fixed with a microphone, the units can be set to automatically increase or lower the volume of its signal according to ambient levels of noise. In addition, the units can be tuned to different time periods, for instance at night the signal can occur at a lower volume. The audible signal itself is designed as rhythmic beating or pulses that vary in volume, sound type, and rate so as to convey whether it is appropriate to walk or not at a given time: generally, the faster beating conveys it is safe to walk, whereas the slower signals mean one should wait for traffic to stop.[11] The slower pattern is like a form of relaxed breathing whereas the more rapid rhythms support if not propel the movement of the body forward during a green light while also giving slight warning that time is running out. (This finds an exaggerated form in Australia where during a recent visit I was immediately struck by their unique crosswalk signals, which sound like a rapid-fire taser gun upon initiating walk mode, making one literally jump into action.)

The movements and timing of the pedestrian, existing within individualized yet common time signatures, are interlocked with the urban pattern, from the length or dimensions of city blocks marked by traffic signals, road signs, and numbering to the signaling of stops and starts, comings and goings. Crosswalk design aims to support the pattern of the walker by lending rivets and breaths to pedestrian life. Forcing one to stop, the crosswalk also allows instances of pause, to relax, to tie the shoe, to reposition one's bag, or take a sip of to-go coffee. These undulations and rhythmical marks operate as patterns within the environment that stimulate forms of alignment or entrainment. The rhythm of the walker steps in line, falls behind, or runs over such existing patterns, formulating a counterpoint to the time signature of urban systems. The unconscious registering of crosswalk signals punctures the vague spatiality of an average urban soundscape, demarcating through patterning and electronic signal points in space and time: one anticipates the starting and stopping of traffic, and the subsequent movement of bodies, incorporating this into one's own rhythm of thinking, gesturing, or daydreaming. The signal acts to coerce the body into rhythmic alignment—it acts as a line around which the step circulates.

Alongside the increased pedestrian life found in cities like Copenhagen, as well as the intensification of traffic occurring throughout modern cities, crosswalk signals lend to shaping the fluidity and sense of free and safe movement within a city. They address the walker increasingly as a sensing body, with current sign-aling often also including vibration plates for tactile sensing.

Within the established ordering of these signals, a timing that regulates the flows between pedestrian and automobile, and between opposing traffics, other forms of being on the street appear. The body in the midst of signals not only follows the patterns of warning or messaging, but also those of individualized sonorities. From ghetto blasters to iPod usage, Discmans to mobile phones, the body on the street often seeks to personalize movement by adding customized ingredients to the regulatory humdrum of the street and its manage-ment. In particular, the iPod has come to impart new dimension to both sidewalk acoustics and the related rhythms and time signatures enacted by the city.

Michael Bull's valuable studies of personal stereos and iPods give wide access to this terrain. A number of key observations surface from Bull's empirical studies, notably, the suggestion that the use of these auditory technologies aid in individual negotiation with the inherent "fragmentation" of urban experience. Personal stereo use acts as a strategy for "managing time and experience whereby [the users] construct sites of narrative and order in precisely those parts and places of the day that threaten experiential fragmentation."[12] As my description of sidewalk acoustics suggests, the blending of all that input radically places demand on the senses, often challenging one's sense of self with an excess of public presence. The urban if anything is that condition of excess on so many levels. Personal audio technologies provide a performative shelter for the senses by both filtering out the undifferentiating flood of sound as well as empowering individual agency in controlling what comes in. By grant-ing such control they also assist in sculpting a new form of sidewalk presence, countering the repetitive signaling of the crosswalk, and its related order, with a seemingly autonomous addition. Users set their own pace through a choice of music, inserting themselves into the time signature of the sidewalk according to personalized rhythm that often appears *out of place*—the user moves down the sidewalk as an alien figure hovering somewhere between presence and absence, locating their sensory attention on an unsteady fulcrum between here *and* elsewhere.

The wired-up walker enacts a sort of *ghosting* of the sidewalk—we may never know what sonic matter is floating through the ear of the iPod user, whose step occupies the vague threshold between zombism and activism. The spiriting of electronic technology finds a new host within the contemporary walker, taking hold within these new forms of mobility to draw out phantasmic bodies.[13] Might the iPod user script a new mythology of the urban, giving narrative to augmented life now spanning the globe?

Turning it up, conducting soundtracks, or smoothing out the pressures, acts of *musicalizing* the sidewalk function to add other forms of rhythm, audition, and sonic experience to city life, creating subjective nests within the social pattern—a supplemental layer of timing to those designed for mass movement. "New sonic territories are composed in the course of this mobile listening experience. As the body moves in synch with the music, the listener transforms the public scene and provides a new tonality to the city street."[14] Jean-Paul Thibaud's observations of audio technology use give further shape to Augoyard's *step-by-step* analysis of the pedestrian. For Augoyard, the step acts as a lever for expanding a relational integration with one's environment, explicitly operating as an "expressive" gesture to forge a mesh of connective threads. Enveloping such a mesh within a sonic rhythm enlivens the step into a personalized "gait," which "transposes the rhythmic qualities of sonic time at the level of the walking expression of the listener."[15] The gait marks out in an expressive manner the meeting point of private listening and public space—it pumps up the step to make the sidewalk a zone of freedom, or to detune the sonic script of patterning with a meandering beat. (Though we must not forget the ever-present jogger, who races down the sidewalk, across the park, cutting here and there the space of the city—and who most often than not is equipped with an iPod. No doubt the sonic accompaniment fills the jogger with great energy, supporting their sportive movements.)

As a pre-echo to the iPod performer, I'd like to recall the opening scene to *Saturday Night Fever*, as a sidewalk moment where music and the body fall in line to a certain beat. With the Bee Gees "Stayin' Alive" hovering around Tony as an omni-directional soundtrack, the scene weaves together the body, the music, and the city into unified composition. There's something dynamic, suggestive, and sexy about Tony's strut, the way in which the street seems to flow around him, supporting his desires, his appetites, his fantasies: the street is there for Tony, and he easily glides, eating pizza, buying shirts, checking out the chicks. The music supports his bold smoothness. It becomes a cradle, a structure that brings Tony in line with the city—he walks to the beat, and the music seems driven by Tony's youthful grace. The music we might say stitches him and the city together, granting Tony incredible confidence. The scene immediately reveals that Tony is part of the Hood, with the Bee Gees singing:

> Well, you can tell by the way I use my walk,
> I'm a woman's man, no time to talk.
> Music loud and women warm,
> I've been kicked around since I was born.
> And now it's all right, it's O.K.

Following Tony down the street, it becomes apparent how music supplies a deep psychic and emotional medium for how to negotiate urban life, and how to compose daily rituals. As Tony demonstrates with his strut—the strut is pure rhythm, propulsion, confrontation, and erotic confidence all in one; it is an urban rhythm shaped by flows of multiple glances, perspectives, and possibilities *as event*.

The time and movement of rhythm builds out and expresses this spatial and emotional event, giving flexibility and points of contact to all that comes to bear down on the city and those who inhabit its spaces. Music steps in, time devolves and develops, rhythms give movement and potentiality to what it means to be *in place*: to drum along, to stomp the foot, to tap the table, to wait in line and then exit, coffee in hand and the street ahead, is to carve out a *journey-form*.

Taking a step and finding oneself on the ground is answered by the subsequent sensation of the ground rising up, to form a steady contact lending to knowing where and who we are. Walking is a dialogue flexed by rhythmical propulsion.

The sidewalk, as site for such energies and dynamics, is also a space where bodies strive and struggle. For rhythms are also directed by tensions of force and movement, of reciprocation and break-down—negotiations with other bodies and their authority. As Steve Pile seeks to remind, "the psychodynamics of place . . . are [also] actualised through interrelated regimes of vision, power and sexuality."[16] Tony strutting down the sidewalks of Brooklyn expresses not only the freedom of youthful beauty in full public view, but, as the film further portrays, the tensions of what it means *to belong*. Yet against the coding of visuality, and the related power dynamics, music and sound appear as a contouring medium for possible routes out or around strict readability. From the disco to the street, music in the film gives shape to a narrative of transformation, of finding hope—to continually relocate the step, into other moves. The geographies promulgated by sound then give dynamic space for ducking and diving the writing occurring between body and law, which may support understanding of the intensification of iPod use and the emergence of sound culture as a counter to the semiotic, imagistic, and ocular demands of modern society.

Extending the drive and flex of the acoustical step, the project *Sonic City* developed in Gothenburg, Sweden, seeks to make more complex the very potential of sonic experience to redesign the patterns of walking and the flow of signals.[17] The project is based on using live sensor technologies and fitting these to the body through a customized vest, so as to create mobile opportunities for collecting, processing, and transforming live input. "The goal of the project is to enable people walking in a city to create electronic music in real time through everyday interaction within the urban environment, literally playing it as a musical instrument."[18] Consisting of microphones, light sensors, accelerometers, and metal detectors, the project becomes an elaborate prosthesis, extending the body and its perceptual and sensory range. Yet significantly, it allows a user to collaborate, through a sort of musical dialogue, with the environment, making a game out of exploring the city as a form of interface. Body and city meet in a generative interaction, where "The users actively directed sensors with their body. In order to produce input, they often got closer to fixed artefacts at hand such as metal or walls."[19] Turning the street into an expanded field of input, musicality and noise, embodiment and emplacement unfold through improvisatory actions—"one of the players started jumping around and playing his body against shadows and metal objects, improvising musically while waiting on a corner for the traffic light to change."[20]

These movements extend walking as a poetical rupture, harnessing the syntactical overwriting notably marked out by Augoyard and de Certeau—the Sonic City Body makes explicit walking as not only a form of inhabitation, but importantly as configuring through tempo-rary displacements the lines and demarcations of the urban milieu. Through headphones a listener hears not the selected tunes of their iPod, but the environment around them captured and processed by an array of digital effects. This process slowly unfolds into a sonic potential, as the user (or player) develops an instrumental under-standing, opening up to more elaborate integration. In doing so, it also unsettles the defining parameters of optical space, the space of the *text*, and the features of self-image by making the body a fidgeting sonic mechanism: one has to move in unexpected ways, to gyrate in search of noises and tonalities surrounding the body, captured as signals in the air or electromagnetic clouds, to explore this invisible acoustic space. Such a shift also creates dynamic interaction between vision and hearing, tuning a listener in to all the complementing and contrasting signals surrounding what they see. The presentation of the self and the forms of pedestrian life unfold to an inclusive and expanded feeling for emplacement, which also locates the user in their own universe of experience. The Sonic City Body on the street comes to supplement the breaking of the urban text by acting as noise-machine, beat-box, and pirate radio all in one, defining a sonic geography with an excess of dimensions.

Whereas the street musician stands in full display, as a supplication to the urban crowd, the Sonic City Body samples, collects, and literally embodies its local soundscape, sonifying secret constructions of time and place. Electronically wired, the user becomes a secret agent on the field of sociality. Wandering in the city, the user discovers a form of body language that exceeds both the step and the gait to include an entire range of gestures.

Sonic City comes to bend the structurations of the built environment, and the contours of the sidewalk, creating an augmented weave of signals. From pulses to clicks to static to washes of sound, the body is an extended instrumentation finding points of contact within the fields of energy swarming through the city. Wireless signals, mobile networks, radio transmissions, the medial flow of input and output zooming, as aerial strata all around—itself a new kind of syntax in the structures of the city, official and unofficial alike—is brought against and into the body, as auditory matter, supporting this reimagining of one's place in the city.

Such a project finds echo in various works of media artist Jessica Thompson, which further support the liberating expressions of the individual walker. For example, her project *Walking Machine* (2003) consists of applying small microphones to the shoes of participants, and fitting them with amplifiers and headphones, thereby allowing a user to hear the city from shoe level. Walking then turns into a small act of auditory pleasure, giving larger space to the momentary instance of placing one's foot on the sidewalk. Step by step, the work comes to impart or let loose an acoustical delight in finding place. Thompson presented the work in 2004 in New York City, during which time "each group of participants became more inventive in the way that they were experiencing the environment; stomping on sewer grates, splashing in puddles and crunching garbage."[21]

IMAGE 10 Jessica Thompson, *Walking Machine*, 2003 (omni-directional lapel microphones, mini amplifier, headphones), at Psy-Geo-Conflux, New York City, 2004. Photo: Joshua Weiner, courtesy of p|m Gallery, Toronto.

As with the *Sonic City* project, *Walking Machine* amplifies the relation of body and space, forming a prosthetic extension to physical points of contact. As the artist proposes, the physical space of the walker is supplemented by a virtual addition, where "technology becomes an enabler, facilitating a heightened sonic experience that liberates the wearer from normal conventions of 'public behavior'." Lacing an auditory thread through the simple experience of walking, "grass becomes a swishing soft carpet, gravel grinds and pops, and ice and snow creaks and groans under the weight of your feet." To hear one's footsteps brought forward in all their tactility and granularity grants an immediate pleasure, giving recognition to the material frictions of the underfoot.

In following such works, and the structuring device of the crosswalk signal, the acoustics of the sidewalk can be heard as an economy of signaling and counter-signaling. From the pulses and repetitions of the crosswalk to the differentiating rhythms supplied by personal audio technologies, the pedestrian threads their way. Yet sound and walking have a longer historical coupling, as with the practice of soundwalking. Developed predominantly within the field of acoustic ecology, soundwalking is a practice that encourages a deeper, more sensitive approach to location based on actively exploring specific environments through walking and listening. "A soundwalk is an exploration of, and an attempt to understand, the sociopolitical and sonic resonances of a particular location via the act of listening."[22] Usually functioning as a guided tour by a leader, the soundwalk quietly probes a given place, appraising the subtle and dramatic movements of sound as they come to filter in and through the walking group. Notably, soundwalking has become an active and rich base for enlivening acoustical understanding and appreciation, appearing within a variety of festivals, conferences, and gatherings. It captures the general drift of the meandering body, focusing the poetical drive underlying the walker as a creative agent, and redirecting or suffusing this with an acoustical project. What such instances aim for is a deeper tuning of self and surrounding, lending to the pedestrian project of making malleable the sense of place and feelings of relatedness.

The Brazilian artist Romano further highlights this relation, while adding certain tension with his *Falante, escultura sonora itinerante* (2007). Consisting of a self-made backpack fitted with a single audio speaker and playback mechanism, the work is essentially a performative action designed as a walk through the city. With the phrase "Não preste atenção" ("Do not pay attention") repeatedly playing out from the speaker, Romano walks around, taking various routes through the city. As a stroll, the work draws out an uncertain line between the sounding body and those who hear. On one hand, it calls attention to itself through an amplification that immediately bursts onto the public scene—people turn, looking, wondering . . .—while demanding that one also ignore the meandering figure. Such a confusing gesture plays havoc on the scene of the sidewalk, and the mediation between private and public.

IMAGE 11 Romano, *Falante, escultura sonora itinerante*, Rio de Janeiro, 2007. Photo: Edouard de Fraipont.

Rather than a participatory and instrumental redefining of the body—as a liberating gesturing movement—Romano as walker numbly circulates as an acoustical pest. His sonic city is an instrument that stages the difficulty of finding autonomy or integration, and instead, performs as an antagonistic nuisance. His noise-machine enacts its own failure by producing the conditions it seems to aim against. *I don't want your attention* leads to *I can't get rid of your attention*. Locating his walk within the city, as a meandering step, Romano supports the project of the free walker as well as complicating this with his own script. He circulates as a daily stroll that shuns the intimacy Alÿs finds in the space of the walk to dislocate forms of social construction. Such actions further contribute to the rhythmical vocabulary of the step, accentuating the beat as means by which to negotiate the time signatures of place.

The Sonic Body

Stepping out from the house, the acoustical view of the sidewalk opens up, which is dotted with rhythmical patterning drummed out by the step in all its metered and fluctuating dynamic. To follow this is to track the marks and scuffs amidst the urban texture, forming a map of so many itineraries. From the daily stroll to the determined walker, the cartography of the step also traces out the audible events surrounding and aiding pedestrian movement. Rhythm, in piecing together the heat of the sound wave with the materiality of the built environment, sculpts out a time-space figure whose energies temporally demarcate the city.

What then might be found in these sonic projects that supplement or shape pedestrian practice with audibility? How does the interlocking of differing rhythmical patterns lend insight onto the social relations oscillating within public space? Henri Lefebvre, in his *Rhythmanalysis*, proclaims that in order "to grasp a rhythm it is necessary to have been *grasped* by it."[23] Thus, the beat is a forceful exchange built from multiple input; a sliding back and forth, an expanding and contracting structure broken and remade by the frictions of the private and the public, of being in and out of sync. This relation in turn comes to locate the body, to fix one within particular orders. As Lefebvre further observes, "Everywhere where there is interaction between a place, a time and an expenditure of energy, there is rhythm."[24] The walker *mobilizes* such triangulation, putting it into the world and against the street to occupy the full breadth of its beating drama. Walking makes a discourse out of the step, whose rhythmical language coheres as a "journey-form." According to Nicolas Bourriaud, the "journey-form" is a contemporary compositional principle based on a "cluster of phenomena" evolving from within the mechanics of globalization.[25] It composes into artistic objects, actions, and investigations built from the rhythms of global movement. From the continual shuffle of networked society arises such a mode of cultural practice, aimed at performing the very conditions of displacement—to fashion an endless itinerary out of the transient condition one is already called to occupy. The journey-form thus "takes account of or duplicates a progression" whose rhythm stitches the local body into a greater network of relational exchanges.

Lacing this back onto our sonic walker, the acts of entrainment, and the dynamics of rhythm—from the step to the gait and finally, to the journey-form—leads to what I want to call *the sonic body*, as the effective dislocation and reconfiguration of the body under the mediating spell of a sonic event. That is, the body totally reconstructed according to the dynamics of listening and in search of a new city. The journey-form of the sonic body is an improvisation seeking out possible entrainment within the soundscape; to drum out, through the step and the gait, a progression ahead of or behind the mapped itinerary—*a splinter, a fragment, a dislocated center*. The sonic body as step-by-step journey-form, whose walk rubs against the patterning of urban systems, and the ebb and flow of exchange, to perform an orchestration of emotional matter—of the psychodynamics of being *in place* and already somewhere else. For the triangulation mapped out by Lefebvre—of place, time and energy making contact—beats out the surge and syncopation of a body cutting through and being cut into by the urban, as so much emotional vitality. De Certeau's counter-scripting, as a ruse and as a tactical antagonism, can be heard to beat from the sidewalk as raw aggression, humor, or love; in the interweave of the rhythmic, the step is prone to digression. As Tony demonstrates, dancing may teach us how to elaborate the step into a journey-form of transformative power.

Riots, Street Fights, and Demonstrations

The city as a topographical condition, as a set of structures and systems, spaces and cultures, bodies and rules, is also, because of such intensities and their mixing, the site of perennial change. The city is a sort of barometer for the confrontations, radicalities, and imaginations that may be said to define history. For the city not only brings together the forces which in their meeting create rich experiences, but in turn resounds with their celebrations and arguments. Though the historical may be examined through textual record, accounts, written archives, and documents, it is equally an audible echo taking shape through material forms, cultural markings, and geographic flows. History is also movement. The auditory then may lend dynamic appeal to the historical imagination to not only fixate on archival pages, but to supplement such reading with a sense for what is buried within, for history is also made concrete through initial articulations, interactions, frictions, and the vibrations of bodies, voices, movements, and their expressiveness. To read then might be to also hear what lies somewhere between the words, inside the white blanks, or over and around the languages that were once scratched onto paper, as an emotional energy.

As Mark M. Smith has commented, the absence of archival sound recordings of particular historical periods does not undermine historical examination of sounds from the past, for these would not necessarily reveal the way a society experienced and received such sounds.[26] How sound comes to circulate, lend meaning, and give shape to social processes and attitudes for Smith may still be found in written documents. The question becomes not so much to seek the original sound, in pure form, but to hear it within history, through an extended ear, as a significant phenomenon, material, and shared experience participating in the movements of history.

The city is also a noise as well as a text, a culture as well as a map, a reverberant terrain as well as a space full of signs; a history surfacing through government policy as well as the potent sonority that envelopes everyday life. To return to the sidewalk as a space mediating between inside and outside, private life and public organization, the meeting of city policy and private use might be glimpsed.

Mitchell Duneier's engaging study of sidewalk life in New York City reveals this relation. Following the daily life of various homeless men, informal book vendors, and panhandlers, Duneier unfolds a detailed understanding of the men who live from this sidewalk economy and the city laws from which they are always under pressure. Interestingly, sidewalk life comes to develop its own set of regulations that conform to city law while seeking ways around it. As Duneier documents: "The Administrative Code of the City of

New York states that no street vendor may occupy more than eight by three linear feet of sidewalk space parallel to the curb. Since most tables are six to eight feet long, generally no vendor can have more than one table on the street. So those vendors who wish to use more than one table pay some of the men without accounts to stand behind or 'watch' their second and third tables."[27]

Sidewalk life acts as a key to understanding the interactions between social norms, as public language, and their upsetting through diverse appropriation or use, marking the sidewalk as a space for expression, argument, and fighting. The riot, the street fight, and the demonstration may be understood as dynamic instances of conflict and debate, as well as an audible interaction between writing (the dictates of law) and noise (the suspension of law), an interaction that lends to defining history: on one side, the law as a signature of written record, decree, juridical account, and on the other, a drive toward its overturning, whose momentum relies upon, is initiated, or calls for the development of a separate language, one that stands in opposition, or that brings the law into its own hands. This other side seeks to resist written record and to supplant it with its own, one that is initially often shaped by the political speech, the verbal slogan, the passing of secret messages, as an orality whose power resides in speaking out, rallying, and having a say. Thus, riots, street fights, and demonstrations produce an audibility that seeks to overturn or overwhelm the written record, the law, and house rule with a meaning determined by volume and the promise embedded in making a noise. Such actions in turn instigate new patterns, aiming to reconfigure set rhythms with other timing. To *break* the law then is to also break the functioning order of a given system.

A set of examples of instances of rioting, street fighting, and demonstrating may lend to this proposal—of listening in while also letting out the nested audibility and emotional force within history, and the tensions intrinsic to pedestrian spaces. In this case, walking and the space of the sidewalk are understood as operating within practices of social transformation. Shifting from the individual walker and to the forces of collective gathering, I want to extend the beating movements of the sonic body, as an emotional and embodied geography, as a journey-form, so as to appreciate how the step manifests in more overt political actions. In locating the flexibility and malleability enacted through the individual walker at the center of an acoustic politics, the verve of rhythmic propulsion must also be heard in the cascade and harangue of collective gathering, which utilizes the mediating line of the sidewalk.

Atlanta, Mob Rules

The inconsistencies, disparities, and imbalances at the core of the Atlanta race riots of 1906, as David Fort Godshalk has examined, point toward complicated social and psychological relations among blacks and whites at this time, in this city. As white mobs brutally sought out and attacked blacks throughout the city, firstly in poorer neighborhoods and later in more middle-class areas of the city, both black and white civic leaders struggled to give articulation to ideas which in the end were neither for or against, but rather sought to understand the complexity of the situation and all the underlying histories and values embedded therein. Thus, "In Atlanta, public words imperfectly reflected underlying ideologies partly because enormous social and economic disparities dramatically influenced both what blacks and whites could say and how they could say it."[28] As with most riots or demonstrations, the power of the spoken word takes on profound importance, along with the ability to capture the public imagination through the use of the voice, language, and related media platforms. The riots in Atlanta were marked by such dynamic, and more so, by the intensities of who spoke, lending to the voice and its meaning the presence of the skin and its color.

Throughout 1906 in Atlanta, the white imagination of the black threat was emblazoned by the ongoing debate of the racial situation, and the endless newspaper reports of attacks by black men on white women, all of which carried threats not only to white society, but

specifically to an inherited code of chivalry carried by white southerners based on defending white women. Such social unrest and report-
ing eventually turned the Atlanta streets into a cacophony of shouted
headline reports, gossip, verbal fighting and debate, and finally esca-
lated into mob rule, documented in Thornwell Jacobs' striking novella
The Law of the White Circle:

> "Where's the police?" the countryman with the little red
> moustache on the end of his nose asked a young hoodlum
> who stood by him.
> "Raidin' the dives down on Decatur Street."
> "Listen to that!"
> Again the cry:
> "Third assault! Paper, mister?"
> "By G_d, there's goin' to be trouble here, and right now, at
> that! Come on, boys, let's give 'em h__l!"
> "I just heard two little white boys was held up and robbed
> in the suburbs," the hoodlum answered.
> "And look a-yonder!" a gamin cried. "Did you see that nig-
> ger grab that white woman's pocketbook?"
> "Gee-muny-chrismus! They're fightin'!" he yelled, as a
> white man sprang on the negro and bore him down.
> Two other negroes came instantly to the aid of the first,
> and a rough-and-tumble fight ensued. At last the crowd
> became noisy, the tension began to give way, the lightning
> flashed, and the storm broke.[29]

The collectivization of anger, mounting disregard for law and order,
the feverish organization of immediate reaction, form into a radical
communicational passing where one voice spurs another to ultimately
become a chorus of embroiled emotion that, in this case, also crosses
and weaves together in a complicated fabric the tensions of racial
conflict. The city street as an acoustical partner resounds with aggression, information, pleas and reports, helping to mobilize and provoke,

defend and resist according to territorial demarcations—the voice both passes information while defending territorial boundary: from Dark Town to Brownsville, the black neighborhoods became sites of conflict where the voice was replaced by the sheer force of bodies beating each other, and public squares the site for last minute attempts at reason.

The ideological fact of racial tension finds articulation in the printed word, as with newspapers and legal document. Yet it poignantly presses in on real bodies through acts of vocality, forceful argument, and hate speech. As Judith Butler observes, "a statement may be made that, on the basis of a grammatical analysis alone, appears to be no threat. But the threat emerges precisely through the act that the body performs in the speaking act."[30] The acoustical thrust of speaking, as the Atlanta riot reveals, was paramount in spurring violence. Yet as Godshalk maps out, the riots themselves came to act as a forceful expression leading to an array of attempts to transform not only the racial situation in Atlanta, but for all black southerners. Vocal aggression, as a key aspect to the thrust of the riot, might be heard to also bring forward a new acoustical space not only on the sidewalk, but importantly, within the courtroom.

London, Suffragette Tactics

Though the voice and orality dynamically function within the insurgence of street fighting, like a vehicle carrying threat and ideological struggle all in one, the public street also carries with it other potential tactical sonorities.

The Suffragette movement in Britain throughout the early twentieth century was a sustained political agitation onto established codes of conduct, social mores, and legality, and ultimately aimed to acquire the right to vote for women (which was only fully legalized in Britain in 1928). Throughout their struggle, a variety of tactics were established as means to give expression to their plight that can be understood to supplement or extend the strict use of vocality to carry the message.

One such tactic for the Suffragettes was the method of smashing windowpanes of public buildings, one of the most notorious being enacted by Amelia Brown and Alice Paul during the National Anthem at the Lord Mayor's Banquet in 1909.[31] Organized window-smashing acted to draw attention to the movement, and to specific protests, by not only vandalizing public property, but also by creating an audible scene: while the voice within public debate is a tool for putting forth alternative views, or generating collective emotion, it may also fail to be heard or find reception—to rise above the established order. Women smashing windows in public, as well as throwing stones and also burning post boxes, other tactics of the Suffragettes, amplifies ideological conflict by attacking civic architecture and the established system. Countering, attacking, searching for a route in, the smashing of windows can be heard as vandalism aimed at society at large, underscoring political view embodied no longer in the voice, or on the skin, but in the gendered body making a noise. Whereas later in the century the afro, the black leather jacket, and the rifle would stand as emblems of the Black Panther movement, formulated into a vocabulary of black resistance, the middle-class woman smashing windows in 1909 stood out unmistakably against the backdrop of English society, turning the sidewalk into an acoustical register of political conflict.

Paris/Bologna, Poetic Politics

The taking of the Sorbonne in Paris in May of 1968 stands as a mythical revolutionary instance whose echoes seem to resound throughout the contemporary cultural environment, marking the beginning of our current legacy and the ending of certain modernist views related to opposition and subjectivity. The function and usage of media may be seen to take a shift at this time, whereby questions of representation, political statements, and debate slide into a slippery space of nomadic identities, metropolitan Indians, radiophonic cacophony, poetic graffiti, and multimedia formats hinting at networked collectivities, all of which place language into a state of dislocation. Contoured by the emerging electrified environment of the 1960s, the new stance of revolutionary statements seem sparked by an extensive sonority, whereby words unfolded in multiplied entities, whose reading became a voluptuous act, a promise of subjective becoming.

Following 1968 and the related cultural outpouring, the Autonomia Movement in Italy led to the establishment of various subgroups, one being Radio Alice, which sought to continue the initial rebellion.[32] For two years the broadcasts of Radio Alice in Bologna functioned as an experiment in political action, identity, and language, operating as an open platform where voices mingled and mutated through call-ins, open broadcasts and debate, fantastic reports, noise and music, montages of poetry and newspaper readings, etc. It thus sought to occupy not the streets, or particular institutes and buildings, but an ethereal, electronic space directed at the imagination ensconced within the urban environment: the poetical graffiti scrawled through-out Paris in 1968 was replaced by electrified expressions of total audibility—it was sound on the run, aimed at the social heart, targeting not a particular political party, or government official, but the very structures of socio-political subjects. Radio Alice was a kind of demonstration on the airwaves, an ongoing occupation whose message was difficult to apprehend, and thus arrest. It remained live, electric, free media on the dial, a sonority spread out across the city.

Copenhagen, 2007

In response to the recent "normalization" process initiated by the center-right government under Anders Fogh Rasmussen, Danish police eventually stormed the Ungdomshuset ("the Youth House") in Copenhagen, evicting the squatting community and leveling the house to dust. Such military intervention sparked extensive rioting, unsettling most of the Nørrebro district with nightly gatherings, vandalism, and the storming of various buildings. Throughout the week-long confrontation, the rioters employed a series of modified flat-bed vans. Fitted with PA speakers and a sound system, the vans rolled through the streets at night to lead the demonstrating crowd through the city. Blasting from its speakers was various music, mostly hardcore techno and beat-oriented, along with anti-globalization anthems, underpinning the force of the crowd and lending a dynamic addition to the gathering. Across the neighborhood one could hear the throb of the music enveloped by occasional cheering and screaming, forming into an auditory register of the movements of the crowd and the demonstration. With the van moving through the streets, music functioned as a physical and emotional support galvanizing the bodies on the street into a collective force, literally expanding the presence of the crowd, and the related message of dissent and dissatisfaction.

* * *

In following the noise of rioting, street fighting, and demonstrating, it has been my interest to listen in on history, albeit swiftly, to recognize in what ways pedestrian life, and the individual walker, shift within a climate of political dissent. To take to the streets, or to seek to disrupt public space, reveals the desire or necessity to interfere with established order. Moments of social transformation bring the walking body into an extended breakdown of official scripting, pushing the instrumentality of locating oneself into an orchestration of larger aggression. The syntactical interruptions of the individual walker on the sidewalk spill over into street action. The geographic nesting of personal sound erupts into a collective voice or action, shifting the acoustics of sidewalks into a dramatic noise. This aggression finds its complement in reactionary attempts to cancel, annul, silence, and over-sound such noise, in a fighting whose ideological intensities resound in meaningful volumes. For example, Act-Up's (the AIDS activist group) slogan "silence=death" underscores such perspectives, highlighting the sheer importance of being heard, on any level, within a sphere where sound is more than just decibels.

Sidewalk acoustics gives expression to the steady rhythms of the everyday as well as the transformative intensities of social unrest.

From the walker shifting between crosswalk signals and headphone tunes, from the step to the gait, and further, to the sudden shattering of glass or the gathered voices of collective protest, pedestrian life flows to write those scripts of de Certeau's walking semantic by seeking more pronounced volume. Wind in the trees, a woman's high heels tapping behind, and the puncturing sound of your own laughter suggests this new text marked out underfoot is also an acoustical space gaining definition through beats and their modulating force.

Marching

The rupturing agitation of rioting and street fighting, with its tumult of related noise and acoustical disruption, gains momentum through the disorganization of bodies—impelled by the collective force of bodies confronting bodies, balanced across the threshold of stability and change, control and its breaking, such unrest requires mass force contorting under the pressure of arrest and containment. In contrast, the timed order of military drill (as the other side, of policing and control) necessitates collective subservience to a rehearsed functionality that folds the individual walking body into the historical and political time signature of the march. Against the acoustical matter found in taking to the streets or confounding civic order, one might hear the keynote of political order and control resounding as a counter-acoustic throughout history and the city. Here, walking shifts from the meandering step or the collective surge, and toward timed regimentation.

William H. McNeill, in his study of marching, has shown that the orientation of military drill functions to secure group cohesion through the initiation and control of group muscular movement. For McNeill, the extreme needs demanded by military order necessitates an intensification of emotional and muscular expression, fostering individual ability to do battle and to withstand the extremes of war while participating in an elaborate mechanism of control and command. Thus, the muscular ordering of military drill releases within the individual body a functional relation to emotional investment, ordering the rapture of embodied expression into a greater choreography of marching and repetition, an entire refinement of corporeal organization by which the body is mechanistic *and* potently lethal. The history of military drill is woven through the history of battle tactics, war strategies, philosophies on how to order the inherent chaos of conflict, where invasion and defence, communications and command, rely upon and necessitate the total organization of bodies. The individual energies of the soldier are brought forward by that tangible experience of collective motion, deepening a primarily muscular release that is nonetheless complex. Such mobilization not only expresses ordered direction, but also grants momentum to the individual body in withstanding the extremes of ordered conflict. Yet what propels this intensity of energy rests below the line of consciousness. As McNeill observes, the rhythmical excitation of the body in the heat of military drill "is centered in those parts of the nervous system that function subconsciously, maintaining rhythmic heartbeat, digestive peristalsis, and breathing, as well as all the other chemical and physiological balances required for the maintenance of ordinary bodily functions."[33]

The ordering of military drill tapping into the nervous system and unleashing muscular and emotional force may also find audible expression not only in the passing of information and the signaling of group action, but also in marching bands, and their inherent musical-muscular functionality. The rioting body on the street breaking shop windows, throwing stones or causing trouble is replaced by the march of the military band, which produce and in turn are supported by audible intensities.

Though marching bands appear in different forms, from high-school parades to street festivals, I want to explore them as located within the military. The gesture of walking, as that rhythmical instant of making contact and navigating the line of the sidewalk, takes on additional meaning when participating in the mechanistic force of the military march. Rhythm here is brought into a time signature that expresses an altogether different order, but one that is also interlocked with that of the liberatory expressivity of the step or the gait. As a countermeasure to the spontaneous skip or the personalized sonic, the march fixes the inherent singularity of the body into a contained regiment; it draws in the embedded energy of the walk but restricts it to a set of prescribed measures. This is furthered through an elaboration of material contact: the sonic body as a noisy reconfiguration of embodied performativity, shaped by the emotional flows of pedestrian life, takes on another shape in the march. Initially, the individual marcher is partnered with the musical instrument, extending the body through a device of audible expression, as a second voice by which embodiment finds a new spatial field of sensorial and commanding effect. This is furthered through participation in the band—the rhythmic pulsing and physical exertion of marching in time and collectively literally composes sound and the body into a larger disciplinary system. Lastly, this formation of a musical-muscular organization is placed within the city, as a military force, unifying this expressive conglomeration into an act of occupation. This totalizing, sonic collectivity unfurls the forceful energies that make the military marching band a complex expression: the seemingly cheerful melodies of John Philip Sousa's "Stars and Stripes Forever" carries forth an entire national image of democratic freedom through the robust disciplinary vigor of the US Marine Corps, bending musicological appreciation with forceful patriotism. With the beating of the collective step, as a drumming without alteration— a hammering repetition—the Stars and Stripes are marked out as a symbol backed by the force of a metered order.

The marching band is an elaborated embodiment, pressing into the muscularity of the body and capturing the nervous energies, and finally, unfolding all of this, as a network or detailed choreography of singularities, to hit the asphalt with exuberance. Michel Foucault pinpoints this elaboration as part of a historical instance found in the establishment of "disciplinary power" that was to invade and radically define the Industrial age. The intensity of this shift lies precisely in its effective overlay onto the movements, behaviors, and desires of subjectivity. Thus, within forms of productive labor or within the field of military drill, a precision of calculated movements, the regimentation of timing and energy expenditure, and the internalization of related values brought the body in line with new forms of control. Within the field of military strategy, Foucault explores the development of military manuals outlining means for establishing powerful force through repetition of actions, or what he refers to as "the instrumental coding of the body." From how to handle a rifle to maintaining cleanly appearance, the military brought every detail of the subject into an elaborate order. "Over the whole surface of contact between the body and the object it handles, power is introduced, fastening them to one another" so as to align or "coerce" the body into an economy of power.[34]

The marching band can be appreciated as participating within this organization of embodied energy, placing the march in line with the drum. The drum as an instrument plays a significant and absolutely pertinent role within marching bands, for the drum best exemplifies the power marching bands wield and the force of occupation it seeks to announce. As John Mowitt's engaging study of drumming shows, the interplay of percussion, skins (of drums and bodies), and the beat interlock power with the corporeal and emotional intensities generated by music. The drum acts as signaling device with great command, replacing the voice of the commanding officer with percussive precision in which "particular beats came to assume the status of signals, calling, for example, for infantry soldiers to fire on the enemy, or, when all else failed, to retreat."[35] Music and audible signaling were thus woven into the strategies of the new modern army, appropriating from the earlier Ottoman military bands the dynamic blast of percussion.[36] The history of the drum is interlocked with military history, either by direct involvement or as a rhythmic parallel in which keeping time, unifying single units into collective signatures, and organizing the individual body as an instrument through whose repetitive rehearsal power could be cultivated.

The phenomenon of the Buekorps in the city of Bergen in Norway testifies to the weave of music, bodies, and marching bands, formed as public spectacle that still carries within it patterns of battle. Developed in the 1850s, the original Buekorps emerged from young boys imitating their fathers who formed small battalions or militia to defend local streets or villages. Wielding wooden rifles, the boys copied their fathers marching formations, dress, and manner, replacing much of the actual defensive concerns with that of music and display, the drum becoming the essential instrument. Still existing today, the Buekorps function as social units of young boys (only a small number of Buekorps now accept girls) that take to the streets throughout the spring, to practice in preparation for Norwegian Independence Day on May 17, during which time competitions take place, turning the streets into a cacophony of percussive rapture. The streets reverberate with sudden bursts of drumming with each Buekorps demarcating a part of the city their own, utilizing the narrow streets and hillsides as acoustical partners, with accompanying shouts and verbal signals punctuating the marches. The young boys thus continue traditions built from the interweaving of military manoeuvres and drumming, interlocking their steps with the movement of marching patterns and the collective surge of timed display.

IMAGE 12 Buekorps, marching through Bergen, Norway, 2009.

Drawing upon the tradition of the Buekorps, the composer Jørgen Larsson presented his own version of the march, titled "I Ringen" ("In the Ring") as part of the Borealis music festival in March of 2007. Working with four units of Buekorps drummers, the performance took place throughout the afternoon, starting with the movement of the drummers marching respectively through different parts of Bergen to finally meet in a public square for musical battle, or "slagerkonk." In addition, the artist had set up microphones on the square connected to a series of speakers mounted on building façades. Utilizing computer treatments, Larsson sampled the live drumming and played it back through the sound system, transformed into a series of reverberant rhythms, accentuating the drumming with added beats and electronics. While the performance lasted, crowds gathered from the four corners of the square, drawn by the intermingling of the live and the sampled, the recognizable marching body as known throughout the city and the transformation or supplemental electronic addition echoing over the square. The work underscored the very performative nature of the marching boys, amplifying their public spectacle into a composite of rhythms that also unravelled the order of their march. Larsson's appropriation of the drummers, as identifiable symbols, both seem to accentuate the way in which drum, body, and city space interweave in a complex sonic organization while disrupting this with an excess of electronic treatment and performative energy. With the reverberation of their drumming beating throughout the main square, the work seem to stage the very staging already intrinsic to the Buekorps as performance that acts to bind young boys into tribal units through forms of ritualized synchronization, in which drumming awakens the city to the coming of age of their men. Thus, their music (recognizable within a repertoire of marching music) is an expression of agency given its annual freedom at a specified time of year, bringing the body in line with certain orders that are musical as well as social. For in this act of coming out, the Buekorps also function to grant the public access to the ongoing lineage of male order, which in this sublimated and parodic form may entertain while hinting at a deeper foundation of national values.

IMAGE 13   Jørgen Larsson, *I Ringen* (In the Ring), Borealis Festival, 2007.
Photo: Thor Brødreskift.

The marching band as an intervention onto the street, a disruption onto established rhythm, can also shift from strict military use to
tactical and interventionist appropriation. The Infernal Noise Brigade
(INB) takes up the reverberant form of the marching band to spur
tactical ruptures as part of various activist campaigns. Started as a
protest action, the INB marched through Seattle against the WTO
meeting held there in 1999, forming an assertive expression of sonic
agitation onto the scene. Echoing other activist bands, such as
Rhythms of Resistance, the samba band from London, the INB infuses
the rhetoric of the military marching unit with ironic flair that supports
the ensuing euphoria that comes with collective action. As Jennifer
Whitney recalls:

> Marching in, we formed a circle and played for a few minutes
> to general consternation and astonishment before clattering
> back out onto the streets again. It was one of my favorite

moments of the day, because it was like we were announcing, "Hey, normal life ends here folks, there is a marching band in your Starbucks, you're not going to work today!"[37]

The marching band forms a nucleus around which numerous meanings circulate, and which interweaves music and place in a way that amplifies the inherent power of sound. Drumming and combat, rhythms and fighting, timing and obedience, coalesce into the expression of the march. The pedestrian movements of the walker are restricted into a refined set of actions to articulate the ideals of a specific order. Marching, as a movement somewhere between walking and running, between the meandering step and the dynamics of the gait, serves to remind that to "keep time" is to hold power. The single body, in relinquishing individual expression, participates in this display of power, gathering all the dynamics of the pedestrian into a precise mechanism.[38] The marching band can be understood as means for establishing order while bolstering the intensities needed for it to gain momentum. We might then recognize this weave of marches and music as the intersection of varying forces in whose performance bodies and cities meet, to articulate rhythmical intensities that both topple and reinforce tradition.

Sidewalk Acoustics

Stepping out onto the sidewalk, walking is a simple gesture. Yet, carrying all the stuff of the body, step by step, the action of walking supplies the imagination with the very promise of *mobility*. To walk is to already leave behind one place for another. To search, to seek, to wander, the walk is the making of an itinerary. Sidewalks then serve this process, as a space allowing free passage, a ground for the expressivity found at the base of the step. Pivot, shift, and then release, the stepping body learns the promise of the horizon from the perspective of the sidewalk: this line of pavement, of stone or concrete, acts as a blank page for the imagination. Yet the page is certainly already occupied, by others and by many scripts—an occupation that brings to earth the flight of the imagination. Free passage then is also a continual side-stepping to avoid bumping into others, creating or modulating the gait of the walker by adding a skip there or a hop here to the rhythms of being free. Private *and* public, the sidewalk is a zone for sharing all the small details of what it means to be, to move, and thus, to interact in and against a context.

The mediating space of the sidewalk, as Jacobs meticulously details, by interlocking private lives and public organization delivers an acoustical thrust found in a soundscape that might be heard as a superimposition of all that comes flooding from *without* and all that surfaces from *within*. From street noise that washes over the sidewalk to shouts that break from windows, the sidewalk soundscape is a medley mixing together these two conditions. By extension, inside and outside feature also as fictitious or narrative zones whereby the emotional and psychological experiences of city life intersperse amidst the social and systematic operations of the metropolis. Finding pockets of reprieve or for improvisation—for that intimacy Alÿs defines—or contouring pedestrian life with auditory secrets and technological differences, to walk is to produce a mesh made from repetitions and rituals; to make narratives out of the stroll. It is a rhythmic performance treading a line between dreams and work. Might rhythm teach us how to use our walk, to forge contact, connection and also new patterning? To walk enacts that primary rhythm, as an extension of the heartbeat, of breath and the pulsing of perception, heard as the click and tap of the step made from the *in* hitting the *out*. Sidewalk acoustics forms dynamic immersion for a body attempting to find its own step.

To supplement such steps with the march, I've also tried to suggest complexity to the gait, as a forceful energy brought into an ordering beat. Like the iPod user, and Sonic City Bodies, the marching musician also figures as a sonic body. Wedded to a musical instrument, the marcher is propelled by the urgencies of disciplinary order keeping time to musical composition, and the muscular force of playing while marching. This sonic body, though, finds a further complement, which I have not touched upon, but which must figure, as a figure itself, within the line of the step, the gait, and the march— that is, the dancer. The sonic body can already be thought of as a sort of dancer, as one driven by the beat yet finding its own particular expressive shape, as a responding counter-rhythm that follows the beat while already breaking it. Dancing dynamically expresses how rhythm is a timed order containing the promise of its own rupture—to dance is to follow the beat while fraying its edges; to cut into the beat with feverish steps. This is given expressive shape in the figure of the breakdancer. As a special sidewalk figure, the breakdancer has occupied city space as a location for display and competition, performing as a total sonic expression by locating the step, and the gait, across the entire body, to bring the beat in and let it press out in pops and drops, hops and flairs. Such moves poignantly locate rhythm as means for reordering place, for pushing against the inscriptions marked on the body, and as a production of another kind of public space—all of which give a lead to the sonic body, as a journey-form of rhythmic urbanism. To dance then is to take the step for a long walk.

4

STREET: AUDITORY LATCHING, CARS, AND THE DYNAMICS OF VIBRATION

If the illusion is real
Let them give you a ride
If they got thunder appeal
Let them be on your side

Let them leave you up in the air
Let them brush your rock and roll hair
Let the good times roll
Won't you let the good times roll-oll
Let the good times roll

—The Cars

It's not cool to be in a car that everyone else can get.[1]
—DJ Funkmaster Flex

You are now about to witness the strength of street knowledge.
—N.W.A.

In which the automobile performs within a greater acoustical demonstration fixating on vibratory excess, the pleasures of skin, and community identity.

Drifting from the pedestrian expressions found on the sidewalk to the intensities of the street, one immediately leaves behind the slower and more nuanced movements of the individual body for the mechanized rhythms of traffic. Though "the street" is often conjured as the image of public life, it is more accurate to remember that the street is quite literally full of cars, buses, and other motorized vehicles. Rather than a location for public gathering, the street is more a functioning obstacle to such collective democratic concentration. On an ordinary day, it's difficult to gather in the middle of 7th Avenue. Rather the street operates according to its own particular behavior, rhythm, and expression contoured and choreographed by the automobile.

Yet the street still carries the promise found in acts of demonstrating—as I noted in the previous chapter, the pedestrian body spills over onto city streets in moments of social transformation or collective gathering, infusing the street with an energy always on the verge of appropriation. The street, more than the sidewalk, signals the very hope of collective action, as well as cultural expression. As cultural mythology, the street is where style takes place, where trends are set, and where the movements of vernacular languages— from graffiti to graphics—are made explicit. It is the carrier of sonic messages, a site for musical expressions, and the location for noises to congeal into cultural form. The street is in effect noise's greatest partner. A site for the generative mixing and intermixing of disparity and difference, of interference, the street is an acoustical instrument for the propagation and diffusion of multiple sonorities, which the city itself comes to feedback. (Waking up one early morning in Los Angeles, I went out onto my friend's balcony where I was staying to be confronted by the glowing dawn light accompanied by a mesmerizing wash of sound humming in the distance. In the quiet neighborhood, the sound hovered like a shimmering vapor and seemed to rest over the entire city. Realizing it was the sound of the freeway located about two miles away, I was amazed by the sonority, and began to imagine the vast network of traffic racing across the city and all the sonic vapor resulting.)

Being on the street, hitting the road, or taking to the highway become mythological narratives allowing contact *and* escape—the street, like the sidewalk, mediates between private and public (between Easy Rider and a bus ride to work). In contrast to the walker on the sidewalk, the street propels the flight of the imagination and literally empowers the self with the roar of an engine. Though drivers, passengers, and the vehicle remain deep within the structures of city life, they flirt with the phantasmic energy of the open road. The street, and by extension the motorized vehicle, offers the body on the sidewalk a dynamic set of experiences by supplying new forms of control: to take hold of the street while behind the wheel is to stake out a form of occupation, as well as to sense the mysterious tangibility of freedom. Each part then performs within a unified constellation, where the "highway" or "freeway" is quite literally a space for itinerant production.

Contouring this dynamic constellation, the presence of an accompanying music is easily situated within motoric expression. As with iPod use, to manage everyday life through sonic experience gives the individual body temporal and material support, figuring as auditory scaffolding that grants structure to location, mood, or desire. "Music is not merely a 'meaningful' or 'communicative' medium. It does much more than convey signification through non-verbal means. At the level of daily life, music has power . . . To be in control, then, of the soundtrack of social action is to provide a framework for the organization of social agency. . ."[2] Tia DeNora's examination of the uses of music within everyday life reveals the degree to which self and sound interweave, affording opportunity for security, self-identity, and group sharing.

The surfaces and conditions of the environment, such as the street, operate as tangible features by which to find a sense of footing, locking into existing patterns (as in the crosswalk) while always seeking personal trajectories. One *latches* onto location. Such a view expands understanding of the inter-relation of self and surrounding by appreciating the material world as an elemental partner. Auditory experience dynamically operates within this larger frame, granting music a significantly special place within this exchange. The patterns, repetitions, vocal expressions, and melodic lines of music create points of contact, of *inhabitation*, while also infusing the environment with a palpable energy. Importantly, the dynamic experiences of music that enable one to find security, excitement, and temporal flux further act as effective conditioning by which to construct a sense of timing and spacing *outside* music. As physical energy, music enables one to forge means for opening up a malleable space between the personal and the social. As with the rhythmical exchange between self and surrounding, as a choreography of beats, the body retains the energy of musical expressions, of songs dear to the heart or which excite the step, as a bodily mapping through which to find place within varying contexts.

This finds dynamic expression within the automobile, and its related audio systems. The weave of car and music forms a sonic technology for heightened sonic experience, driving forward a reworking of time and place. "Sonic technologies—with their attendant use and the sounds they transmit—allow for overlapping singular spatialities that are neither wholly random nor neatly discrete, instead coming together at certain points and falling apart at others."[3] Such hyper-spatiality is literally sculpted by the car cruising down the street. Filling its interior chamber with music, rolling down the windows, and charging forward through the urban network, the car carves out a complex topography, of shifting perspectives, overlapping sonics, signifying agency. Such complexity is also radically inscribed with psychic and emotional energies, riveting the car with psychodynamics, of so much desire, expression, anger, and fantasy.

As I explore in the previous chapter, the walker on the sidewalk searches out, through a primary rhythmical alignment, the accompanying environment as points for possible contact. Fixing the step within a particular groove forms a means for entrainment, giving expression to the dynamics of place, as a beating exchange. Extending this to the site of the street, and within the car, driving affords release from the particular frictions of the step—to be on the road is to float free of the social challenges found on the sidewalk, and the brushing and scraping of so many face-to-face encounters. For this reason, the car functions as a space for distraction and drift (as well as numbing boredom). With the insertion of sound technology, this space is brought into a sort of sculptural relief—the car experience is radically shaped through the selection of a musical track—tuning in, or popping in a CD, the drive becomes an aesthetic experience.

The experiential conditions of the car, and its related sonic technology, literally drive a listener beyond the concrete reality of the sidewalk, replacing the acoustical experience of hearing the immediate environment with the construction of an auditory enclosure. With recorded sound, and the craft of acoustical engineering, the car affords a hyper-immersive auditory experience that incorporates the entire body within its propagating and enveloping verve. How does such an experience perform on the street, as a privacy placed in full view? What acoustical territories are made from this enveloping sonic, and might its occasional leakage reveal particular cultural energies?

Vibrations

Sound and auditory experience forms a primary sensual matter in continual contact with the body. The sonority of daily life is a deeply impressionable sensing, impinging on thought and feeling in ways that give accent to the shifting self. The physicality of sound, as a movement of air pressure, of vibration, of interpenetrating exchanges from all around, forms an enveloping and effective influence. Such experience fills everyday life with an ongoing material flux, forming a phenomenal life-force existing here and there in which we are deeply involved. This involvement though also occurs as unconscious contact, where attention moves in and out of focus and yet whose sensing is ongoing. The acoustic world is thus "a world which comes to me, which springs into life for me, which has no existence apart from its life towards me."[4] Sound is a movement that comes forward, and in doing so directs itself toward me, as if always there and to which I am always being called. Yet the movements of sound, as an immersive acoustic, also exist below the line of audibility, in the shape of vibrations. Sound and vibration are intimately linked, forming a partnership that extends the air-borne wave to the material world, as frictions and tactile feeling.

Physically, vibrations occur as oscillations due to frictions or the pressure waves of a sound, resulting in a resonating energy field. For instance, the plucking of a guitar string is essentially a vibratory occurrence whose energy results in a particular pitch or frequency of sound, which we hear as an oscillating sound wave. Sounds are generated by vibrating objects and materials, and they in turn generate, through a sort of reciprocal exchange, further vibrations as they come to touch material surfaces. Vibration is then a primary base of sound, a fundamental material event perpetuating the movement of sounds and extending, as an elaborate network, the connective elemental force of auditory events.

Vibration also rests below the line of audible perception, often occurring as subliminal and tactile shifts in energy and force. For this reason, vibration is an influential, sensual flux performing as a vital contour to the psychodynamics of the emotional self. It folds across the body and imparts a further dynamic to the force of auditory latching—*the passing of a subway train under ground, below this floor of a café where I sit and have soup, a small vibration traveling up through the floor, along the metal base of the table, to arrive finally onto the plane of the table, a sensation caught just under my arm as it rests on the edge of the table, a marble edge tickling my arm with a train many meters below in a vast network of frictions and contacts, to touch my skin and land against the surface of my bones.* Vibration extends the environmental soundscape deeper toward the physical material plane, to link the body into an expanded field of resonating energy.

Beginning with the primary sensation of being in the womb, auditory experience is first and foremost a tactile energy. In the mother's body, the child senses all the fluctuations and modulations that occur from the mother's voice, and related bodily processes, as they vibrate back inside. These vibratory sensations form a deeply sensual backdrop, massaging and caressing the child during months of growth. This continues well after birth, as the sudden energy of the outside world surrounds the child, and in particular, the mother's voice appears now with accompanying eyes and lips, as an entire animate form full of sight, touch, smell, and sound. The child, as Didier Anzieu suggests, experiences the mother as a "first skin."[5] Subsequently, tactile sensing significantly influences the psychic shape of individuality, delineating the body as a sensing surface or "skin ego" through which inside and outside meet. Further, the skin continually responds as it unfolds or is folded upon by all the expansive forces of being in contact, to continually shift the border of the self.

The perception of sound as a vibratory, sensual undulation against the skin follows well into the development of speech. "As we listen to our own voice, we feel as well as hear its vibrations, feel the complex, self-caressing dance of tongue, palate, and lips, counterpointed with the pleasurable muscular rhythms of the breath being drawn in and released."[6] The delight in sensing one's own vocality inside the chest, within the throat and against the lips, as an elaborate resonant experience, as Steven Connor suggests, lends dynamic pleasure to *producing* the self: one senses the power of the voice inflected by the capacity of the body to extend and to give meaning through its own reverberant potential. To *speak up* is to draw forth sound from the depth of the body, as a fundamental vibration—as air forced through a set of passageways—that in turn sculpts the relational figurations and contours of the spoken: speech carries forward the undulating pressures of the inside to an outside, to be brought back down again through one and another's ear canal with its reciprocal, vibrating bone. A network of palpable sound is thus in continual movement, turning acoustics into elaborate phenomenology that exceeds the traditional limits of space. Vibration disregards material boundaries.

The extensive, vibratory sense at the base of vocality is playfully revealed when babies discover the ability to hum or blow against their pursed lips, causing bubbles to fall across their cheeks, and parents to reciprocate, rubbing noses and vibrating together—*brrrrrrrrrrrr* . . .

brrrrrrrrrrrr . . . The vibratory gives pleasure, and in turn participates in a developing vocabulary of sensation and sensing. The fleshiness of speech, as a primary means for not only conversation but a form of self-contact, may be witnessed to expand out through the body, into a medley of tiny instances: the small movements found within the swallow, where the flows of saliva drive an entire choreography of muscular action whose resulting sensations trickle from the back of the mouth and through the throat; the vibratory throttle occurring with the sneeze that shakes the head in a violent and pleasurable instant; to the cracking of bones, each pop and crinkle a vibratory spark thrown through the skeleton; and the various unexplainable spasms, squirts, and torsions that occur as part of movement itself, each of which produces miniscule articulations that tease and tense the body.

What I am seeking here are forms of sensorial latching that operate below the line of consciousness, as well as audibility, from the womb to the motions of the body and speech, and further, to the fundamental embodied sense of being *on the ground*, where footsteps down boulevards or alleys, along carpeted staircases or across wooden floors, make for a primary rivet aligning body with place. Such instances of touching the world may come to provide structure to the ambiguities and tensions of being a self, while lending to more articulate forms of cultural practice.

As mapped out in the previous chapter, walking as gesture may be a site for a radical placement and displacement of self, fixing and unfixing identity to urban structures, locational politics, and cultural form, locking down as well as opening up to the full view of potential horizons. Walking as fundamental rhythm, as metered gait, as pulsional drive, must in turn be sensed along the lines of a vibratory instant found in that moment of the foot hitting the ground and the wind brushing against the skin. Vibration is an energy that often goes unnoticed, undetected within the movements of taking a step, of being in place and against surfaces. Yet vibration acts as a palpable link, for "it is the vibratory essence that puts the world of sound in motion and reminds us, as individuals, that we are alive, sentient and experiencing."[7] To take one's first step is to enter a new field of sensation, where moving into the world causes ripples up from the soles of the feet and through the ankles and shins, to arrive at the knees, which absorb these sensations into the mechanics of self-propulsion and alignment. The vibratory acts as a conducting matter for the generative production of contact, existing below and around audition. In this way, vibration is a primary sensing that unfolds the individual body toward a "common skin," elaborating the relational ontology of sound as deep groove.

Beats below the Skin

I want to extend my previous thoughts on rhythm, and the project of the walker, by exploring the acoustic territory of the street as defined by the movements of vibrations and generated by the conditions of the car. The street shifts the rhythmical coordinates of the sidewalk, as a place of contact, for the full propulsion of automotive experience, as a vibration under the seat. In this way, the street is a sort of energy field overwhelming social contact with speed, pro-pulsion, and the promise of *giving it gas*. The momentum of car life supplements the sidewalk-body with mechanical excess that drives to the core of the body a vibratory acoustic. At the same time, this vibratory experience and the features of car life intertwine to form into social expressions as pointed as the face-to-face encounter found on the sidewalk. The mediating line between public space and private life, as a rhythmical conduit found on the sidewalk, takes on another register on the street, where the car supplies the expressiveness of being public with motoric thrust.

This shift also brings with it a more pronounced relation to music. As indicated in iPod use, the operations of auditory latching are given a further beat or point of contact when walking turns to music, and the foot taps the ground—*following rhythms, the flow of beats, throwing the foot against a surface, keeping time* . . . Such instances of auditory latching, as DeNora proposes, act to create forms of looping whereby embodied presence finds contact through percussive timing. Tapping the ground, drumming the desk, and striking one's knee are gestures of making contact to produce a personalized, musical time. These gestures supplement the more structured or regimented time of the body as it moves through the day by granting flexibility, distraction, and interval. Whether tied to specific songs, or as auditory memories, this "musical time" carves out a secondary rhythm for the body on the move.

Such integrating sonority brings music in and through the body, incorporating it into personalized movements, as fixations and contortions that express a given music: *this music is part of me, it finds its way in*; I align my own movements to its rhythms, its shape, and thereby append it, as a kind of imaginary limb, to the potentialities of how I imagine myself and how I may relate to what is around. It both breaks the body apart, as a dynamic intrusion—*to dance the night away*—and at the very same moment stitches it back together, in forms of expressive movement, dress, and articulation, and importantly, into the making of time.

Musical time surfaces in relation to music heard but also as expressions of *relating*: as the dynamics of audition bring us into contact, "aspects of an auditory environment is afforded by—among other things—perceptible sonic patterns . . . as found in music and in many other soundscapes . . ."[8] In this sense, music serves as a material experience through which we learn how to hear, to detect, and to engage with the auditory environment—as intervals that break up the day, as repetitions that create personal rituals, as sensations that rupture or ease the passing of minutes. Yet, as with the tactile exchanges touching the skin, auditory latching can be appreciated as existing below the audible field, and within vibratory sensing, also granting us a deep vocabulary for how to feel.

Latching onto, making contact, fixing bodily rhythms to surrounding ones, the movements that tap along with or follow the flow of given beats accentuate the degree to which musicality is governed by or remade into explicit formations between self and world. The musical work is found not entirely in the compositional structure, nor in the formation of social groups, but also in the figural reciprocation with self and the place of listening. This finds echo in Henri Lefebvre's *Rhythmanalysis* when he declares that "The relation between musical time and the rhythms of the body is required" in understanding musical experience.[9]

Such embodied experiences are given greater accentuation in drumming. Drumming here should be cast within this larger field of vibratory sensation, embodied gestures, and auditory latching, as a sort of extraordinary project where "hitting the skins" exemplifies the primary contact enacted during ordinary moments, when the body moves against things to locate generative sensations. In this way, I take the drummer as a body especially involved in rhythmic and vibratory labor, engrossed in and living out in amplified fashion the fundamental acts of personalized time and related spacing. The drummer produces not only the beat, but also a pounding that extends inward just as much as it fills space with rhythm. The drumming body, in beating skins, generates an entire field of tactile and psychic energy—the beat returns to the drummer, as trails of energy cutting through the body, moving up from the arms and through the shoulders, down the spine and into the pelvic area, as sensations that also fill space with their driving movements, as sound pressures against other skins.

The skin ego, as Anzieu's primary psychic material, finds a literal complement in the skin of the drum, forming a loop of vibratory, sensing energy. John Mowitt extends Anzieu's theories of skin by elaborating its relational function through the "percussive." The field of the percussive, as a signifying gesture or matrix, supplies the skin of the body with an enveloping meaning that flows from within and from without. Percussion in this case is a form of epistemology driving and mapping ways of understanding and defining the world. Drumming is not only the literal action of instrument playing, but the incorporation of the rhythmic into the body, and returning in acts of making contact. To brush up against, to fidget, to reach for, to repeat, form tactile engagements with what surrounds. The skin, as a shared border between a subject and its exterior, activates a resonating, signifying field locating percussive contact as points of powerful exchange.[10]

In *The Book of Skin*, Steven Connor elaborates on the life of skin. What sparks Connor's enduring curiosity is the degrees to which skin participates in the reworking of an inside and an outside. These ever-shifting tactile experiences, and the touching that passes across so many surfaces, unfold as undulations and abrasions, cuts and scrapes, through which skin comes to life. The "weather of the skin," as Connor suggests, gives indication as to the "climatic conditions" passing between interiority and exteriority so as to shift overly strict "readings" of bodily inscription.[11] Connor's examination of the meteorological epidermis uncovers an altogether different skin condition, giving elasticity to the way in which skin comes to signify.

> The skin always takes the body with it. The skin is, so to speak, the body's face, the face of its bodiliness. [. . .] The very wholeness that the skin possesses and preserves, its capacity to resume and summarize the whole body, means that it is always in excess of, out in front of the body, but *as another body*.[12]

In locating the experience of vibration, as an undulation of pressure, the skin literally surfaces, drawn out by the touch of sound. The contact of flesh, following Connor, can then be addressed as a meaningful sense, plied by the sonic and brought into a tension between pleasure and pain, security and rupture. Vibration can lull to sleep, with the humming melodies of another; it can also force out all sorts of bodily matter. Vibration lets me know you are there, or that someone is coming; it also breaks the calm through thunderous force. Such instances push the skin inward, so as to touch the deeper nerves of sensing, or to make the interior organs an extended skin.

I want to underscore this tactility of sound, as an extension of the beat; and to take the step of the walker, as a fundamental point of physical contact that also surfaces as street culture and street knowledge. The percussive in this regard is not so much the hit but the subsequent surging of energy surrounding it, inward and outward, as rhythms that align certain skins against others. This energy both supplies the body with dynamic support while diffusing its borders toward a field of shared sensation. Such tactile, generative energy inflects sonic experience with palpable force, forming a relational stitch of emotional, physical, and psychical material that sends the skin shivering. As John Shepherd poignantly states, "It is the tactile core of sound . . . that reminds us that the gaps and silences between the delineations of structures, whether social, cultural or musical, are not gaps or silences, but directionally charged fields of meaning and experience that speak to our sense of identity and existence."[13]

Street Smarts

The sensing of the percussive field, as a conduit between inner and outer, through movements vibratory and rhythmic, condition and reveal aspects that I want to hang onto in approaching the street, borrowing from the notion of "auditory latching" and seeking those "charged fields of meaning" within the car. From the perspective of the drummer, as those taking any kind of pleasure in tapping and dancing, auditory latching is not only a means of finding security between a body and its surroundings, but also how such a relation brings surroundings inside, against the skin and deeper. It is my interest to follow these rhythmic forces as they move from single bodies, of drummers and their surroundings, and onto the larger cultural spaces, where beats become powerful vibrations. Beats that eventually end up on the street, as vehicular motion.

Rhythm, in general, as measured time as well as physical sensation, directs a relation of self and surrounding that breaks down their separation as well as affirms it through cultural form: the beat is both a corporeal intensity hitting skins and bones as well as specific expressions of cultural movement by which rhythm becomes a *coded* cultural striking. In this regard, the difference between the rock beat and the hip-hop beat is measured not only in its physical experience, as intensity hitting the body, but as a measured time contoured by cultural structures and their forms of expression, marking the beat as unmistakably particular. To participate in the beat is to subscribe to what it delivers, as a physical force gathered and ultimately harnessed according to musical meaning. The vibratory motions experienced as a child situate themselves in musical taste, rising up within a percussive territory. Thereby, "music comes to have effects upon the body, to function as an entrainment device for bodily processes and bodily conduct."[14]

This interlacing of beats and movements, energy and bodies, may further highlight why cars and music have such a special relationship. The automobile, with its musical partner, has become an intensely sonorous machine, realizing a radical potentiality in creating listening experiences with great momentum. The car becomes a generative space that affords the listening body a private relation to music, as an enclosed space, while also granting volume and vibration to the intensity of the drive. It boosts the presence of the beat through its particular acoustical properties. As a physical space, the car is an optimal music machine, accentuating surround sound, bass vibration, and diffusion. Through an amplification on wheels the car affords musical expression an added kick already embedded in music's promise of movement, driving the drive of music through personalized control and deep inertia.

As a vehicle, the car also lends greatly to personalizing movements through the world, cocooning the self within a stylized interior space each of whose features offers numerous means for directing individual expression while being public. A living room on wheels, a sonic bubble, the car is a total design giving enormous power to the driver. Sonically, it operates akin to the personal listening device, in so far as auditory structures are sought and cultivated through self-selection so as to *deal* with being public.[15] As an auditory field, it supplies the listening body with a refined set of sonic intensities, driving music directly against the body and down into every pore.

The car makes radical additions to such experiences by gathering more fully the ability to control one's own space, and by driving such personalized interior *toward* the public. Both operations take on greater power through the automobile, whereby acoustical privacy (aligned with the very mechanics and rhythms of the car's internal functions) finds rhythmic definition, and controlling public presence is accentuated through the *stylization* of privacy. The car is a *second skin*.

Expanding on his work on personal stereos and iPod use, Michael Bull's account of automobile privacy and its acoustical dimensions are driven by the notion of "habitation," accentuating a car's ability to create domestic comfort and security. Such habitation is furthered through its auditory features, of isolating a driver from the outside while creating conditions for a powerful listening interior. As Bull elaborates: "The aural privacy of the automobile is gained precisely through the exorcizing of the random sounds of the environment by the mediated sounds of the cassette or radio."[16] Such a view lends import to the psychological unease experienced at the threat of external noise.

As Shelley Trower maps out in her thoughtful account of vibration and its related cultural histories, sound impinges on the listening body to not only create comfort and enjoyment, but as well to wield the threat of pain. Sounds of the world form a surging perceptual backdrop, and thereby come to represent, if not literalize, all that remains beyond one's control. In response to the psychological research done by Heinz Kohut and Siegmund Levarie, Trower further observes that "Tones, rhythm and repetition contribute to the sense of order in music which allows the ego to remain intact while dealing with the external world of sound."[17] Music, in structuring sounds, stabilizes the threat of sound and organizes the dynamics of audition around a set of recurring motifs. Such a view supports DeNora's proposal that "music affords a kind of auditory device on to which one can latch in some way or other . . ." underscoring music as "a resource for the constitution of embodied security."[18] Locating the listener within the car, aspects of control and security are bolstered by the mobile thrusts of the sonic experience, as shaped behind glass and within the sensation of being in control. The car is a sort of private domain through which one also displays powerful meaning.

The advancement of auditory design within automobile engineering has over the decades taken on greater importance. The refinement and marketing of luxury vehicles, safety features, and comfort all contribute to an elaboration on the car's auditory features, incorporating acoustical engineering and car sound systems. Yet the two meet around the central concern for minimizing exterior noise, internal vibration, and harshness. To create an improved automobile "seal" is seen to maximize the ability to experience comfort by blocking out exterior noise, particularly related to wind. The car's seal lends dramatically to the privacy of the ride, and the ability to experience the feeling of control. Coupled with this reduction of exterior sounds is the blocking of engine vibrations, which infringe upon comfort and add levels of noise disturbance. Creating forms of insulation against this, by incorporating a level of material blockage between the driver and the engine, isolating the underside of the carriage, the car's base, and softening the material properties of the interior shell, affords a softer and quieter ride. These aspects are deeply extended through larger elaborations of the car's "architecture," along with the incorporation of audio systems. "The automobile manufacturer, by controlling the properties of the interior, can treat aural design as a complete system—positioning the seats, orienting the windows, selecting the presentation format, mounting the loudspeakers, designing the acoustics, and adding signal processing."[19] Accordingly, the car becomes a fully designed experience.

In addition, developments in asphalt rubber, or "silent asphalt," complement the refinement of the automobile seal by minimizing environmental noise created by the car itself. Contemporary highway construction throughout Western Europe since the 1980s often incorporates silent asphalt, aiming to lessen the throw of sound from the road through the inclusion of absorbing material. Layers of rubber are placed within the road structure, forming an absorbent cushion that draws in and retains the automobile noise rather than amplifying it. Such technology forms a counterpart to automobile design, making quieter the road and the experience of driving by up to 10 decibels.[20] This can be further seen in the elaborate construction of "sound walls" that act as appendages to freeways. These barriers deflect the trajectories of traffic noise in order to shield nearby neighbors or offices.

Auditory design participates in this overall field of automotive engineering, adding dynamic input into building cars as experiences, turning driving and the car into a form of lifestyle—to control the stylized aesthetics of being on the road, and the experiences found therein. Such stylizations are furthered in car sound systems. First fitted into cars in the 1930s, initially as car radios, the automobile was quickly recognized as providing not only a space of comfort and mobility, but of aesthetics and style, and along with that, a vehicle for new forms of musical marketing.[21] The better the sound quality, and the more elaborate the sound system, the greater impact on the possibility that drivers will in turn consume the availability of media material. Cars and radios were put side by side in the elaboration of their markets, intersecting with governmental policies surrounding communications and transportation, where the message of the ride was contoured by the intersection of personal use and manufacturing regulations. This relation surfaces in those moments when cars become vehicles for the expression of particular cultural groups, noticeably marginal or in tension with mainstream culture.

Taking It Low

Lowrider car culture in Los Angeles is built upon a history of cultural struggle and expression, gravitating around an appropriation of the car as an emblem of class and race identity. Mexican-American groups in the late 1930s and throughout the 1940s were often without means to afford new automobiles, and so formed social groups in which cars were shared property. With so much driving and collective use, the cars inevitably required personal maintenance. Mechanical repairs on the shared vehicles dovetailed into aesthetic flourishes and stylization, resulting in the expression of group identities through the car. Quickly the car became a medium for seeking transformation, a literal vehicle to ward off the challenges of social marginalization, and to extend the cultivation of an emancipatory aesthetic. Styling the car was equivalent to fashioning social and political identity on wheels—a vehicle not only for needed transportation, but also for the public display of life searching for its own route.

IMAGE 14 Lowrider cars, Pharoah's car show, Los Angeles, 2009. Photo: the author.

Los Angeles has always been a site for the appropriation and modification of cars, leading not only to lowriders but also street racers, hot rods, and car clubs, each cultivating specific forms of car customization, from pin-striping to hydraulic lift-systems. These early days though mark the car as a space for cultural negotiation, upon which might be read the intersecting differences of centers and margins. While hot rods and racing became cultural expressions of a predominantly white male culture, lowriding was clearly the dominion of Mexican-American youths. Throughout the 1940s, the act of lowering the car to the lowest point possible above the ground became an art form that not only marked the car as culturally specific, but also elaborated that specificity in centimeters. Such modifications can be read, according to Brenda Jo Bright, as "performances of self-imagined identity enacted against an inverted background of cultural stereotypes and racially marked experiences."[22] Cars for Mexican-American youth culture became means to work within a prejudiced system, fashioning specific messages through precise alterations. Lowering the car, upholstering its interior with fake leopard skin, intermixing parts from various models, adding side-rails and chrome bumpers, or stripping it down to a stark grey (known as the "lead sled"), functioned as an appropriative act bent on tweaking the codes of luxury commodities, leisure activity, and public display according to the vernacular of Chicano ("pachucos") identity. The car became a site for self-determined labor whose value was gained on the street, where cruising formed social activity, and competitiveness lent to the formation of group rituals and codes.

Lowering the car below a legal limit also set the stage for a confrontation between Mexican-American youths and the extraordinarily white police department of Los Angeles at this time.[23] Cars were then at the core of a battle within the social ordering of the city, in which the ability to be mobile formed a cultural struggle. It also became a way to stay ahead of the law, as hot rods and other racers took the streets in illegal racing to in the end gain enough speed to outrun the cops.

In competition, in 1931 the Los Angeles Police Department (LAPD) became the first police department in the United States to develop an extremely efficient radio communications system.[24] Initially structured around a single radio transmitter, and eight City Hall switchboards that dispatched information to 44 patrol cars, by 1938 the system allowed two-way communication. Fitting police vehicles with radio devices, and creating the first call and dispatch system, police could monitor the streets, relay information to other cars, and centralize all this through a switchboard system, ultimately allowing greater control of the streets and their related cultures.[25]

The customization of the automobile thus sweeps both ways, allowing for better policing as well as for the expression of cultures that remain already outside. The tensions existing between Mexican-American immigrants and the local authorities in Los Angeles at this time were an operative influence upon related social unrest. We might glimpse the degree to which automobiles were at the center of cultural clashes by recalling the Zoot Suit riots of 1943, in which Navy personnel assisted by police (and their vehicles) as well as taxi drivers, drove through downtown Los Angeles grabbing Mexican-Americans at random and severely beating them before hauling them off to jail. Stemming from an overarching public paranoia of "cultural invasion" mounting throughout the United States during the War, in this instance the policing infrastructure of mobility and radio technology enabled the hooliganism of agitated soldiers to cruise the city with great fluidity in pursuit of "outsiders."[26]

Audible Identity

The expressiveness of car culture spans the globe, finding extreme manifestation in forms of self-styled design and personalized usage. With lowrider culture this takes the form of car-body modifications, including hydraulic systems enabling the owner to lift the car up so as to "appear" legal (which quickly gave way to competitions known as "bouncing"), to the total aestheticization of engines, suspension systems, and all such related parts (which at times appear in plated gold, and other chrome finishes), to pin-striping and other paint applications. In addition to these customizations, the installment of extreme sound systems within the automobile performs within the cultural vocabularies the car comes to enact. Introducing sound and related audio technologies into the style of customization only elaborates upon the existing relation between sound and cars. As auditory design reveals, the car itself is a sound emitting machine, as well as a sonic potential awaiting animation: the car creates noise and vibration through its impact and contact with road surfaces while musicalizing what it means to be on the road through its own entertainment systems. While windshields provide a cinematic perspective to ultimately encase a driver within his or her own dramatic performance, audio systems provide necessary soundtrack to the world as it zooms by. As earlier mentioned, the car allows an increased stylization to public appearance, where the body, through the extensive machinery of the automobile, may slip across the lines of criminality to produce a confrontation with dominant culture. How often the car participates in criminal actions, leading to those innumerable car chase scenes in which cops and robbers are tested as to their driving skills, and the city streets are turned into a dizzying maze. This finds greater sonic amplification in the trend to fit cars with mega-bass sound systems that totally undo the insulation and auditory design of the car.

Automobiles are vibratory machines that not only provide forms of tonality, but a deep bass that is more tactile than sonorous: the automobile is a conducting mechanism that, when fitted with 15-inch sub-woofers in its trunk—itself a resonating chamber—may produce frequencies ranging below 20 Hz and decibels well above legal limits. In Los Angeles, such sonority takes on magnificent proportions, turning the entire car into sonic technology. Originating mainly within Mexican-American and African-American youth groups involved in rap and hip-hop culture, the mega-bass sound systems continue a tradition of modification and customization, aligning the automobile in the making of cultural identity that, in this case, is not only visual but dramatically sonic.

The privacy of habitation that Bull outlines as particular to the automobile, and its related listening habits, is overturned by a sonic leakage that definitively drives the car toward its ultimate public broadcast—the car literally *booms* down the street. Mega-bass sound systems literally announce stylization by being heard before being seen. In this way, the lowrider car, as a blank canvas allowing symbolic expression through paint jobs and murals outlined by Bright, is also an audible machine granting cultural identity a deep form of amplification. The rumble of bass and beat, which are mostly felt and heard as surprising vibrations, as sound pressure and oscillating wave, as *throb*, function as part of the identity of the car and its driver, or the crew, directing, according to a rhythmic pulse, so much energy against all those that overhear. The car is thus a staging of the production of beats that extends the skin—of the drum, the body, and now, the car—to the resonating mould of the street. Getting in, and turning up, delivers a unified message that finds its energy in the unifying throb of this sonic vibration; the car creates a common skin for all those that occupy its interior, brought together by the shared groove flowing and rippling across body, to make the car a machine for crafting the deep energy at the heart of culture—to draw out the deep pulse that longs for expressive form. To unfold, to carve out, to violate, the car is literally a vehicle for probing what lies ahead, and the sonic boom, an echolating device used in seeking the open road, or the crowded street. Might the mega-bass, vibratory energy of this sonic-body-machine be heard to further *beat back* the violence streets have come to force onto Mexican-American and African-American youths within this city, as a deflecting shield turned into bass culture?

The outfitting of the car with mega-bass sound systems may echo back to the LAPD's radiophonic additions, which supply the individual cop with prosthetic potential that makes man and machine come together in powerful ways. Allowing communications between vehicles, police sound systems also supply means for their own amplifications, this time with the voice from inside the car that, through the introduction of megaphones attached to the roof or sides, can address from behind the wheel. That the car shifts into an extension of the authoritarian body is expressed in the experience of hearing the car speak, extending the body of the cop to greater proportions, as voice of command. Such potential though is folded back through its application by migrant farm workers in Los Angeles guided by Cesar Chavez to create "car caravans" through the community— Chavez enlisted the help of lowrider car clubs in the 1960s to honk horns and speak through loudspeakers in order to *spread the word*. In this sense, the car literally occupies a two-way street, moving between official and unofficial scripts; like the walker, drivers look for their own route through the grid of the streets.

Boom Boom Boom

Though the practice existed well before, the term "lowrider" was only coined around the time of the Watts Riots in 1965 to refer to cruising youths who not only lowered their cars but who also sought to remain out of sight of the cops, that is, to keep a "low profile." From its beginnings in the late 1930s to today, lowriding continues to evoke images of gangs and youth violence, making the very sight of the lowrider automobile a threat to mainstream culture.[27] Howard and Barbara Myerhoff's field studies of middle-class gangs conducted in Los Angeles in the early 1960s underline the sort of conflation occurring between cars and gang identity: "The car, in fact, permeated every aspect of these youngsters' social life. The size of groups which gathered was usually limited by the number a single car could hold . . . Radios in cars were never off . . . (and) after school and on weekends, many of these youngsters could be seen slowly cruising in their cars . . . The cars were the location for nearly all social events engaged in by these youngsters . . . It was at once the setting and symbol of much of adolescent deviant and non-deviant sociability and sexuality."[28] The car comes to offer both deviant and non-deviant behavior a space of gathering, marking it with a series of interpretations, from within differing cultural perspectives. To a white middle-class cultural perspective, the sight of the car operating within Chicano culture is readily identified and equated with gang culture, as threat, while within Chicano culture the car slides more gradually from gang to non-gang practice, functioning in turn as a space for productive labor and the positive expression of cultural identity, specifically as an alternative to gang culture. Interestingly, the car can also offer a safety zone within Chicano culture, as a form of alternative lifestyle to the "gang nation." As Bright explores, the formation of car clubs and car competitions can function as alternatives to gang participation, allowing Mexican-American youths the possibility of escaping gang violence through providing productive and creative exchange and social networking.

Yet from each side, the manipulation and modification of automobiles comes to signal a form of class and cultural consciousness as to the specifics of Mexican-American identity. As the journalist Ted West has pointed out, lowriding culture throughout its history has been imbued with a political energy articulated through automotive expression: "As surely as long hair and dirty clothes in 1967 expressed young America's contempt for its government in war, 20×14 tires on tiny Cragars supporting a 1964 Impala with no ground clearance express the refusal of a young Chicano American to be Anglicized. There has never been a clearer case of the automobile being used as an ethnic statement . . . This isn't just engineering, this is community consciousness."[29]

With the introduction of mega-bass sound systems into lowriders, the movements of such ethnic statements become a booming and vibratory throb. The added sonic beat to the car's modified presence clearly bespeaks attempts at occupation, a sort of territorial claim gaining force through the sub-woofer while also remaining mobile, and potentially beyond arrest. The boom of the bass aids in the cruisin' vehicle to search out possible routes through the city, to capture attention, and to compete. The car then is also a drum, delivering the beat as street culture on wheels, which, through an intersection with hip-hop culture, makes mega-bass a racial and social statement. Accentuating the "sound of the funky drummer" originating in James

Brown's 1970 hit and reiterated in Public Enemy's "Fight the Power," the mega-bass sound system intensifies the embedded dynamics of skin, and the percussive as signifying strike: cutting through the triangulation of drum, body, and rhythm, mega-bass is a tool for the production of an expanded skin, placing all the vibratory plenitude under the seat of the driver as well as blasting it out, as a beat racially marked.

Putting Public Enemy's *Fear of a Black Planet* on wheels, pumped through double 15-inch sub-woofers and driven by 4 amplifiers locked inside the trunk turns the car into a message machine, where customization expresses social and cultural dissent through appropriative tactics, to announce—

"1989 the number another summer (get down)
Sound of the funky drummer
Music hittin' your heart cause I know you got soul
(brothers and sisters, hey)
Listen if you're missin' y'all
Swingin' while I'm singin'
Givin' whatcha gettin'
Knowin' what I know
While the black bands sweatin'
And the rhythm rhymes rollin'
Got to give us what we want
Gotta give us what we need
Our freedom of speech is freedom or death
We got to fight the powers that be
Lemme hear you say
Fight the power"

Beats that turn the history of beaten bodies into counterattack—

"As the rhythm designed to bounce
What counts is that the rhymes

Designed to fill your mind
Now that you've realized the prides arrived
We got to pump the stuff to make us tough
From the heart
It's a start, a work of art
To revolutionize make a change nothin's strange
People, people we are the same
No we're not the same
Cause we don't know the game
What we need is awareness, we can't get careless
You say what is this?
My beloved lets get down to business
Mental self defensive fitness
(Yo) bum rush the show
You gotta go for what you know
Make everybody see, in order to fight the powers that be
Lemme hear you say . . .
Fight the power"[30]

The pump of the rap, pumped through with mega-bass all sculpted and amplified through cars and culture, is not only a vibratory self-massage, but importantly a calling out. "Lemme hear you say" turns the street into a political space, replacing the movements of demonstration with a cruisin' narrative. "Rap music centers on the quality and nature of rhythm and sound, the lowest, 'fattest beats' being the most significant and emotionally charged."[31] As Tricia Rose further describes, the rhythmic intensities of rap music finds particular force in drumming traditions within African music, which through its complicated importation into African-American cultures is given power by its ability to symbolically break the law. "The thing that frightened people about hip-hop was that they heard rhythm—rhythm for rhythm's sake—and that's why it's so revolutionary."[32]

Such dissent may also give narrative to an auditory latching supplying disenfranchisement with another mode of carving a space for itself, one driven by the resonating space of the car. Hip-hop's rhythmic signatures driven by the rapping voice, locking into the beat's pendulum movements, finds support in the cruisin' automobile. The car literally becomes total mega-phone for the pronouncement of a certain racial pride that seeks the resonance of the road. The sound of *Boom Boom Boom* then is both an acoustical thrust, a vibratory bed bringing the driving body deep into reassuring, auditory pleasure, as well as a sonic image of canon fire directed back out to culture at large. In Los Angeles, such booming grabs attention to form triggers of identification—*I dig this song*—ultimately registering the makings of gang culture aimed against those who get in the way—*this song is our weapon*. Rhythm is not only a form of organizing time and space, but means by which such organization is in tension with others. Bass Culture put on wheels is a potent weapon for broadcasting in full view the legendary aggression at the heart of rhythm, a signal preceding the potential use of the gun. Vibration, in providing a key base for entrainment—those undulations and waves found from childhood—also becomes cultural energy to cohere group identity, or shared skin, and threaten those outside the car.

This blending of beats and roads finds its own brand of hip-hop in the formation of "Jeep Beats" spawned in the early 1990s designed around the cultivation of Jeep vehicles, notably the Suzuki Jeep. As the track listing to Bassman's *Jeep Beats* from 1995 demonstrates, the vehicular potential of cars is not only found in the acoustical shell, but in the quake of the vibratory: "Intro To Boom, Wicked, What U Want, Bass Pie, Deep Thrust, Doo Doo Bass, It Takes 2—(The Bassnamic Duo), Bass In Your System, Bass Dawg, Bass Junkies, Here Cums The Bass, Quake Of The Month, Trunkshakers"—*Jeep Beats* constructs a bass-language sited as part of automotive volume, as a quaking space enveloping the driver in palpable beats.

The vibratory phenomenon of locating the self in relation to surroundings is thus a form of embodied work that seeks to fix the primary sensation of being immersed within a cultural and social structure in which sensations can turn into violation—where Public

Enemy's "Fight the Power" turns into Bassman's "all I want to do is go boom-boom, pump the bayou, let's shake the trunk" to oscillate between cultural aggression and sexual fantasy, radical dissent and punning lyric. The boom of the bass is also then an expression of *taking pleasure*—an erotic energy unfolding from the car not only as sonic machine, but also as sex engine. The rhythmic is thus both embodied rap that delivers a hard punch, as well as a vehicular fore-play that fuses hip-hop culture with the legacy of sexual identity the car has always generated. The cruisin' car is also a stealth weapon enacting the power of the (male) body to claim territory. Rhythm, sex, politics, music, violence, and the degree to which these are custom-ized according to particular cultures form a complex force that turns the road into an economy of cultural negotiation and resonance.

Extending the legacy of funk and hip-hop music, the modified mega-bass car is an engineered *funk-production*—a drum machine for the production of the Phat Beat for an altogether different set of grooves. The car might be said to take on the status of the turn-table, as a sonic technology casting a new mix that is equally new epistemology. The language of scratching shifts to a language of mega-bassing, relocating the breakbeat as "hyperrhythm," which ultimately "scramble the logic of causation" to forge a "new illogic of hypercussion and supercussion."[33] The signifying field of the percussive outlined by Mowitt shifts once on wheels, altering the rock beat for the throttled vibe—a vibration that takes all the psychic energy found in the percussive and places it within the sub-woofer.

Kodwo Eshun's sonic analysis of the forces of funk and hip-hop elaborates the rhythmical, sparking a dynamic vocabulary that seeks to embody the very energies of this scrambled logic. As he continues, "Hyperrhythm generates a new physics of physicality," aligning Mowitt with the spinning decks of Dr. Boom, whose "Count-down to Super Boom" is an interstellar interlude readying the skin for the mix of the big beat with an accompanying African groove—a boom with a *thwack* to loosen the skin, as a flaying sonic. With the force of the car, this hyperrhythm is shaped not only by the particulars of musical structure, but also through the resonating modifications of an automotive instrument driving frequency everywhere. The Phat Beat then is rhythm becoming vibration, turning into sonic object as sculpted by the car and highlighting the skin of the driver—the Phat Beat forces the skin from within the car outward, onto the surface of the customized vehicle, and further, against the street as a form of *skin culture*.

The contemporary sounding of the car brings back to the ear another set of tunes, those accompanying earlier lowrider culture. Though predating the mega-bass addition, lowrider cars in the 1960s brought forth their own musical soundtrack, in the form of Cannibal and the Headhunters, Johnny Chingas, Freddy Fender, The Jaguars, and Ritchie Valens. The cool tunes of the West Coast scene found a particular setting within the lowrider car, giving Chicano flair to surf culture. (Every weekend I used to overhear my neighbor David, an ex-gang member in Highland Park, Los Angeles, playing doo-wop tunes from his parked car, while he and his buddies would stand around the car and drink back cans of Bud Light. Even for the retired gang members, the car, the music, and the scene of the street were their territorial site, as an important constellation by which to find home.)

We might hear the customized car, and its sonorous aesthetics, replete with vibratory bass, as a vehicle for reclaiming a right to the street. "The car's humanity lies not just in what people are able to achieve through it, not yet in its role as a tool of destruction, but in the degree to which it has become an integral part of the cultural environment within which we see ourselves as human."[34] The seeking out of identity and human relations, as found through automotive experience, is forcefully given expression in lowrider culture, where borders of racial violence and the automotive skin superimpose in the making of community. The lowrider car is fundamentally a space for sharing; a communal object, it performs, through ongoing maintenance, as a tribal ritual by which familial and relational ties are secured.

The do-it-yourself customizations at the heart of lowrider culture find more corporate rendering in Toyota's recent concept car "Pod."[35] Including an elaborate system of IT sensing devices, the Pod operates as a living organism, replete with decorative exterior lighting that registers different "moods" at a driver's command. This hyper-designed, hi-tech automotive object fixes the car as an elaborate extension of the body, functioning more as a lounge chair to aid in the contemporary networking of the subject. The Pod brings to mind lyrics from "Let the Good Times Roll" by The Cars: "If the illusion is real / Let them give you a ride," which replaces the vitality of "Fight the Power" with an altogether different vibe. Thus, the car swings between energetic message and cushioned illusion, between cultural weapon and private drift.

Alongside the latching customizations of the car, the culture of dB drag racing turns the automobile into an object not only for new forms of display and relation, but also as a device for sport. Developed over the last 10 years, dB drag racing, also known as Bass Racing or Sound Pressure Level (SPL) competitions, is a competitive sport utilizing the automobile as an acoustical shell by which to drive or "race" bass frequencies. Competitors customize their cars for optimum sound pressure levels—often eliminating superfluous elements from the car, filling car doors with cement, and packing the trunk with an array of amplifiers, the competition is designed to reach sound levels over 170 decibels. In 2005, Scott Owens became the first person to break the 180 decibels barrier with his Ford vehicle. Sponsored by Pioneer Audio, Owens' car was fitted with 13 Pioneer sub-woofers powered by 52 Premier amplifiers. Such incredible power produced a sound equivalent to that of a rocket launching and louder than the take off of a jet airplane. Such extremes of course make the car uninhabitable, turning the customized mega-bass sound system into an elaborate technical intervention, and ultimately shifting musical expression and sonic identity to the sport of vibration.

IMAGES 15 AND 16 dB drag racing, event held at Media Markt, Flensburg, Germany, 2009. Photos: the author.

Slow Groove

Rhythm, vibration, and the dynamics of auditory latching bring the street to life, and find deep expression in the momentum of driving. "He who walks down the street, over there, is immersed in the multiplicity of noises, murmurs, rhythms . . ."[36] The car might be said to complete this sensorial trajectory of the walker mapped out by Lefebvre, literally driving the dynamics of vibratory contact and self-propulsion to a mediating height: the car as technology is an aesthetic totality, lodging the body within an elaborate network of devices and effective potentialities. *To drive is to project oneself.* Sound and music dramatically support this projected embodiment, marking the street as a space of transformative amplification.

The network of the automotive experience can be heard as a sliding and throbbing of so many surfaces. From the surface of the street to the rubbery point of contact with the tire, and further, to the surfaces of the car cutting through the wind, all forming a vibratory undulation to trail across the many surfaces and planes of the car, deeper, into the car itself; the vibratory movement races through seats and along the steering wheel, ultimately touching the skin of the driver and passengers, massaging, caressing, in a complex of sensation, to ripple the skin and send it into sympathetic release. The car literally mobilizes the dynamics of vibration to create particular skin experiences.

Against all this vibratory energy though, I also want to take a step away from the speed and rush of the automotive high, and the social and racial challenges that have come to infuse the car with degrees of sonic meaning. *To slow down* . . . Easing the foot off the gas pedal, the car in turn provides a smooth ride—the city street slips into a dreamy zone and the car eases the body across its surface. Only a minimum of texture scores the seeming glide of the ride. In this slow lane, I want to linger for a moment, to register the rhythmic and vibratory beyond the bass race (and the race bass), and within the movements of traffic that find the humdrum of daily life puttering away. For the car, like the rhythmical break of musical time—the moment of creating or finding contact within and among all the features of the world—in turn constructs another spacing. The privacy of the car also keeps the body off the street, literally away from contact, to form poignant isolation devoid of those murmurs and noises Lefebvre points to as experienced by the walker. Though the car, through all its modified expressions, can operate for cultural and territorial dispute, the acoustical interval it imparts to being on the road might also be heard to numb the senses with isolating verve. For if auditory latching comes about according to the dynamics of finding place, therefore charging a relational dynamic in continual flux, to be in the car is to potentially hear only oneself, and the selected tracks of too much available audio. In this instance, the car sound system becomes a surrogate for all the direct contact passing by—turning up or quieting down, the interior stands in for the soundscape one is ultimately separated from.

As an interval, a spacing within time, the car is a machine of fantasy—shielded from the street, the body floats freely. Driving generates that illusory sense of possible escape while often delivering back the harsh reality of the concrete. Though one can go anywhere, the street seems to lead only to more of the same. Selecting a soundtrack for such a slow, mesmerizing ride, the auditory space of the car is a modulating stance against this dynamic—to fill this vague space of the automotive with an excess of comforting features. To help keep one's eyes on the road, the booming bass or smooth melodies supply the imagination with psychic relief. Vibration unfolds the skin beyond its singular shape and body, to touch additional surfaces, as the making of a sensual elaboration. Vibration also helps to ease one back into reverie, into the deep memory of primary caresses—to draw the skin in, affirming the body as a sensing whole and the street a space of acceptance.

5

SHOPPING MALL: MUZAK, MISHEARING, AND THE PRODUCTIVE VOLATILITY OF FEEDBACK

I'm all lost in the supermarket
I can no longer shop happily
I came in here for the special offer
A guaranteed personality

—The Clash

. . . the landscape has ceased to be a backdrop for something else to happen in front of: instead, everything that happens is part of the landscape. There is no longer a sharp distinction between foreground and background.[1]

—Brian Eno

How psychoacoustics and the history of modern shopping came to meet, producing smooth backdrops for distracted listening, to give way to ambient relations.

The potentiality for sound to act as building material finds expression in a variety of disciplines and within varied fields of science. Notably, acoustic design as a profession maps out the behavior of sound phenomena in relation to architectural space. The work of acoustic design fundamentally aims to shape the movements of sound through space to either minimize excessive noise or disturbance or to harness the characteristics of specific sound phenomena to heighten the appreciation of their presence, as in the case of concert hall design. Barry Blesser and Linda-Ruth Salter, in their detailed account of acoustics and aural architecture, examine the profession of acoustic design, locating points of contention and histories of acoustical experimentation. In a discussion on listening

165

environments, Blesser and Salter suggest that an understanding of spatial acoustics can be viewed according to two perceptual processes—"modifying the direct sound to produce a primary sonic event with increased size and intensity, and creating a separate slave sonic event [secondary event] that is experienced as enveloping reverberation."[2] Therefore, spatial acoustics generally addresses an existing or anticipated sound event (music, voice, ambient, etc.) while crafting architecture to converse with such event. It both accentuates the intensity or meaning of the primary event and also supports its spatial spread through a secondary event, that of reverberation, which carries forward the primary sounds further into space.

Aspects of sound phenomena, such as vibration, disturbing echo, and loudness are generally subdued by related architectural adjustments within acoustic design. This can be seen particularly within domestic and working environments. Understandably, the disturbing effects of sound to extend between apartments, either from appliances or from neighbors, has led to degrees of acoustical work, importantly in terms of sound insulation. Regulations throughout the UK require sound insulation against both airborne and impact sounds between walls, floors and stairs, stressing that these "shall have reasonable resistance to the transmission of sound."[3] When placed within the home, spatial acoustics shifts its focus from that of aesthetic pleasure or communicational clarity to health and safety.

In conjunction, a great deal of spatial and acoustical research has also occurred within the fields of music technology and electroacoustic composition, particularly with works that incorporate a dynamic sense for sonic movement. The manipulation and shaping of sound matter in the electronic studio often unfolds alongside questions of architecture and spatiality that when coupled to elements of music composition activate the ear in multidimensional ways. The psychoacoustic figures that arise through the integration of acoustical features with electronic sound have generated a history of sonic art that continues to expand and unfold in numerous ways. The legacies of electroacoustic music and sonic art since the 1950s still echo in contemporary practices that put to use sonic-spatial understanding. Forms of current sound practice often incorporate or presuppose sensitivity to architecture, and to questions of locational sound in general, leading to an overall recognition of sound's potent ability to act spatially. This has found additional application in the use of surround sound technology in cinema and home theater systems since the 1990s, making multichannel audio available for general use.

Extending this appreciation for sound and space, I want to turn to the shopping mall. The mall offers an extremely familiar yet also surprisingly complex instance of acoustic design that incorporates a number of sonic and spatial elements. From my perspective, the mall gives expression to an "ambient architecture" that, while being caught up within the verve of consumer culture writ large, utilizes the physiological and psychological dynamics of audition (among other sensorial events). It does so in turn by considering the specific locative conditions of a given architecture, forming a rather elaborate construction of sound and space. In this way, it offers a compelling point within the acoustic territories of everyday life, highlighting a history of spatial politics fully wed to sonic experience.

As space the mall is often open and reverberant, catering to a variety of public needs and interactions. In many cases, the mall acts as a central public space for local neighborhoods or regions for not only shopping, but importantly for gathering and for public involvement. Incorporating many entertainment facilities, the mall often provides a customer with an extraordinary range of activities. Thus, as an acoustical situation it is highly active and generally full of ambient sound that contains numerous elements. From play areas for children to food courts, dental facilities to fitness centers, the mall reverberates with a number of interactions set within a systematic structure of management. It organizes and caters to the sense for public meeting, acting as social center, hang out, and consumer fantasy all in one. Additionally, the mall incorporates an active presentation of electronic and recorded sound by way of extensive intercom and speaker systems, which generally amplify background music to effectively contour the atmospheric shape of the mall. These amplifications aim to accentuate the fluidity of the mall experience by supporting a feeling for mobility and relaxation which shopping entails—customers should find the needed object or item without obstruction while also experiencing a feeling for consumer experimentation through browsing, trying on, imagining. The mall in this sense is deeply scripted and predetermined while relying on an architectural vocabulary of atmospheres and ambiences to which music and sound play a vital role.

In examining the mall, as an atmospheric, psychoacoustical public environment, I also want to consider the sonic figure of feedback. Whereas the driver in the car is situated within the potential range of vibratory sensing, the shopper in the mall is conditioned by an elaborate ambience designed to *give back* the image of one's desire. The shopper arrives in search of clothing, furniture, or electronic appliance from which fulfillment or satisfaction is partially gained or imagined. In this sense, the mall anticipates the desiring flows of the individual body, as a network of psycho-emotional force; it harnesses the energies of the shopper while returning such energies in the form of consumer delight and fulfillment. This *feedbacking* though operates as a volatile, tenuous effect, shifting according to so many fluctuating particles of production and consumption, as an enveloping mesh.

As a sonic energy, feedback is tenuously drawn out. It rises as a sonic thread, appearing between an electronic sound source, such as a microphone, and its amplification source, such as a loudspeaker, and their close proximity, to result in a looping, humming effect. Feedback is cause and effect united in a self-contained coupling, where an input gives an output that comes to influence the input again. This might be said to function as part of any system or production, shifting in degrees of positive and negative influence.

These operations of feedback also appear within studies of communication. In Barry Truax's important study on "acoustic communication" the author emphasizes the "feedback" of acoustic information, which "is necessary for orientation, and in the most general sense, the awareness of self in relation to others."[4] Feedback, as a communicational channel, affords an audible understanding for self and surrounding as they flow together, defining a positive channel for environmental sensitivity; feedback is a sort of registration of this acoustical interaction, indicating points of contact and connection as well as breakage and interruption. Feedback generates a locative sense for place and emplacement—how my own presence is an active participant within the larger acoustic ecology.

Engaging these understandings of feedback, the mall provides an environmental situation for exposing acoustical communication on a number of levels. In following these I wish to consider how the mall utilizes all the effective materiality of sensing to generate a production of subjectivity. Yet this production occurs through an unsteady balancing between flow and break, excitement and disappointment, giving way to a relational dynamic between body and surrounding, self and object. That is, the feedbacking found within mall life occurs as an unsteady flow of acoustical information and exchange, rising at times in acts of secret performance and falling at others in moments of mishearing. The mall is a scripted space that, in weaving together varying intensities, acoustically sounds out multiple routes within its seeming monotony.

The mall acts as a galvanizing container for a number of performances. Such performances both reinforce the view of mall culture as symptomatic of a general withdrawal of social values outside forms of consumerism, an anonymous and impersonal space of pure capital, while also spawning curiosity as to the greater weave of architectural effects. In approaching the mall within this study of everyday life, I linger within its corridors and shops so as to bring forward possibilities for reappraising often-negative understandings of mall culture. I wait for the next tune to play over its speaker systems while overhearing a conversation between a sales clerk and a customer on the current problems occurring within the local baseball league. From this perspective, the mall comes forward as an elaborate meeting point between a fully scripted acoustic and spatial design and the multiple forms of public experience occurring therein. In this regard, the mall can be viewed as a production that draws out the psychological and social effects of sound and audition arising from within a culture of management. Within this totalizing sonic experience, the movements of social bonds might also be heard, as a lateral or nested coordinate within the script of the mall. In this way, I want to also hold up the mall as a space that generates complex listening formed from the effects of background music *and* the productive ambiguities found in ambient architectures.

Muzak

In considering the mall as an acoustic territory, it is my aim to detect the movements of sound and music as they come to shape the spatial and social experience. For it is clear upon entering shopping malls that music is key to designing the particular environment. As Jonathan Sterne notes in his account of programmed music in the Mall of America, "music becomes a form of architecture. Rather than simply filling up an empty space, the music becomes part of the consistency of that space. The sound becomes a presence, and as that presence it becomes an essential part of the building's infrastructure."[5] Thus, the shopping mall offers a dynamic account of a particular sonic architecture that has come to pervade so much of quotidian life. Yet, by listening in to the mall as a complex acoustical space, the trail of background music and the ambient din of shopping all point to a larger history related to consumerism, labor, and sound reproduction. Walking through the mall then is to participate in the here and now, as well as a lineage of sonic research and social history.

The psychological and physiological effects of music have been widely researched and documented as part of the history of industrialization within the Western world. Jerri A. Husch's study of music in the workplace provides a rich analysis of how music was taken up within the larger industrial management culture of the early twentieth century. At the core of such history was a growing understanding of the relation between capitalist production and the health and mental state of the worker. "In other words, neither the machine, nor the mechanical mode of production could be stabilized and maintained until the social and psychological processes necessary to sustain them had been internalized by the workers."[6] To aid in the process of internalization, the placement of music within the workplace became an operative ingredient. A dramatic rationalization was mounted to examine and define every aspect of the workplace, exemplified in Frederick W. Taylor's studies of time and motion, and his "scientific management" theory, which led to the design of production machinery based on the movements of the working body. Ideas of efficiency and production management were coupled with growing scientific examination on the vitality of the individual worker (which presented a deepening challenge to the growing industrial core of US and Europe at this time as seen in labor disputes and the development of the unions). The efficiency of production was increasingly understood to presuppose the comfort and standardized labor of the individual worker.

Locating music within the workplace gained credibility throughout the 1920s as psychologists increasingly entered the field of labor management, being hired to examine the space of work, the response of workers to various conditions, and the question of standardizing the movements of production, which had come to radically replace earlier forms of labor and a worker's relation to his/her craft. "It was agreed that the growth of purely mechanical and other routinized forms of labor had indeed diminished opportunities for self expression, but the effects of this loss were seen to be offset by the actions of business management in humanizing the work process."[7]

The development of Muzak in the early 1920s is radically linked to questions of the workplace, and the feverish reality of labor disputes and union aggression. Following the developments of radio and telephone technology, the possibility to wire in sound from a central control led to a systematic appraisal of music's effect on labor and the psychology of the worker. It was found that the tasks of work could be better supported by providing background music in the workplace, giving workers an auditory frame through which bodily rhythms, the repetition of physical tasks, and the often monotonous passing of time could be eased.

The effects of music were generally recognized to increase metabolism, strengthen or modify mood, and importantly, to "increase not only the intensity of sudden effort, but also the duration of sustained effort and the power of renewing it."[8] In addition, the rhythmical structure of songs was discovered to aid in the repetitive movements often found within modern work, and to reduce the sense of monotony experienced from such actions. The muscular expenditure of energy finds a literal source of support with the presence of music, giving subliminal nourishment to lessening the fatigue of the workday. In addition to supporting and easing fatigue, music had great effect on a worker's attention span. As Husch outlines, the early studies by Wyatt and Langdon (1939) conducted in England revealed an increase in production output with the insertion of music into the working environment. The sheer quantity of output rose as music allowed workers a sense of distraction to the banality of their surroundings, while also reducing the level of conversation occurring between workers.[9]

Such psychological and physiological tests continued well into the 1950s, often linked to military testing, where the question of alleviating undue stress and fatigue while increasing attention and productivity is key. With the development of Muzak (originally by Major General George O. Squier, a decorated veteran and then Chief Signal Officer of the United States Army), locating appropriate music within the workplace became a dynamic reality. Reorganized in 1934 as the Muzak Corporation, the company operated through the use of electrical cabling (later replaced by telephone wire), sending out programs of recorded classical compositions to workplaces. The light pattern of melodies, the recurring movement of soft rhythms, the forms of harmony accentuating song structures, all cradle up against the body in the midst of work to aid in its efficient output. These psychological and physical effects were incorporated into the Muzak program, eventually leading to an extensive network of clients and musical repertoire aimed at specific spaces and work situations. As a Muzak researcher commented in the late 1940s:

> Factors that distract attention—change of tempo, loud brasses, vocals—are eliminated. Orchestras of strings and woodwinds predominate, the tones blending with the surroundings as do proper colors in a room. The worker should be no more aware of the music than of good lighting. The rhythms, reaching him subconsciously, create a feeling of well-being and eliminate strain.[10]

Muzak was immediately understood as a form of "atmospheric architecture," conducting mood and behavior through sonic material. Yet Muzak's original relation to the workplace quickly shifted to other environments. Already by 1934 the company was installing their system in residential households, originally in the Cleveland area. By 1946 Muzak was heard in restaurants, offices, transit areas, factories and supermarkets, and eventually finding its way to the White House (in the 1950s), providing "functional music" to postwar America. Might Muzak's success be attributed not only to the demands of labor management, and the burgeoning industrial production of the early twentieth century, but also to the emergence of a domestic culture seeking stability against the malaise of the economic depression followed by the social intensities of the Second World War? If music has the ability to effect psychology, and to support the fatigue of physiological expenditure, can we hear Muzak as a form of environmental conditioning to aid in the general mood of the populace?

As Joseph Lanza has noted, Muzak also pervaded musical productions and sound culture throughout the 1950s and 1960s, leading to moodsongs, elevator music, and an auditory diffusion of compositions for emotional life. "Along with Muzak and elevator music, there is moodsong to accompany our favorite movie scenes, tickle our subconscious fancies on television and radio commercials, alert us to the next network news station break, and lull us in our home entertainment centers."[11] Moodsong appears in numerous media and situations, to effect a given experience through emotional and psychological intervention. Such sonic experience resituates our relation to figure and ground, foreground and background by operating on the peripheries of perception, and through conditioning the atmosphere of place, granting the design of space a dynamic psychoacoustic supplement. In this way, Muzak became an intensely sited production by understanding the listening body in relation to specific environments.

One dramatic location for the implementation of background music can be found in the shopping mall. Muzak has appeared as a material addition to mall architecture since the 1950s, pervading the vast and reverberant spaces with an extensive network of speaker systems to pipe in a controlled program of light tunes, versions of popular songs, and instrumental renditions of jazz classics. As Sterne further notes, music in the mall is key to scripting the architectural experience: "Programmed music can be said to territorialize the Mall: it builds and encloses the acoustical space, and manages the transitions from one location to another; it not only divides space, but also coordinates the relations among subdivisions."[12]

Muzak's scientific research, though initially arising in relation to the workplace, finds application within the spaces of consumption and the growing consumer culture of the 1950s. The psychological and physiological drama of the shopping body might in turn find support through a steady stream of music, programmed in relation to the architecture of the mall, and the ebb and flow of energy attached to the movements of spending.

Margaret Crawford has poignantly observed that the history of the mall incorporates a steady accumulation of architectural and spatial effects aimed at engaging the consumer. As she notes, the "Malling of America" from the 1960s to the 1980s radically shaped the physical and social landscapes of the nation, aligning real estate interests, commercial production, and local economies with a culture of consumption often masked as "the demands of the consumer." As she queries, "If the world is understood through commodities, then personal identity depends on one's ability to compose a coherent self-image through the selection of a distinct personal set of commodities."[13] From this perspective, the mall can be understood to fuel the manufacturing of desire. To do so, the mall structures its entire development and success according to the particular laws of consumption, which make an unsteady weave from the flows of capital and the flows of personal identity. Thus, the seeming banality of the mall can be read as a dynamic register of the meeting of the individual body and a fully scripted system of management. "As central institutions in the realm of consumption, shopping malls constantly restructure both products and behavior into new combinations that allow commodities to penetrate even further into daily life."[14] To perform such combinations the mall balances "products and behavior" by providing tangible goods related to local demographics and lifestyles ("real needs"), as well as stimulating a prolonged fantasy of associated goods ("imagined needs")—that is, the mall gives comfort while always already unsettling one's sense of fulfillment; the mall satisfies immediate need while suggesting, through a perpetual presentation of associated goods, that one does not have everything.

To return to the notion of feedback, the mall instigates a level of feedback so as to loop the customer and the shopping condition together, weaving them into a psychodynamic structure. That is, as a customer one must find what is needed while at the same time be given additional input, as a constant production of lack aimed at the imagination. The mall draws out this need for more by balancing the feeling for harmonious mingling—*this jacket is perfect*—with an ever-so slight coming of change or rupture—*I'm sure there is something just ahead.* Consumerism interlocks a sense of completion *and* a feeling for desiring more. By locating such fluctuations within the space of the mall it might be viewed as an architecture for the promotion of longing, housing the ongoing fantasy of possible identity while giving support to the mood swings of consumption.

The mall offers what Guy Debord termed "shimmering diversions" of capital made explicit in the architectural environment, which incorporates individual fantasy while mirroring back one's own image as on the verge of collapse—the horizon of the mall, as an ambient spatiality perfumed by the tempo of musical form, holds steady the ever-new with the banalization of the always the same. The fragmentary nature of shopping—*of trying things on, of getting carried away, of wishing for more*—thus puts the shopper into a subdued frenzy, a desiring flow continually seeking fulfillment through what he or she sees and feels. Thus, the shopping mall is "calculated to organize the disorienting flux of attributes and needs" and to balance "the limited goods permitted by this logic and the unlimited desires released by this exchange."[15]

Muzak's initial program of quarter-hour music (15-minutes of music followed by 15-minutes of silence) was designed to support the worker, stimulating the energy expenditure of muscular movement and the fatigue of attention by specifically intervening within the time frame of production. Music could re-animate the expenditure of energy while silence could aid in reducing the monotony of a steady stream of information. Such a concentrated structure demarcates an acoustical horizon where one is conditioned by the appearance and disappearance of musical stimuli over time. Following Muzak into the space of the mall, we can identify how it comes to perform within the logic of consumerism by aiming to mollify the unsteady balance between "goods and behavior" and the labors enacted by the consuming body. From Frank Sinatra to the boy band Blue, the mood swings of shopping are anticipated in the shifting shades of musical textures.

Phil Kotler's ideas of "store atmospherics" from the late 1960s draws early attention to the effective capability of lighting, crowding, music, and even scent, to induce various moods conducive to the experience of shopping.[16] Store atmospherics give spatial conditioning, creating degrees of comfort or stimulus, which also find parallel in the architectural ideas of Victor Gruen. An Austrian architect, Gruen immigrated to the US in the 1930s, along with many other architects, notably Mies van der Rohe, Walter Gropius, and Marcel Breuer. Establishing himself in Manhattan as a leading store designer, a job many of his architectural colleagues viewed lowly, the story of Gruen is interwoven with the story of mall culture. His store designs for such shops as Barton's, Ciro's Jewelry of London, and Lederer de Paris, all located in the growing high-end retail section of 5th Avenue, revolutionized the notion of shopping. Drawing upon his Viennese roots, Gruen's shop designs were based on elaborating the shop façade into an arcade where passersby could stroll into and absorb the extended glass display cases recessed into the walls before entering. The arcade became a site for the presentation of goods, turning them into museum displays replete with special lighting, mirrors, and elegant fabrics aimed at highlighting the uniqueness of the objects. "Employing innovative store layouts, brand-new materials, strategic lighting, and shocking façades, the partners [Gruen worked alongside Morris Ketchum] fashioned a retail experience that surrounded the viewer with glittering goods."[17]

Gruen's elaborate store designs thus aimed to create a retail experience, stimulating the shopper as a viewer and lending to the movements of consumerism a dynamic architectural backdrop. Such expressions though carried with them an innate sense of fantasy and desire. As Gruen commented in the early 1940s, "we want to influence emotional rather than rational powers."[18] The shop architecture was an illusionary space designed to stimulate and promote equally the goods for sale and a shopper's curiosity. This led to a number of spatial effects, notably extending the shop out onto the street, or bringing the street into the shop to create a seamless effect.[19]

Gruen's designs were notably commented upon, receiving praise for their innovative use of materials in creating retail experiences as well as being criticized for their apparent trickery. Lewis Mumford blasted Gruen's designs as an "assault on the senses" that turned architecture into "parlor pomp."[20] Mumford's criticisms were already out of touch with the emerging culture of consumerism that would lead to further assaults on the senses, shaping the built environment through a vocabulary of pure effect. Gruen's early designs in Manhattan lent persuasively to future retail developments, providing a model for how to attract customers, and further, to profit from the increasing expansion of the real estate market that emerged alongside the American suburbs.[21] Gruen's architectural ideas were eventually replaced by pure economics. As he states, "Loans for buildings which are to be leased are based not on the structural soundness of the building but on the financial soundness of the tenants; not on the thoroughness of design detail but on the thoroughness of lease writing; not on the aesthetics of the structure but on the beauty of the financial statement."[22]

The work of Gruen runs parallel to the development of "store atmospherics" to signal a continuation of the psychological and physiological reach of Muzak in understanding the complex interweaving of muscular energy, personal desire, and economics. Muzak's "stimulus progression program" participates in conditioning the atmospherics of shopping, where "All the familiar tricks of mall design—limited entrances, escalators placed only at the end of corridors, fountains and benches carefully positioned to entice shoppers into stores—control the flow of consumers through the numbingly repetitive corridors of shops."[23] Music not only adds to the formal design of the mall, but interlocks with the energies of the shopper. This occurs through a number of effective musical dynamics, most notably, tempo and volume. For instance, Smith and Curnow's "arousal hypothesis" (1966) examined how certain volume levels influence how much time shoppers spend in stores. It was discovered that louder music results in people spending less time in the shop, whereas softer music generally resulted in customers spending more time. "Arousing music" essentially made customers shop quicker. Tempo of music was further understood to function similarly to volume, with the quicker music stimulating a customer to move more swiftly through a shop.[24] Such studies were even conducted to gauge how many bites a customer in a cafeteria takes during a meal—the faster the music, the faster the chewing. Yet, moving quickly through a shop does not necessarily result in a customer spending more—while it may help to stimulate a steady flow of shopping, it was also found that customers who shopped slower generally spent more money. Therefore, the dynamics of the shop must balance between customer flow and customer spending, resulting in a "stimulus progression" applied to spaces of consumption. Volume and tempo come to impress themselves upon the shopping body, as a contouring intervention onto the energy flows and expenditures, continually modulated so as to structure or contort the movements of spending.

Distracted Listening

Barry Truax takes note of how systems of electroacoustic audio have come to pervade the environments of everyday life. "In many situations, electroacoustic sound *imposes* its character on an environment because of its ability to dominate, both acoustically and psychologically."[25] Muzak dramatically participates in such electroacoustic domination, and as Truax further observes, results in an environment becoming "a designed, artificial construct."[26] In this case, the listener is located as a "consumer" of an auditory environment, which in the mall structures the aural sense through an electroacoustic system of audio dominance, resulting in a "distracted listening" experience. Such distractedness for Truax lessens our ability to discern environmental information, undermining the communicational feedbacking of self and surrounding as key to aural sensing.

Following this perspective, and the related effects and electroacoustic technologies, I want to also claim or insert an element of *ambiguity*—to shift the clear form of audition, which seems to hear in the mall a steady line of active auditory dominance. In contrast, or as a shadow, I want to reflect on Muzak and what other kinds of stories might be told from the mall experience.

Akin to Joseph Lanza's own positive appreciation for Muzak as participating within a more general history of music, I want to hear the mall also as an architectural situation in which an array of sonic experiences play a significant role. To do so, I draw upon Paul Carter's evocative essay, "Ambiguous Traces, Mishearing, and Auditory Space," which gives a compelling examination of the auditory through the theme of "ambiguity." Claiming that listening as a communicational channel incorporates the pleasures and potentiality inherent to ambiguity, Carter stakes out a productive territory in which mishearing opens audition up onto a rich process. As Carter states, "Listening, unlike hearing, values ambiguity, recognizing it as a communicational mechanism for creating new symbols and word senses . . ."[27] The dynamics of listening unfold as a productive volume by explicitly "evolving out of ambiguity and mishearing," thereby retaining "these signs of what cannot be fully communicated."[28] Listening forms a dialogical activity, full of slippages; a set of maneuvers that in nurturing communicational clarity also incorporates all the subtle gradations, challenges, and misapprehensions of relating.

I want to adopt such productive mishearing in approaching the mall, so as to not only hear the drive of Muzak as a force of (negative) distracted listening, but also as a sonic materiality adding richness to the overall oscillations of place. As I've tried to map out here, Muzak uncovers a range of potentials for manipulating and engineering physical and emotional experiences. Yet such totalizing visions, when placed within the mall, also give rise to an unstable structure—surely within the balancing act of the mall, the flows of desiring and imagining contoured by the extravagant rendering of consumer production also generates an array of misguided information, prolonged agitation, tiredness, enthusiasm and other forms of distraction that I take as *positive and multiple*. The script of the mall is also prone to slippages, generating boring tedium as well as sudden flirtations, both of which supplement the directness of spending. These disarrayed experiences might be based on ignoring the humming of background sound altogether, or by finding pleasure in simply listening along.

To return to the model of feedback, the looping that occurs between self and surrounding is also a volatile thread of acoustical exchange— feedback is by nature a *wavering line*, in constant motion, and oscillating in a glissando that rises and falls according to the dynamics of proximity, air pressure, or outside influence. This wavering oscillation imparts an elemental dynamic to the exchange of self and surrounding, as a deeply significant flexibility, and on a communicational level must be heard to give way to moments of intimacy and mingling, or intense proximity, as well as alienation and estrangement. Feedback is relationally productive precisely by functioning as such a sensitive, tensing link prone to fluctuation.

A study by Bing Chen and Jian Kang of a shopping mall in Sheffield reveals that customers appreciated soft or quiet music as part of their surroundings. Interestingly, they discovered that the sounds of other people were the loudest in the mall, indicated by interviewees as the "most annoying."[29] Such a comment highlights the mall as an immense acoustical stream to which background music contributes while surprisingly providing an element of smoothness. As Jeffrey Hopkins further notes in his study of the West Edmonton Mega-Mall, "Although malls were originally hailed as a quiet retreat from the sonic congestion of downtown streets, sound levels in some mall corridors now, paradoxically, exceed those of a downtown city sidewalk."[30] In his empirical survey of the Mall, Hopkins further found that among "the 576 negative words used [in describing the Mall], the term with greatest frequency of occurrence was *noisy*."[31]

From such perspective, the soundscape of the mall could be heard to fulfill the generally negative view, of an environmental break that overwhelms the communicational feedbacking of self and surrounding. Yet, in a curious twist, Muzak and the field of programmed music comes to supply a sort of "masking" to the noise of the mall, brought forward on top of the many voices echoing throughout. Background music thus imparts a degree of security or relief from the contemporary crowded mall. Its recurring fluidity and repetitive stream provide a safety net to the otherwise noisy environment. In this way, the mall brings forward an elaborate input to the aural sense, which involves Muzak as a conditioning background woven into the increasingly noisy environment, to generate various anxieties as well as pleasures. In short, sound and music perform in multiple ways, suggesting the aural environment of the mall may not be as static, or as singular, as at times assumed.

IMAGE 17   South Coast Plaza, shopping mall in Orange County, California, 2009. Photo: the author.

In contrast to the notion that "listening is always listening *for something*," Carter suggests that listening instead "respects the erotic power of ambiguity, the generative potential of a representation that exceeds every determination."[32] Therefore, listening should be appreciated not solely as a plentiful act locating the individual within the power of meaningful exchange. Rather, listening situates us within a relational frame whose focus, clarity, and directness are endlessly supplemented and displaced by the subtle pulses, mishearings, and fragmentary richness of relating. That is to say, listening may be so intensely relational by operating as a *weak* model of subjectivity, to ultimately nurture more horizontal or distracted forms of experience.

From this perspective, I want to also highlight the background as participant within the model of mishearing: to overlay ambiguity upon the built environment so as to appreciate how the senses are always navigating through a spatial or geographic network of the present, and gaining multiple experiences, sensations, and knowledge from the *entire* social field. If audition and sound teach us how to engage omni-directionally, to find points of contact underground, at home, and on the street, then surely the renderings of Muzak, in supplying spaces of consumerism with material support, can be listened to as bringing into relief the background as an environmental feature, to add to the acoustical field of experience.

* * *

The thrust of mishearing comes to continually realign the feedbacking of self and surrounding; from primary to secondary events, from background to foreground, mishearing creates new points of contact. In Don Ihde's *Listening and Voice*, the author sets out a compelling consideration of the significance of sound and its relational energy. In a section on language and listening, Ihde recognizes two polarized tendencies, crossing between a "Cartesian linguistics," which locates meaning already in the word, as idea, and a purely "phenomenological listening," which hears the word as fully embodied. On one side, language supersedes the physicality of the spoken, while on the other, meaning is found in the variations of embodiment. As he states, "The infection of a 'dualism' of the 'body' of language in abstract sounds with its presumed disembodied 'soul' of meanings pervades our very understanding of listening."[33] In the midst of such dichotomy, between the abstract body and the meaningful soul, Ihde explores the fluctuations that displace or unfold the "center" of language. This center is thus buffered by two poles, what he calls "the near and the far." Accordingly, the "near to language" is understood as *musical signifi-*

cance, and the "far to language" as *silence*. Between these poles, the act of listening continually oscillates, veering between the plenitude of musicality, as that sensorial richness of sound, and the sharp absence of silence. Through such consideration, Ihde underscores a dynamics to listening that are also co-productive of meaning: "Word does not stand alone but is present in a field of deployed meaning in which it is situated," suggesting that "what is said always carries with it what is present as unsaid."[34] Echoing Carter's appreciation for ambiguity, to listen then is to participate within a field of dynamic audibility, shifting from near to far, from abstract sounds to linguistic meaning, and from the said to the unsaid. This *geography of meaning* gives way to a range of experiences, of ways of relating, which ultimately under-scores listening as an important means to "hear the *otherness* . . ."[35]

Following these views on listening, the ear veers and slips, focuses and drifts; I follow your words, and at times, I grow distracted, by the sounds outside, by my own thinking. Rather than strictly occupy the clear channel, the center of language, to engage the primary spatial event, listening imparts meaningful experiences through a fluctuation of focus that brings one in and around the mass and verve of so much sonic materiality, of *otherness*. The audible spatiality of the near and the far endlessly shifts attention from what is in front to what is behind, bringing the abstract and the concrete, the said and the unsaid into fruitful contact.

Marking the background as participant within the full range of acoustical feedback, listening in the mall might be a *distracted form*, but distraction often uncovers a surprising array of thoughts and feel-ings, epiphanies and meanings. Distraction may act as a productive model for recognizing all that surrounds the primary event of sound— *to suddenly hear what is usually out of earshot*. It allows or nurtures the ability for one to appreciate the sounding environment in all its dimen-sional complexity. Distraction may in the end function as means for undoing the lines of scripted space, loosening our sense for perform-ing within a given structure, and according to certain expectations; to exceed or to fall short of the assumed goal. To be distracted is potentially to be more human.

The production of background music, as I want to suggest, following my own course of distracted listening, may provide a key understanding onto the importance of the background, as participant within
the production of effective input. Might Muzak be actually heard to
uncover the background itself, as such a forceful and signifying elemental feature within the modern environment? And further, to introduce
distraction also as a positive vocabulary for (un)scripting the self within
social spaces? The background may stand as the very site for the nurturing of new contact, performing to draw out peripheral and minor
energies, and to give residence to the overlooked. Muzak, and other
ambient technologies (to which I will return), occupies the background
precisely because it functions to generate or trigger new subjectivity.

Interestingly, background music may be set within the general
electroacoustic developments of the twentieth century, as part of the
sonic arts' involvement in spatiality.[36] The electronic and technological experiments conducted by Pierre Schaeffer and Pierre Henry in
the studios in Paris in the 1950s find curious parallel in the work of
Ray Conniff, an innovative arranger and composer associated with
the Muzak Corporation. At Columbia Records in the late 1950s for
instance, Conniff started to compose voices as part of the main
orchestral instrumentation, scoring female voices alongside trum-
pets and soprano saxophone, and male voices with trombones. This
led to his highly unique "ethereal" sound, with wordless voices mixed
within the instrumentation. In addition, for his debut album, S'Wonderful
in 1956, Conniff attempted to capture the reverb of an early church
recording session by playing back each of the tracks from a speaker
mounted at the bottom of a stairwell in the studios, and rerecording
this up on the sixth floor. In doing so, Conniff created an airy interweave of voice and instrument to the point where the two indetermi-
nately hover in dreamy unison. This compositional vision shifts the
traditional view of voice appearing on top of instruments, leading to
an early ambient sound bringing the background and foreground
together, to elaborate what he understood as a core sensation to listening: "All I can say is that it's a sort of pulsing. The average persons
like to hear a pulsation, not obvious, but reassuringly there in the

background."[37] Conniff's particular use of voice and instrumentation was complemented by his interest in stereo recording techniques. This led to his innovative live stereo concerts in the late 1960s, utilizing a three-channel set-up to deliver a surround sound experience. Such sonic experiments and twisted spatialities open up a perspective on mall life that might begin to hear in this acoustic territory an actual promotion of listening. Though the mall at times is certainly a dreary place, its psychoacoustic project, the feedbacking dynamics, with the airy works of Conniff hovering in the background, along with all the energy flows found therein put into play much of sound's enveloping and effective verve.

Acoustic Politics

The mall forms a complex audible perspective. The perfuming of its corridors with sonic matter, in conjunction with the ambient din and social exchanges, give way to a politics of acoustic space, where decibels often exceed local ordinances, and the labor of listening is balanced between social integration and monetary expenditure. The mall then is an amalgamation of multiple economies, embodying an acoustical tension pitting vocal fatigue against background music, auditory advertising against the joys of listening, and the technologies of production against the technologies of consumption.

The legacy of Muzak has instigated more contemporary approaches toward scripting space acoustically. Audio branding and sonification are currently active design strategies dramatically participating in the total aestheticization and crafting of contemporary social space. From advertising jingles and sound logos for particular brands or companies to ringtones and sounds for gaming devices, as well as sonified weather reports, the play of sonic memory and auditory sensing are rapidly mobilizing much of Muzak's core ideas. Such a pervading development runs in tandem with the elaboration of global capitalist structures, with mobile and personal technologies opening the way for a myriad of new shopping encounters.

Such acoustic politics can be further glimpsed by investigating developments in recent audio technology. For instance, The Sonic Teenager Deterrent, or the Mosquito, has been installed in numerous shopping centers and pedestrian zones across Europe and the US. Designed to discourage loitering, the Mosquito sends out high-pitch frequencies, roughly around 16,000 Hz, which mostly effects loitering teenagers—given that the range of hearing decreases with age, frequencies above 12,000 Hz are often only heard by young listeners, turning the Mosquito into an anti-youth weapon. As the developer Howard Stapleton commented, "I got it so that only my kids hated it and my fianceé and I were completely unperturbed. We put up the prototype outside the [test] store and almost immediately people stopped congregating. The beauty of it is that the noise does not have to be loud, just pitched at the right level which affects teenagers."[38] Placed within shopping centers and pedestrian zones, such technology enables partial crowd control, dissuading loitering youth from blocking the flows of shoppers and disrupting the movements of buying within the mall.

Complementing Mosquito technology, the development of Whispering Windows technology has enabled the use of surfaces, such as large windows, to be turned into audio speakers. Manufactured by Etrema Products in Ames, Iowa, the technology is comprised of a small round transducer made from Terfonal-D alloy, a composite of rare alloys, which can be attached to flat surfaces and connected to an amplifier (operating through "magnetostriction" which is a property of magnetic materials that can change shape through magnetic transduction). The transducer essentially acts to sensitize the surface, making it vibrate up to 20,000 times per second and allowing it to function as an amplification surface.

These recent technologies extend the range of sonic effectiveness. As Steve Goodman provocatively suggests, "It could be argued, in fact, that Muzak pre-empted our submersion into a generalised surround sound culture, with the ambient purr of control and the digital modulation of affective tone that forms the ambience of contemporary urbanisms."[39] Thus, the amplification of a highly crafted melody by Ray Conniff swinging through the department stores, arranged as an elaborate psychoacoustic and multi-speaker event specific to the airy lightness of perfume counters, begins a steady electroacoustical conditioning of the everyday, leading to the contemporary flood of sonic pervasiveness.

The ability to transform storefront windows into sounding surfaces grants the retailer an additional outlet for attracting attention and drawing customers into the shop. Therefore, two acoustical signals occur, though running in opposite directions aid in the construction of consumer design and retail functionality. The Taylorist analysis of efficient production finds its complement in the contouring of the spaces of consumption with their own set of sonic tools designed to condition the shopping body, with the Mosquito forcing unwanted bodies out of the corridors and Whispering Windows inviting others in. Muzak thus finds expanded iteration in the form of whispering windows and mosquito signals, not to mention Surface Sound, a technology which enables any surface to be turned into a sounding zone. From here, the mall itself (and any other architectural surface or space) can be made a sensitive membrane for the conduction of electromagnetic signals.

The totalizing of the contemporary sound environment also brings with it counter-narratives designed to reinstate or thwart the complete occupation of public space by the directives of consumer culture. The collective Radio Ligna has generated a series of performative interventions designed to explore and open up public spaces to other forms of occupation. Founded in 1995 by media theorists and radio artists Ole Frahm, Michael Hüners, and Torsten Michaelsen, Ligna has worked to put into question prevailing structures of how public space becomes demarcated. Most notably, Ligna's work reveals the degrees to which commerce has come to condition the built environment, leading to a normalized sense for commercial interests and economic gain as defining factors for public interaction.

IMAGES 18 and 19 Ligna, Radio Ballet, Leipzig Central Station, 2003.
Photos: Eiko Grimberg.

As an example, their Radio Ballet from 2002 staged at the Hamburg railway station is a critical manifestation of Ligna's approach and strategy. Structured as a radio transmission of pre-recorded voice and sounds, the work invited listeners to participate in a series of unified actions and gestures to take place in the railway station at a designated time. Participants were asked to bring portable radios, and earphones, so as to tune into the radio broadcast while at the station, and to follow the instructions spoken by the broadcast voice. The performance essentially requested participants to occupy the station, appearing as an unidentified collective, and brought together through the invisible transmission, each participant listening and responding to the given instructions, which asked them to dance to music, to hold their hands as if begging, to lie down on the floor, to look up or to look down, etc. Through such actions, the Ballet was specifically designed against recent laws passed by the local government, which enable police to remove any person loitering in the station without purpose. The identifiable gestures of the loitering body were brought into play through the Ballet, from the homeless sleeping on the ground, the one begging for spare change, others just sitting or standing around—such bodily appearances were enacted as intentional yet ambiguous signs of criminality as an attempt to rupture their signifying meaning.

Ligna sought to point to and question the station as a now-privatized space, newly renovated to incorporate a shopping mall with stores, restaurants, and hotels. By integrating commercial shopping into the station, the city redesigned its legislation so as to appeal to businesses and to aid in controlling the station as a seemingly public environment. The insertion of the Radio Ballet, and its subsequent generative transmission, brought forward a tangible albeit undercover counter-narrative.

This strategy has also been applied in a number of performances designed for shopping malls. Staged since 2006, Ligna has sought to specifically address the space of the shopping mall, as a "laboratory" for encouraging individual exploration. Their shopping mall interventions, also operating as covert radio transmissions, function on the threshold of the visible, with participants blending into the crowd and performing very simple, subtle gestures. For instance, their "Transient Radio Laboratory" in Liverpool was structured as a series of four "research modes," namely, movement, speed, communication, and interior. Each mode functioned as means to intervene and tease out a performative rupture, operating as a "secret conspiracy against the normal behaviors in homogenized zones of consumption."[40] By instigating a set of countermovements, Ligna sought to promote a subtle but palpable form of deviation—to enact a set of possible alterations on the "normal" functioning of the mall, as a space of subjective experience. Such gestures inevitably rubbed up against mall security, leading to a number of confrontations:

> The next exercise was in "disturbing walking" by walking in slow motion. One of the securities took his chance and asked me, nearly standing, if I knew one of the other participants. I said no, I do not know her, hoping she had not said something else. The guy went back to his colleagues and after another short discussion he approached me again requesting that I should leave the shopping centre immediately.[41]

The Laboratory performed alongside the structures of surveillance, management, and coding at work within the mall. These systems actively control the mall, as a social space, delimiting modes of behavior while also supporting the integral pleasures needed to support the flows of the shopper. Again, the mall performs a constant balancing between too much and too little, seeking to harmonize the feedback of consumer culture—*of finding what one needs*.

A combat of signals might be heard to take place, between the effective architecture of consumerism replete with loudspeakers, whispering windows, and mosquito frequencies and the secret transmissions and social choreographies aimed at splitting the acoustical hold on the individual body. Ligna's work inserts a shift in spatial experience, carving out a zone for other forms of inhabitation and conduct—to appropriate or shift the given feedback. For Ligna, intentionally occupying the background becomes a route toward supplanting the invisible yet no less determining directives often defining public space.

Their work brings to mind the legacy of silent discos, which were designed as a means to have parties without disturbing local environments and neighbors with excessive noise. Through wireless headphone transmissions, people could dance to a private and shared music, leaving behind only the residual sounds of their own movements. Such technologies have subsequently been used for mass demonstrations, allowing the passing of information to go unheard by those outside the group. The wireless headphone then acts as support for organizational needs, spawning tactical potentials for maneuvering through given conflicts and subverting the omnipotent hold of scripted space. The secret transmissions of Ligna set in motion a series of rupturing background movements that, when choreographed into a sudden collective body, appear out of place, ambiguous, and suggestive. They both carve out possibilities for other behaviors while marking an identifiable break for those who witness, wonder, and stare perplexed at the disturbing walk or the raised arms of strangers.

Airports

The contemporary airport has come to also function or mirror the form and content of the shopping mall. As many contemporary airport developers have discovered, shopping is both an easy way to help travelers pass the time and a productive opportunity for generating revenue. Airports and shopping malls form part of the contemporary network of what Marc Augé has termed "non-places"—

those contemporary zones in which identity and social relations are relegated to a pure functionality within the "landscape-text" of travel, credit card exchanges, and duty free spaces, lending to the experiences of "super-modernity" where "the only face to be seen, the only voice to be heard, in the silent dialogue [the traveler] holds with the landscape-text addressed to him along with others, are his own: the face and voice of a solitude made all the more baffling by the fact that it echoes millions of others."[42]

In contrast to place, non-place is thus a condition of super-anonymity, where identity is replaced by passport numbers and digital read outs, leading to a landscape of chain stores and controlled movement. Yet non-place and place intertwine as polarities, each invading the other according to a greater choreography of social interaction and event. Thus, within the space of the airport sudden exchanges may take place that become personal while the familiar streets of one's neighborhood are suddenly infiltrated by a corporate design found throughout the country. For Augé though, what may mark our contemporary experience is the intensification of the non-place, as a growing coordinate dotting the landscape, and feeding experiences of common space.

Such hyper-depictions, of solitude and the terror of codified space, though might not be entirely dichotomous with more personal experiences of place. Arjun Appadurai equally explores these contemporary movements and intensifications amplified in the networks of global marketing that unsettle identity, place, and history in favor of a smooth, codified, and super-modern mechanics. Yet what surfaces in Appadurai's thinking is a sensitivity to not so much the oppositional or dichotomous accents inflecting place from non-place, that overarching and gripping solitude, but the co-productive ways in which contemporary cultures slip in and out of such spaces. "Thus, to put it summarily, electronic mediation and mass migration mark the world of the present not as technically new forces but as ones that seem to impel (and sometimes compel) the work of the imagination." The "work of the imagination" forms a relational dynamic, which is "neither purely emancipatory nor entirely disciplined but is a space of contestation in which individuals and groups seek to annex the global into their practices of the modern."[43]

In following the reverberant acoustics of the shopping mall, my attention has been turned to the history of Muzak, and the defining research that came to mark the background of modern society with a set of deeply codified sounds. It has been my intention to undo the often-negative or singular understanding of these sounds. Rather, to hear in background music a larger understanding of sound, music, and audition that might operate as a "work of the imagination," figuring the flows of a global, corporate sound in tandem with local nuance and experience — to carve out within the spaces of consumerism a productive break for supporting other practices of listening. These practices — from Ligna's radio ballets to the distractions promoted by Muzak — suggest a more productive means for recognizing the auditory slippages and ambiguities that surface from within the systems of the super-modern: though Muzak may fill our ears with highly designed acoustical matter, it may also participate in the auditory cultures of the contemporary that generate surprising moments of juxtaposition and fantasy. (Recently, at the South Coast Plaza Mall in Southern California, a competition was held to see who could identify sounds found in the Mall. From the fountain on the first floor to the sounds of Abercrombie & Fitch, contestants were provided with audio recordings through the Mall's blog and asked to send in their answers. Sponsored by the Mall, the competition suggests a light-hearted reflection upon its own acoustical spaces, and an appreciation for its visitor's listening experience.)

The local and the global, place and non-place, thus form a continual process of exchange and mutation further echoed in Michael Taussig's anthropological narratives through which he locates "the magic of the state."[44] For Taussig, the general "fetishization" inherent to capital delivers in turn a matrix for surprising appropriations, counter-narratives, and supplementary energies often running parallel to the very systems they seem to oppose. That is, the "magic of the state" is both its ability to disguise capital for need, while charging the desiring flows of bodies and imaginations with generative force. It is thus *through* the very forms and mechanism's opened up by global production and consumption that one may also locate forms of appropriation, personal narrative, and sharing. Overlaying such ideas onto the mall, riveting its corridors with the work of the imagination, and filling its food courts with the magic of the state, the ongoing humdrum of the shopping spree may shift the flows of feedbacking energy into a channel for multiple projects.

To return to the airport, that space of vagueness and boredom, of the super-modern, we hear again the pervading trickle of background music mixing with a reverberant bed of acoustical events. The space and conditions of the airport recall the shopping mall by locating the traveler in a maze of consumer opportunities that run parallel to architectural elements producing ambient effects.

At the Oslo airport in Norway, the condition of the traveler gliding through the non-place of transit is also addressed through the permanent installation of "sound showers." Produced by the artist and engineer team Anna Karin Rynander and Per-Olof Sandberg, the showers were installed at the airport in 1998 and allow a visitor to stand underneath a parabolic speaker and listen to a series of sound scenarios. The eleven showers are located through the main concourse, distributed as points of relaxation to the waiting traveler. Stepping into one of the showers triggers the playback of audio, enveloping the listener in a disjunctive sonic environment that contrasts sharply with the sounds of the airport in general. Sounds of waves, birds, giggling babies, or stories whispered by selected individuals feature as counterpoints to the tensions often derived from travel. As the work suggests, a "sound shower" might function as a cleansing opportunity for the individual traveler, a secret rupture within the fricions and exhaustion experienced while waiting at the airport— essentially as *a form of distraction*.

IMAGE 20 Anna Karin Rynander and Per-Olof Sandberg, Sound Showers, Oslo airport, installed 1998. Photo: the author.

In contrast to the directives of Muzak, the sound showers aim not to generate a light yet influential background for the spirit of shopping, or a musical structure to support the productive actions of workers. Rather, the shower uses sound as a counterbalance or spatial break within the often-linear movements of travel and the long stretches of waiting. The sound shower might be a form of sonic therapy suggesting other ways for sound to be installed in public spaces, where it acts as private or secluded enclave. Yet sonically the shower seems to in turn draw upon stereotypical motifs of pleasurable or appealing sound. From baby sounds to ocean waves, bird calls and whispering voices, the poetics of the Oslo showers run parallel to the sonic palette of Muzak by appealing to a notion of the common public: no challenging or provocative sound, or dynamic range of frequencies. Though this does not belittle the presence and opportunity the showers present, it may remind our listening habits of the difficulty raised when locating sound in public—to negotiate the line between provoking the ear with stimulating audio material and avoiding the level of noise to which public space remains sensitive. How might one open the ears of the public, as many sound artists and projects seem to aspire, without relying upon an existing aesthetic vocabulary that can only follow in the tracks of an already scripted pleasure?

Such a question may find preliminary answer in the developments of ambient and generative music. As Joseph Lanza points out, particular forms of avant-garde musical aesthetics often aim for the background, as a dynamic and generative location for sonorous presentation. From Erik Satie's "furniture music" to Brian Eno's *Music for Airports*, composing work for the background shifts musical structures and materiality to another level of attention: to occupy the background, to function within the ambient details of audibility, demands a softer, less tense, and more horizontal form of composition and sound. Ambient music is thus a sound aimed at subliminal hearing, where, in the case of the airport, it slides into the ears of the semiconscious traveler to lightly stimulate or relax the imagination. By extension, generative music, based on random looping of independent tracks, or algorithmic systems drawing upon a database of sounds, creates a bed or weave of sounds whose relations never repeat in the same pattern. Such work greatly extends the ambient project by in turn operating as spatial installations. For instance, Arne Nordheim's permanent installation, *Gilde på Gløshaugen* (2000), located in the Science Faculty Building of The Norwegian University of Science and Technology in Trondheim, Norway, creates an alteration of the public environment while fully operating within its given functionality. The work is essentially a 24-channel audio system mounted throughout the open hallways and atriums of the building, amplifying a database of composed sounds according to different live parameters, such as the amount of people in the building, or weather and light conditions outside.[45] Through digital sensing and computerized systems, the installation generates a continual sonic atmosphere, blending with the existing soundscape and environment.

Might ambient and generative music chart out a *magic of the state* by operating well within the movements of technology and consumption, and in doing so, to uncover potentialities in mystifying spaces of public interaction with a set of imaginary coordinates? In listening to *Music for Airports* (1978) the ear inevitably drifts toward a zone of ambiguity, where the free-floating tonalities supported by the gliding of smooth voices push the listener onto another level of attention—away from *listening for something* and toward reverie, fantasy, and distraction, as a listening that remains open and prone to wandering. Nordheim's sonic infiltration of the University building also delivers subtle input into the comings and goings of students, offering momentary distraction while functioning within the found structures and parameters of the educational institute. This poetics of distraction seems to suggest alternative itineraries for inhabiting space in which the feedbacking of self and surrounding becomes concrete; like Muzak, such work flirts with influencing the emotional and psychological state of the public, while in contrast seeking to challenge the overly-determined conditioning of the built environment. From Ligna's mall actions to an ambient aesthetic of sound showers and musical overlays, the undoing of the strict distinctions of figure and ground, back to fore, aims for a distracted subjectivity that might productively find new points of contact and alternative narrative within scripted space.

Atmospheres

The history of architecture intertwines with a history of the senses. As built forms have evolved and developed through history, the particular experiences of embodied presence might be said to shift accordingly. The expressions of architecture, in signaling particular cultural beliefs, press back upon the experiences of individuals a conditioning structure that surrounds the senses as effective input. The built environment, in giving form to a cultural system also receives sensual input emanating from those who put to use a given architecture. Such a process can be appreciated as supplementing the understanding of architecture with the *experiential* and the continual process of sensorial energy and involvement that follows. As Peter Zumthor suggests, "If a work of architecture speaks only of contemporary trends and sophisticated visions without triggering vibrations in its place, this work is not anchored in its site, and I miss the specific gravity of the ground it stands on."[46] The vibratory gravity of a site, as a poetical image, points to a sense for not so much the identifiable, primary elements of a place—*I like those windows*—but rather an atmospheric and suggestive energy pervading a place, as a sort of secondary, reverberant texturing.

Notions of the *event* of architecture awakens the perception of the built environment to this performative unfolding every body and building come to enact. This must be emphasized as a dialogue passing back and forth on multiple levels, and bringing into its weave a network of associated systems, practices, and histories. Architecture is thus a technology *and* a living system pushing and pulling under the dynamics of multiple forces, thereby reflecting the radical energies and ideas that play out as the social and political. From this perspective, architecture might be appreciated more as an *atmospheric pressure* modulated by visible and invisible forces—a kind of weather effected by and causing effect onto the everyday. As Jean-Paul Thibaud suggests through the theme of "ambience," "Each ambience involves a specific mood expressed in the material presence of things and embodied in the way of being of city dwellers. Thus, ambience is both subjective and objective: it involves the lived experience of people as well as the built environment of the place."[47] Through such a perspective, sensing the built environment involves an array of experiences, feelings, and qualities that shift through the temporal and seemingly immaterial registers of the everyday.

In addressing the mall as a sounding architecture, I've wanted to underscore listening as a highly active component. In doing so, the effective influence sonic experiences come to enact is brought forward in dramatic ways, drawing out the ambience of place inflected by a psychodynamic accent. To uncover this drama, my own listening has sought to not only follow in the well-tread lines of the schizophonic argument, of a *Moozak* that aggressively infringes on "freedom" by manipulating the senses.[49] Rather, by introducing ambiguity into the equation, and letting the ear *mishear*, I hope to accentuate back-ground music as one of many auditory experiences through which we still may learn to listen.

As a physical and spatial movement, sound carries a collection of information related to the conditions of the original object or body, the source of sound, along with the related environment. It creates what Truax refers to as a "feedback" of acoustic information. Yet, as a communicative medium sound carries information that is inherently temporal and evanescent—it can only communicate by always already disappearing *into* the environment. It thus supplies communication with a vital medium—*to truly hear the world and each other*—while unsettling signification with instability—*to listen is to also confront the voluptuous richness of ambiguity*. In this regard, "feedback" is a continual process that teeters on the line to becoming noise or to tapering into silence—it rises and falls in intensity according to the near and the far of audible events, building spaces of intimacy and distraction, togetherness and dislocation. Such a communicational model vitally introduces a relation of self to others that is not necessarily harmonious or steady, but full of continual negotiation and surprise—and which may introduce into the scripting of audible spaces an ever-present shadow.

6

SKY: RADIO, SPATIAL URBANISM, AND CULTURES OF TRANSMISSION

The sky fell down when I met you
The green of the countryside has turned to blue
I had the moon right on my fingertips
And when first we kissed, there were stars on your lips
To be with you just made it seem
That walking on snowy clouds was not a dream
You gave to me all this and heaven too
When the sky fell down and I met you

—Frank Sinatra

. . . the towers become beacons of information transfer. They become physical, material sites that deliver us to what is hyper-real. But rather than displaying a sharp dialectic of materials on the one hand and hyperspace on the other, the towers, with their ominous, distancing, and cancer-causing presence stand as confused signs for the constant intermingling of the imagined and the seen, the tangible and the abstract, the organic and the artificial.[1]

—Ken Ehrlich

In which a flood of signals charge the air with projected subjectivity and generate radiophonic cultures full of voices, spirits, and the threat of war.

I have distinct memories of lying in our front lawn in Michigan as a kid with my brother and sister to watch the night sky on summer evenings, marveling at the tiny lights above. I'm sure this must have been my brother's idea, giving us the motivating push to run outside into the night and consider the larger world. I always followed him, knowing he was brighter, older, and more adventurous. The memories are extremely faint, but I can still picture it, the warmth of the night, the sharp summer grass pricking my skin, and the blackness above peppered with these mysterious glowing points, like nails jutting out from a dark wood.

Thinking about it now, I'm not sure what we imagined it being all about, these stars, but I do know the immensity of the sky gave me a sense of the poetics of all that matter above my head. Clouds, rain, stars, and lightning, along with the mixture of ever-shifting blues and grays, blacks and purples, these things had always set my mind dreaming. The great emptiness above as a continual picture slowly encasing all the activities below: how could the imagination of a child ignore this great immensity, in which the shapes of clouds endlessly produce an array of characters, from dragons to seahorses, and whose colors shudder with the intensely nuanced alterations of time? The *sky* . . . even the word sparks a myriad of possibilities to push up from under this writing: I immediately want to leave behind the intellectual thrust of this text to land on a fecund earth of total dreaming. That is, it brings me to what Bachelard understands as "childhood," which is not only a distant time in one's life, but importantly, the drive of the imagination itself.

And so I end here, within this nebulous matter rich with so many resonances to locate a poetics, the point of departure not only for imagining but for sound as well: to leave behind the underground, the streets and sidewalks, even the homes and the city, to leap into the void above and into the medium by which sound becomes. For the sky is also the space of air—the two are inseparable; one holds the other in a vague, shimmering embrace. Yet curiously, the sky leads the imagination back down to earth, and back into city life; the projected energy tossed up from below comes to reveal more about terrestrial life. All the vastness above acts as the primary condition of spaciousness itself, lending to visions of habitation, projection, and motion, as well as containing fundamental forces of nature, the cosmos, and breath itself. *To look up is to also take a deep breath.* The sky then acts as a mysterious conductor for subliminal and elemental orchestrations, unfolding air as its medium, which "is neither on the side of the subject nor of the object. It has neither objecthood nor essence . . . The air is impression without presence."[2]

Entering this vastness, this rich medium, also tunes us to the quivering of so many frequencies, filling the seeming emptiness with a multitude of energies and forces. Too many to account for in the end, which paradoxically makes concrete that undulating sky above, giving it structure, form, territory. As a kid I certainly did not see all the radio in the sky, or even consider the stars as part of an elaborate energy source beating through the ionosphere. The poetics of the sky grants the imagination a vital medium for fantasies of oblivion or hope as well as for material constructions. As Joe Milutis elaborates in his compelling account of the ether, "one might want to call the ether . . . a fabric of signs that is both material and phantasmic, an electronic rain that is continuously decoded and received in common or poetic ways."[3] Such dynamics marks the sky above with anxious visions— its emptiness is subject to colonial take over, which even the smallest of imaginings might perform. The sky receives all the projections of human fantasy, while also answering back with a set of radical responses: the crashes of thunder that make houses shake still might terrify with its messages. Richard Cullen Rath marvelously documents how early American settlers looked toward the sky above, along with indigenous Americans, as an animate field full of voice, where "A clap of thunder was the act of a specific being, a personal act that helped establish the identity of its source. . ."[4] These beings, referred to as "thunderers," occupied the sky as a community of mystical intelligence. Thunder was to be heeded, its palette of sonority a vocabulary of anger, warning, and command.

Thus, what one sent out into the ether might be said to come back to mark a dialogue where sound and air intertwine into material animation, leveling all expression and presence to a shared condition of breath. An ethereal syntax glides above and through the flows of inhalation and exhalation, as a system of vaporous coding. Further expressed in Victorian obsessions with draughts, contagious winds, and miasmic odors, the ether was matter moving in and out of bodies to carry unseen entities, or the mesmeric conductions of magnetic energies in acts of healing, spirit channeling, and hypnotism. An enveloping medium, the air is susceptible to contagion, to contamination, and take-over, and to the powers of emanation.

The sky is both an image of absolute freedom and a vague territory able to deliver thunderous wrath of the supernatural. Or in the case of military battle, the terror of aerial bombardment. The air raid signal of the Second World War piercing the urban environment sends the population underground, while the sky fills with tons of lethal metal. The German military knew well the dynamics of the sky, designing their operations around the "Blitzkrieg," or "lightning war," which relied upon the precision striking of its Stuka dive-bomber. The Stuka was equipped with a set of automated functions, thereby enabling a pilot to focus exclusively on aiming while in full dive. The terror of such a machine was further animated by the addition of a screaming siren to its wings, which sent out a high-pitched frequency when diving through the air. The lightning strike was a fully constructed event, announcing impending destruction to the population below through sonic intensity. The whirling sound itself echoed the glissando of falling bombs—the descending pitch leading to the inevitable moment of silence, giving way to a reverberating pause of suspense as one anticipated the explosion. Such aerial signaling defined a psychological terrain equal to that of the bombed out city, turning the poetics of the sky into a space where life and death were held in the balance.

The terror of impending bombardment found its complement in early radar detection based on audition. The Hythe Sound Mirrors located on the east coast of England were part of the country's early attempts at radar defense. Built as concave discs projecting eastward toward the continent, the Mirrors functioned as listening devices allowing the engines of German bombers coming in from the English Channel to be heard. The arsenal of military conflict came to locate sound at the center of its sensorial experience, impressing onto the sky a feverish sensitivity.

This ethereal topography can be appreciated as a primary site of sound, for it acts as a supple and ambiguous materiality, while being overlaid with numerous meanings; it is the primary source of sonorous becoming as well as consisting of the body's own vitality—*breath and sound occupy the air while being constituted by it*. Sound and air move in and through each other, acting as voluminous spatialities that invisibly surge across the terrestrial.

To follow this ethereal poetics then bends the ear toward the forceful emanations that traverse both earth and individual body. What kind of geography might this be, and how might we begin to trace this weave of airy happenings? To do so I have chosen to focus on radio as a contouring of the sky. For radio brings forward an intensely anxious perspective onto the potential of sound to disrupt or cohere given orders; it further occupies the sky with a set of aerial fantasies whereby transmission features as means for emanation and transformation. Yet, radio comes hand in hand with the radio tower—the tower marks the landscape as part of infrastructural networks, while stimulating the aerial imagination with material promise. The tower, and its related antenna, are objects that generate aerial figures—like thunderers, aerial figures are manifestations of terrestrial projections that in turn come back down to haunt or invade life on earth. Transmission is equally about such imaginary emanations as well as national infrastructures of communication networking, dramatically aligning the sky with the earth. Radio hovers between fantasies of transmission, of sonic emanation, of airy imagination, and the possibilities of making concrete such projections through ideas of nation and community. Thus, it provides a platform for listening onto everyday life as it searches for new forms of construction and collectivity.

Towering Visions

The radio transmission conducted atop the Eiffel Tower in July 1913 not only made possible the standardization of time for the Western nations, it also radically transformed, and set the stage for an architectural object: the Tower as a symbolic expression of modern engineering now electrified to form an elaborate electro-communications network.[5] The Tower, in reaching for the heavens, now also radiates horizontally, reaching out in all directions to make connection on the ground, to signal and transform the landscape from a visible field to an invisible network.

Turning the Eiffel Tower into a transmission tower inaugurates new forms of distributed and participatory architecture, which would lend significant energy to the twentieth century urban project. Infused with the pulse of time and the dynamics of space, the Eiffel Tower as radio tower completes the drive of the ultra-modern and opens out onto the larger projects of spatial urbanism (to which I will return in greater detail).

Already in its moment of construction in the 1880s, the Eiffel Tower signaled the total upheaval of the urban skyline with its radical implementation of cast iron framing developed for bridge and factory design. As Sigfried Giedion observed, "Viewed from the standpoint of construction, the whole tower is an adaptation of the lofty supports of iron bridges, increased to cosmic dimensions."[6] Such cosmic dimensions take on even greater promise with the capping of the Tower with transmitting antennae by projecting outward beyond the earth as well as by bringing back down signals from above. As Moholy-Nagy's montage photographs of the Tower suggest, the jointed tapestry of metal framework gives expression to a technological rationality, itself the basis for new modern poetics. Such rationality is participant within a spiritual mythology that, according to Kandinsky, interweaves geometry and abstraction with the depths of the sensory.[7]

Though modernism's techno-spiritualism spawned fantasies of universal languages, a metaphysics transcending the globe in the potential of connection, it also found balance with the practicalities and entertainment possibilities of reaching the masses, as witnessed with the broadcast of the first regular television programming in the world beginning in 1935 from the Berlin Radio Tower.[8] Synaesthetic plenitude and the inner resonance of spiritual bodies, which for other modernists, such as Velimir Khlebnikov, find further potential in the promise of mass transmissions, are counterbalanced by an appeal to the quotidian, in which news reports, radio dramas, and commercials address the average citizen. The potentiality of transmission is thus occupied by the fantasies that govern avant-garde utopias as well as the imagination of television producers. As a 1935 radio report from Berlin attests, the "radiating" dynamics of transmission wield mysterious hold on the imagination, while giving way to multiple content:

> Four hundred and fifty-three feet in the air, rising slightly above the top of the well known Berlin radio tower, with its famous restaurant, two copper rings appear to be growing in the sky. Each has a diameter of about ten feet, and their surfaces shine in the early spring sun like spun gold. They are symbolic of a new era—television is no longer a mere technical problem, but is being made available for the use of the general public. The golden rings are the antennas of the Berlin Television Station.[9]

In Japan, such relations find articulation with the construction of the Tokyo Television Tower in 1958. As a symbol of the new Japan following the Second World War, the Tower gave expression to the country's ascendancy as a global power and openly drew upon the Eiffel Tower as a model for its design. Measuring 13 meters taller than the Eiffel Tower, the Tokyo Tower is constructed from an iron frame reaching 333 meters high and has served as an important transmitting relay.[10] The symbolic importance of the Tower can be further understood in relation to the tensions embedded within transmission: while seeking to signify the nation's future promise, the Tower was regularly featured as the site for fantasies of destruction in Japanese films, with the likes of Godzilla smashing it to pieces in the various monster films made throughout the 1950s and 1960s.

Transmission towers become galvanizing beacons around which intersecting perspectives converge, bringing together the belief in the power of transmission to spawn new forms of being—democratic, spiritual, fantastic — while offering new modes of gain to the forces of commercialism and military might.[11] As architectural forms they are suggestive of new possibilities for inhabitation and urban experience based on the atmospheric and the connective, and at the same time, they come to burden the spaces of living with the weight of their messages. The ways in which social relations take shape might be seen then to find projected imagining in the energies of transmission — *to look up is to also seek another configuration of what is down on earth*. While tuning into the radio brings sound forward to fill the living room or car, it equally delivers, in muted form, the infrastructural networks that put sound out there.

"The interpenetration of continuously changing viewpoints creates, in the eyes of the moving spectator, a glimpse into four-dimensional experience."[12] Giedion's descriptions of the Eiffel Tower resound equally with the advent of radio communications, which were to amplify the "interpenetration of viewpoints" and realize a bolder glimpse onto four-dimensions through live media. Architecturally, the steel frame constructions exemplify the very condition of transmission: as light-weight, structural, and without interior, the frames are pure form, seemingly immaterial and extending from the earth. They rise to rivet the sky with a punctuated suggestion, that of immaterial force; as hardware they hold out the promise of disembodiment, displacement, and amplification. Spatially, they come to provide an imaginary map for an elaborate network of expressivity, drawing out the breath of the broadcast individual, while making concrete a sense of national or communal security. The towers, in their potent spatio-temporal energies, act as monuments to the nation, granting identifiable and enigmatic images: the tower draws in and projects out the spirit of nationhood, aligning the mysteries of radio waves with national security.

One might look toward the Berlin TV Tower located in Alexanderplatz to recognize this interplay. Constructed between 1965 and 1969 after extensive debate throughout the 1950s, the TV Tower aimed to facilitate two functions, namely, to provide necessary transmission capabilities to East Berlin as well as to act as a symbol for the German

Democratic Republic.[13] While the GDR struggled to locate the necessary funds throughout the 1950s for such projects, in 1964 Walter Ulbricht, the party leader, was inspired by the city proposal by Herman Henselmann from 1957, which located the TV Tower in the heart of the city (a rare gesture in European cities). Ulbricht's enthusiasm finally led to the construction of the Tower and its opening in 1969. The Berlin TV Tower did succeed in providing television programming to East Berlin, combating the heavily watched West German television stations, as well as boldly marking the city as a living, modern monument to the Communist state.[14]

IMAGE 21 Berlin TV Tower, Alexanderplatz, opened in 1969. Photo: the author.

Transmission Culture

The development of electronic transmission, and related infrastructures of towers and networks, uncovers a culture of aerial imagination.
The suggestive beaming of signals enacted by antenna creates a
medial space, nurturing ideas of freedom and communications, power
and magic. Such imagination is sparked by as well as initiates
technological fantasies and products, fusing eccentric visions to
quotidian forms. By following the aerial signal back to its transmission
tower, I'm interested to engage transmission culture, as auditory
intensities that come to fill the sky and, importantly, to trace the
energetic passing between transmission and the urban imagination.
Transmission carves out a space and in doing so generates a sense
for new forms of occupation and inhabitation, of power and dispute.

The development of "spatial urbanism" and the cultures of city life
following the Second World War led to programmatic shifts in understandings of architecture, diffusing the built across a greater set of
spatial and social coordinates that find support in the material and
imaginary force of transmission. Modern architecture, exemplified in
the CIAM group (initially established in 1928) and the work of Le
Corbusier, sought to find suitable form for postwar conditions of the
new city. Le Corbusier's earlier proposals for the city of tomorrow,
with its combination of vertical towers and open green spaces, found
its criticism by those seeking more direct, embodied routes toward
contemporary life. The fantasy of the rational city, though lending to
a culture of spatial thinking, ran the risk of inculcating a systematic
leveling of the inherently dynamic and textured conditions of everyday life. The emergence of spatial urbanism in the 1950s would come
to suggest a wider architectural perspective, whereby the city was
understood not as objects fixed within a functional field, but rather as
relational movements and energies physically as well as emotionally
defining space. "Space" would then become a multifaceted theme, a
material base for exposing the experiences of individuals within the
urban. "The space of spatial urbanism was not the space of void or

absence but rather a space projected onto a terrain as a structured and structuring entity . . . Space came to be seen as a kind of field of synthesis, hosting the convergence of those dichotomies that had defined modern architecture's internal tensions since its beginning — freedom and standardization, art and science, structure and spontaneity, monumentality and rigor."[15]

The potentiality opened up by the advent of new electronic communications and technologies of transmission lent to this spatial imagination by unfixing architecture and the geometric cube. In its place came the energetic, mobile, and connective, where "hyperbolic paraboloids, space frames and grids, plastic pods, concrete shells, and massive megastructures spread across the landscape, connecting, communicating, overlapping, and integrating."[16] Exemplified in groups such as the Situationist International (SI), Team 10, Archigram, and the Metabolists, questions of urbanism, architecture, and space became infused with the suggestive implementation of electrical circuits, network technologies, communicational structures, and the potentiality of the immaterial and the unfixed so characteristic of broadcast media. Though Le Corbusier and the related CIAM group focused largely on built forms, traditionally gravitating around the image and notion of the home, the new spatial urbanism found greater inspiration from social and urban spaces, and their related cultures and systems. To engage such spaces entailed a more thorough glimpse onto the infrastructures of city life, such as transportation networks and communication devices. A number of elements align themselves within this perspective, notably the automobile, which was to become an object of continual inspiration (and disgust), leading to projects such as David Greene's *Living Pod* (1965) and Ron Herron's related *Walking City* (1964), which overlay vehicular design onto urban planning: the city was envisioned as a continual shifting of bodies and buildings fused in a mobile metropolitan system.

These infrastructural visions curiously echo the increasingly present image of the transmission tower and its antenna, relay stations, and networks of cabling, circuitry, and transformers that dynamically inter-sect with buildings and their related landscapes. The integration of electronic and communication technologies into the fabric of architec-ture following the Second World War lent inspiration to the idea of the future city. In addition, the Cold War was to bring forward a hyper-consciousness onto the design of everyday objects, making the emerging suburban home itself a highly functional, automated electronic environment.[17] Such developments though were poignantly predicted already in 1928 when Buckminster Fuller announced that "There will come a time when in our individualistic harmonious state all work will consist of thinking and crystallizing thought into sound or directionable spheres which will set in motion machinery or controlled fourth dimensional design."[18] Domestic life would be replete with hidden wiring and invisible signaling, making the city the very hub of not only centralized control, but also individualized freedom and mobility.

In contrast to architecture as an object located within a fixed landscape, the de-aestheticized, proto-proletariat steel frame tower harnesses the image of libidinal desire, and the flows and slippages of unconscious projection that city life came to represent in the 1960s. The *Walking City* was itself a mechanistic functional structure as well as a support for the potential fevers promulgated through contemporary interaction. The importance of psychological states was to settle within the core of spatial urbanism, contouring the new relational understandings with a sense for the unseen and sensual forces feeding city experience. Exemplified in the SI's theory of "psychogeography," the flows of subjective rhythms and fevers were appreciated as defining the urban situation; it recognized the two as interlocked phenomena, whereby psychological and emotional life were both determined by and determining of the built environment. The city was viewed as a controlled and structured territory ordered by the material aspects of its continual construction and decay, while at the same time receiving and conducting a heightened sense of embodied flow, rhythm, and social interaction, modulating the imagination with mobility, energy, and the sensuality of fleeting exchanges.

Psychogeography articulated a belief in the primary rupture the city came to offer; an intrinsically rapturous force whose movements were at odds with the modern "system city." The SI sought to harness this fundamental force—to exaggerate the psychological component to the city through intuitive and spontaneous actions (such as the *dérive*, or drift) that underscored the body as a differentiating break onto the mechanistic functionality of modern life. "Drift therefore became a transgression of the alienated world,"[19] allowing the appropriation of existing systems and official structures for the pleasures of the experiential.

Georg Simmel's work from the 1910s fundamentally maps out this relation, highlighting the city as an "extensive" emanation whose "total effects" go well beyond its physical borders. Such emanation for Simmel functions as the "actual extent in which [the city] is expressed," which he goes on to equate with the emanation of the metropolitan individual. Within the forces of the metropolis the range of individual expression comes to exceed the physical limitations of the body, whose effective reach extends "temporally and spatially."[20] The city and the body thus intertwine to operate as an emanating, medial network through which the here and now is immediately augmented with the potential of elsewhere. Being in the city is to not only experience the physical and direct environment, but to sense the extensiveness of functioning dynamics surrounding and invading the body. The geographic contours of urban life are thus networks between material environments and the intensities of perception, imagination, and fantasy, creating a feverish topography.

By and large the city came to represent and offer itself as a magnetized, energetic field by which the new behaviors of contemporary life would demand new architectures. What this new architecture would be found its operative language through the notion of "the atmospheric." Psychogeographic drifts sought out particular regions

216 • Acoustic Territories

of a city, highlighting the ruinous, the local, the informal, against the terrain of the bureaucratic, following intuitive sensations and modes of feeling that often relied upon a sense for the atmospheric or the ambient (as well as the drunken): the atmospheric is more an overall condition determined not solely by architecture or specific materiality, but by the organization and modality by which space is *occurring*. As Gernot Böhme suggests, "Atmospheres stand between subjects and objects . . . their great value lies exactly in this in-betweeness."[21] The atmospheric thus interrupts as well as complements and completes architecture, and importantly urban experience, by *emanating and projecting*: where architecture and urbanism fall short, atmospheres lend dynamic, voluminous support.

The ambient and atmospheric undulations that would form a material vocabulary for spatial urbanism can be understood to high-light the feverish topography of the modern city, acting as a live medium influenced by and further effecting the sensitized realm of this body-city network: the surface tensions of urban life flood the city environment with a plethora of temporal movement, to immerse the individual in its agitating and complicated charge. Atmospheres and ambiences are diffuse sensorial coordinates that create spatial extensions, from the ocular nuances of particular rooms to the audible events that give particular environments a given mood. As with Muzak, and the conditioning of store atmospherics, urban ambience lends effect to the experience we have of space. Forces of emanation, ambiences suggest an airy contour to the demarcations of space, no less pivotal to its formation.

All such instances, of atmospheres and psychogeographies, find expression in related architectural and urban proposals, such as Constant's well-known *New Babylon* project begun in 1958, which was an elaborate urban vision consisting of sectors determined by mood and ambience. *New Babylon* was an imaginary city aiming for the total undoing of the urban plan in favor of a spirited fragmentation. Bordering on quasi-science fiction, *New Babylon* finds early iteration in Constant's drawings and diagrams related to playground designs he was developing (alongside Aldo van Eyck) in Holland in the mid-1950s, which consist of labyrinths and ladders networked together to form a maze of intersecting lines, arcs, and trajectories. The playground comes to suggest spatial structures that are more half-objects than architectural forms, defining a set of parameters by which individual movement and activity may take place, all of which would be operative in *New Babylon*. Such work functions more as skeletal architecture, recalling the steel frames of transmission towers and the infrastructures of the modern city. In this way, there forms a suggestive link between transmission and spatial urbanism, infusing this architectural culture with the radiophonic and its associated signalling. Thus, for Constant and his visions for a new urbanism (termed "unitary urbanism"), the city was but a network sewn together by a series of girders, ladders, and potential movements, which came to articulate, through a material language, the reality of broadcast media. The city was a medium for the networking of desire and its related play, and the means to amplify such elements was to make the city, as Yona Friedman terms, an "extensive infrastructure" open to adjustment and readjustment.[22]

IMAGE 22 Constant, *New Babylon* project (metal, plexiglass, wood), 1958. Photo: Jan Versnel.

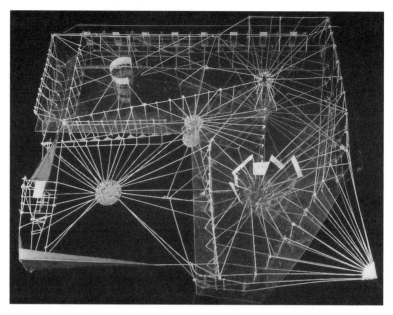

IMAGE 23 Constant, *New Babylon* project (metal, plexiglass, wood), 1958.
Photo: Jan Versnel.

Echoed in the psychogeographic maps produced by Constant and others, notably Debord and Asger Jorn, the cutting up of the city map resulted in nodes and connective lines, splotches of ambiguous terrain alongside tense vectors, where "parts of the city that lack atmospheric intensity are simply removed" and "zones of intense ambience float free on the blank page, linked only by unidirectional red arrows that define flows of attraction."[23] As Mark Wigley's description of Debord and Jorn's *Naked City* (1957) publication outlines, the psychogeographic map was a redrawing of the city according to a circulation of ambient presence.

New Babylon, psychogeographies, drifts and ambiences, all provide an echoing resonance with the infiltration of electronic media following the War, and cultural visions of the new city. The SI applied broadcast media as a metaphor for an ambient city networked through a conveyance of emanating sensations and conducted through an elaborated infrastructural architecture. Their drifts were primary radial tools for the bolstering of a rapturous lifestyle, finding expression in the proposed SI exhibition for the Stedelijk Museum in Amsterdam for the fall of 1959. During the exhibition, which was to take the shape of a labyrinth built inside the Museum, it was proposed that participants were to roam the city over the course of three days communicating through radio transmission.[24] The Museum was to act as a kind of hub around which vectors and drifts would be inserted into the city by the force of attraction and repulsion, a sort of primary magnetism by which urban space and embodied experience would converse, and the streets would come alive as avenues of transmitted communication.

* * *

Fitted with disk platforms, directional and mirror antenna, and aerials for wireless and television broadcast, transmission towers symbolize an oscillation between the power of state control and the potentiality of personalized expression, which may be said to reside at the very heart of radio and other broadcast media, marking, as Michele Bertomen proposes, "Transmission towers [as] tangible manifestations of our immersion in this cosmos of communication."[25] For Bertomen, such cosmic depictions subsequently undo the ability to fully apprehend, from a single perspective, a field of knowledge, replacing the authoritarian panopticon with a vision of fragmented and multiple points in a leveled field of exchange. As she continues: "In the dispersed electromagnetic medium, this singular glance of authority has been fragmented, democratized by the multitudes that now participate in its formation. The radio network might be considered the physical heir to the workings of the moral consciousness."[26]

Radio comes to embody the possibility of sharing beyond the particularities of nation-states, governmental offices, and social demographics, and it does so partially by formalizing networks through the spindly appearance of the transmission tower. For "Transmission towers and the network of communications they support are paradigmatic of a distinctively new conception of the world, one that also demands new strategies for perception."[27] Though Bertomen locates this radical alteration against the single perspective or apex of knowledge, governed by an architecture of tangibility and visibility, such perspective falls short in recognizing to what degree communication networks—of towers and their ultimate transmission—are fully regulated by an infrastructure of control and policy: what information can be transmitted and who has access become immediate questions that undermine the belief that "modern transmission towers suggest an antithesis to the understanding of knowledge as an immediately comprehensible overview in favour of one in which all points in the system provide equal and compatible points of access and comprehension."[28] This is poignantly glimpsed in the mounting of personal transmission devices for the broadcast of illegal signals. To erect one's own transmitter not only infringes upon the landscape of existing towers, it further trespasses on the territorial field of frequency and related law. Transmission towers may indeed point toward an upheaval in the paradigmatic base for the production of knowledge, but they equally do so by spawning new forms of control. Thus, the radial drift of urban adventures, while seeking to generate and fully occupy the networked, ambient city, run parallel to new modes of surveillance that eclipse the full possibility of a New Babylon. Transmission is equally about power and propaganda. The ability to control media channels certainly has proven dramatically operative within acts of social and national dominance, as well as forming a strong foundation for combating such dominance. To transmit is to tap the political heart of social connection.

Media

Constant's development of the ambient city finds early influence from his meetings with the sculptors Steven Gilbert (an earlier

member of the Cobra group, along with Constant) and Nicolas
Schöffer between 1953 and 1956. Schöffer's ideas on the future city
in particular are radically suggestive of what would later become the
New Babylon project. The early sculptural works of Schöffer consist
of steel frames and supports enlivened by the incorporation of kinetic
movement, sound, and light projections, expressing his theories
of "spatiodynamism" that began to surface in 1948. The use of
steel frames for Schöffer provides an optimal structure by being
"transparent" and "airy, penetrable from all sides."[29] Transparent
and airy, they function to support the application and amplification
of temporal media, such as light and sound, or what the artist
called "radiation."

IMAGE 24 Nicolas Schöffer, *Chronos 8*, installed
1982, Kalocsa, Hungary. Photo: the author.

IMAGE 25 Nicolas Schöffer, *Chronos 8*, installed 1982, Kalocsa, Hungary. Photo: the author.

Schöffer presented these sculptural works to Constant, whom he invited (along with Gilbert) to collaborate on a large-scale project, which turned into a manifesto titled "Neo-Vision." The manifesto was an attempt to establish a concentrated forum on the intersection of art and architecture informed by new thoughts on communications and related technologies. Following these discussions and meetings, a collaborative team was formed for the making of a sculpture to be exhibited as part of the International Building and Public Works Exhibition in Paris in 1956. Consisting of Schöffer, the architect Claude Parent (who was to later collaborate with Paul Virilio in the Architecture Principe group), composer Pierre Henry (whom Schöffer would continue to

IMAGE 26 Nicolas Schöffer, *Tower of Liège*, installed next to the Congress Palace, Liège, Belgium, 1961.

work with throughout his career), engineer Jacques Bureau, along with art critic Guy Habasque, the *Spatiodynamic Tower* project echoed Schöffer's earlier sculptures, particularly his *Spatiodynamic City*. Like the *New Babylon* project, the *City* was a model construction (along with drawings) depicting a networked city of long translucent volumes accommodating a variety of functions, transportation arteries with helicopters roaming the skies, and cars traveling underneath, all stitched together by an elaborate system of communications and structural supports allowing the city to grow, and even become mobile. With the new *Tower* work, the patchwork of steel framing gave support to animating light beams, sound systems, mirrors and motorized sections, all of which were to suggest a new vision of urbanism. With music by Pierre Henry, based on analysis of the surrounding environment, the *Tower* was also imagined as broadcasting antenna, to be further located in front of various apartment buildings. Schöffer was thus envisioning not only an art of transmission, but its full incorporation into the new city. As Guy Habasque wrote, "The possibility of animating space in an entirely new way is indeed coupled with the introduction of a temporal element which had never been taken into account in the conception of a work of art."[30]

Schöffer's work was to become an integral part of Cybernetic Art, providing an important early model of not only how technology might be utilized in sculptural form, but also how sculptural form might become suggestive of a future built in tandem with computer technology. As Schöffer imagined, the plastic arts were to become spatialized and radiant according to the promise and urgency of atmospheres and networks, systems and their organization— communicational bonds that further remodel how cities are imagined and built. In this regard, Schöffer's work runs parallel to the critique of modern architecture appearing at this time, as in the work of Henri Lefebvre.[31] According to Lefebvre, architecture and the emerging discipline of urban planning had succumbed to an emphasis on opticality, relying upon notions of the "visible" and "readable," all of which deeply mobilized groups such as the SI. As a consequence, visions of the urban future were complicit with a mode of production that overwhelmed and overshadowed what Lefebvre termed the "tactile" and the "experiential." As Lefebvre argued, opticality essentially supports an understanding of space as inherently "abstract" thereby alienating the more organic intensities of everyday life from the sites of their occurrence.[32] As Steen Eiler Rasmussen further proclaimed in his *Experiencing Architecture* in the late 1950s: "It is not enough to see architecture; you must experience it. You must dwell in its rooms, feel how they close about you, observe how you are naturally led from one to the other. You must be aware of the textural effects . . ."[33]

Rasmussen's tactile emphasis echoed the SI's "atmospheric" and situational poetics, as means to undo the reign of opticality in city planning. In contrast to CIAM and its systematic rationalism, Rasmussen and Lefebvre describe an additional perspective, whereby space *occurs* through sensual relations to materiality that ultimately supplements ocular dominance.

The concern for the temporal and tactile, the ruinous and the animate, finds expression in a vocabulary of moods, atmospheres, and ambiences. This suggestive vocabulary was to find quick support in the increasing emergence of electronic media, communication networks, along with televisions and early computers, circulating through the everyday terrain of urban life. Electronic media, transmission, and live circuits might aid in turning space into temporal media sensitive and sympathetic to the fevers of the everyday. To refuse the abstraction of city space, and the subsequent notion of the "spectacle," the street was to become a live wire for the passing and exchange of ongoing play and imagination, to form "the only authentic communication," which "is the one presenting itself from the outset as a form of common action, of everyday life collectively reinvented, in an immediacy dispensing with all representation . . ."[34] In this regard, Schöffer's *Tour Spatiodynamique Cybernétique* exhibited in 1961 in Liège may similarly express such themes by building a transmission tower not only for broadcast, but for the self-generative organization of a feedback system. Consisting of a 52-meter orthogonal steel tower fitted with 33 rotating axes, driven by motors to put into motion 64 mirror plates as well as polished steel blades that reflect and refract light into a medley of projections and reflections, the Liège Tower became a living system. No longer a strictly representational art, the work functioned as a live interactive vehicle for generating relational exchange. In addition, the Tower was fitted with microphones and other sensing devices, which responded to the environment, feeding the electrical brain of the Tower (developed by the Phillips Company) with information that in turn structured and influenced its movements. Such cybernetic workings suggest methods for the production of atmospheres and situations that Constant's *New Babylon* proposes in model form. "In a sense, the boundless games of the SI are meant to be played out not in urban space but in the sky,"[35] accentuating the embedded aerial projection found in the work. Feedback systems, informational links, and communicational networks thus have at their core a restructuring of urban life in support of temporal sharing and airy modulation.

Airy City

The construction of atmospheres, the networking of sectors, and the circulation of flows of desire and communications gather into a formal language reminiscent of transmission towers, circuit boards, and playgrounds. The steel-framed tower structures, which were to increasingly fill the landscape following the War, are a material vocabulary for the imagining and modeling of future cities. As *New Babylon* expresses, along with works by Schöffer and Friedman, infrastructural supports provide a key spatial syntax for nurturing the play and spontaneity of the metropolis. Their works appear more as structural supports than completed volumes; they are a series of beams and girders, frames and ladders, by which to support the movements and circulation of bodies and interactions. In this regard, transmission towers provide a key image for reimagining the production of space that need not result in static form. For they are objects whose form can only be understood in considering what they generate more than what they statically represent. They stimulate the imagination in exploring means for inhabiting not so much the volumes of the new home, but the working city, as a space always somewhere else. In addition, they seem to suggest a radical form of integration with technology, parallel to the development of cybernetics beginning in the late 1940s (with the publication of Norbert Wiener's seminal *Cybernetics, or control and communication in the animal and the machine* in 1948). Cybernetics was to wield an important influence upon following generations working not only with computer science, mathematics, biology, and zoology, but art and its involvement with electronic systems, networking, and transmission taking off throughout the 1960s with the works of the art-technology groups such as E.A.T. and Pulsa. Prior to the actual utilization of electronics and circuitry, we can glimpse sorts of proto-constructions in architectural projects and proposals, as with the SI, where the fusion of bodies and architecture would take on bolder systematic visions. The works of spatial urbanism link individual behavior not solely to an architectural object, but to an urban plan that held in its wake a new relation to the electronic imagination. That Le Corbusier would analogize the home as a "machine for living" underscores a greater inertia within modernism, marking technology as a new frontier not only of tools but modes of behavior—the SI attacks against the Corbusian vision highlight a subtle yet poignant difference. For the SI, machines for living were not only about rational planning and systematic design, but also about breakdown, noise, dreamy effect, and drunkenness. Thus, notions of transmission (desire and code), the built (network and architecture), and their synthesis would appear on both sides of an ideological fence that sought to define in what way the modern environment was to appear and in itself behave.

The SI's antagonism toward administrative culture did not miss the field of communications technology: "Sociological and cultural theorists so well hide the question of power that experts can write thousands of pages about communication or the means of mass communication in modern society without ever observing that this communication is unidirectional, that the consumers of communication have nothing to respond to."[36] The SI's critique of urban space goes hand in hand with a critique of mass media, and more generally, mass culture, echoed in understandings of Schöffer's work: "The sensations produced by Schöffer's sculptures belong to a real therapy for the 'mal du siècle' and, in addition, they accord with other processes, psychophysiological ones, which also exert an influence on exchanges and blockages of circuits of information."[37]

Constant's *New Babylon* is thus a model of a future city, which will "make possible the creation of an infinite variety of environments"[38] through technologies of atmospheres, as well as a circuit board for the construction of a new form of mass media, whereby people will have something to respond to, for "communication is only ever found in action undertaken in common."[39]

Prior to the SI experiments, the city and electronics find articulation in the work of Buckminster Fuller, whose architectural and engineering visions sought to integrate theories of mathematics and communications with questions of manufacturing and design. Fuller's eccentric projects progressively sought to include a sense for communications and time, aiming to model new architecture in support of modern lived experience. Curiously, his 4-D Tower from the late 1920s functions as both an apartment block, designed to support free movement and the management of affordable housing, as well as structures of communications technology. Fitted with radio transmitters, the 4-D Tower was to operate as a communications device, stitching the inhabitants together into a network of related towers and fusing life with extensive contact. As Fuller describes, "In our individual homes no matter where we may be we can speak into our combination radio-telephonic-recording-dictator recording our commands graphically (word or picture) to our machines which will involve only real thinking and study of statistics by the directors of industries machines."[40] Living would be infused with the potentiality of technological connection. Apartment blocks seem to hover in the sky, flowing down in modular patterns to support a great deal of flexibility. "A room should not be fixed, sound not create a static mood, but should lend itself to change so that its occupants may play upon it as they would upon a piano."[41] Such open-ended and individualized architectural visions point toward an overarching cultural perspective, which would continue to find argument throughout modernism: the built environment necessarily comes to support as well as limit the glimpsed potentialities of freedom.

Pirate Radio, Pirate Territories

At the time Constant's *New Babylon* was surfacing in 1958, and Schöffer's tower projects were being developed, offshore radio broadcasting was initiated off the coast of Denmark. Converting an ex-German fishing vessel anchored off the coast between Sweden and Denmark, Radio Mercur started broadcasting in the summer. Following the steady development of radio broadcasting throughout Europe and the United States since the early to mid-1920s, with the British Broadcasting Corporation being established in 1927, offshore radio transmitting is part of a general culture of pirate radio broadcasting that aims to usurp the larger media structures. The early Baltic offshore radio ships, from Radio Mercur to Radio Nord and Radio Syd, ran from 1958 until 1962 when joint legislation was implemented among the Scandinavian countries officially outlawing offshore radio transmission. Though pirate stations developed in tandem with state control of radio, and the emerging network of commercial stations appearing in the United States at this time, offshore transmissions offer a compelling version by also occupying and setting into relief the very question of spatial and national borders: offshore broadcasts both insert additional content to media flows while disrupting the management of national borders. Appropriating and converting ships into transmitting vessels, dodging the authorities on the seas, and sending out signals toward coastlines, offshore transmissions function as physical and medial additions to given nations: they literally append to the edge of countries as part of their own extensive communications infrastructures. In doing so, they also begin to perform as manifestations of spatial urbanism: the Walking City or 4-D Towers find materialization in the modified ships whose broadcast signals would come to generate a social and medial space full of cultural vitality.

The offshore transmitter interrupts the signal space of national broadcasting to inaugurate new forms of connection and knowledge.[42]

Pirate listeners form alternative communities, demarcating a distinct space within the greater medial environment. Such recognition ultimately led Ronan O'Rahilly to launch the infamous Radio Caroline in 1964. As a record producer and manager, Ronan had sought to promote the recordings of the artist Georgie Fame, but was continually turned down by the major radio stations whose airtime was sponsored by the major record and publishing companies. To combat such restrictions, Ronan had the artist independently recorded and a record released, and finally developed his own broadcasting channel.

Anchored in the Thames Estuary, Radio Caroline was fitted with a 168-foot tall mast topped by antenna aimed to withstand the harsh environment of the sea, a 10-kilowatt transmitter, plus generators, record players, tape machines, and a mixer, all of which were housed in a studio built into the ship. Run by a crew of 10 Dutch sailors, the ship maintained a continual circulation in and around the Thames Estuary, with the crew working for six weeks straight, with DJs being transported to and from the ship by the use of a small shipping vessel, which also brought mail and supplies. After one week of broadcasting the ship received 20,000 letters of fan mail, along with complaints from the Belgian government that it was interfering with maritime broadcasting.[43] Radio Caroline was a floating medial vessel, interrupting not only the circulation of transmitted signals, but also transfiguring the very means by which signals were sent and broadcasting sustained.

The immediate success of Radio Caroline in 1964 (which continued well into 1967 when the British government passed the Marine Offences Act, erupting into often fierce battles between offshore stations and the police, and even among competing pirate vessels) can be understood in relation to the cultural revolution emerging within music in the mid-1960s, to which it ultimately catered. Playing records by the Rolling Stones, The Animals, The Hollies, and the Beatles, to name a few, striking up a steady base of listeners dissatisfied with the likes of the BBC, whose monopoly assured diluted and generalized programming, Radio Caroline essentially galvanized the cultural momentum at this time—countercultural music required countercultural transmission. The promise of transmission from an offshore perspective is also the promise of hearing something one cannot find elsewhere, fully embodying the mythology of the pirate vessel appearing as if from nowhere, thereby participating in the movements of radical autonomy.

Such instances of pirate radio broadcasting contribute to a perspective on the aerial imagination by not only supplying alternative content, but by mapping radio's borders with terrestrial tension. The poetics of transmission towers, in piercing the sky with a potentiality of electrical extension, finds its complement in the lateral, watery broadcast: the tower sends the imagination up into the sky, while offshore transmissions liquify the spatial demarcations of borders and bandwidth. Thus, radio may be understood to negotiate the spectrum of the imagination and its realities, granting energy to those who seek the outside through an ethereal fugitivity.

Spirits

Electrifying visions of other worlds, galvanizing the interchange between earth and sky, and charging the air with a radical ambiguity, the transmission tower sets the scene for alien communications, utopian fantasy, an interlinking of minds, and a general unease and paranoia as to what may come speeding through the radio, the phone lines, the television, the broadband, to locate itself within the home. Thus transmission towers vacillate within the imagination to lend support to the fantasy of communicational technology—to extend the limits of the body, whether individual or political, social or aesthetic. Such extensions though are not without their dangers, for transmission might also deliver viral infection. Contagion and feverish contact take on manic proportions when fitted to electronic media. Whereas the physical germ may extend from a single body to another, in acts of contact, speech, or airy proximity, the medial germ infects through extended electronic diffusion. The voice or sound on the radio beams itself directly into one's environment, taking root in the folds of the ear to contaminate the host body. As a potential contagion of frequency, the radio wave gathers up all the cosmic dust swirling in the ether, lending vitality to lost, hovering spectral entities.

The *ghost in the machine* delivers alien input, balanced unsteadily between infection and healing, corruption and guidance, temptation and enlightenment, conditioning electronic media with degrees of dangerous influence. The tower is thus an open symbol for the sheer potentiality found in transmission, veering across the spectrum of signification and giving to mass media means for psychological control. William Burroughs reflects on the potential for such control, recognizing that "The control of the mass media depends on laying down lines of association," which penetrate the unconscious with influencing effect. The threading of the nation with infrastructural hardware literally pictures these lines of association, with the circuitry, cabling, antenna, and related elements charging the psyche with unease as to who or what might be listening, monitoring, or implanting. Yet, "When the lines are cut the associational connections are broken,"[44] thereby disrupting the connective patterning. In this regard, the dream machine device developed in 1961 by Burroughs' associates, Brion Gysin and Ian Sommerville, is a sort of counter-hardware designed to break the lines already implanted within; with the flickering lights hitting the closed eyelids, the dream machine unleashes unconscious energy to subvert the weave of psychic imagery promulgated by mass media.

Extending the greater history of contagion aligned with metaphors of the air, electronic media are germ warfare, forcing a moral perspective onto the right to airspace. Airspace "becomes a metaphor for the shared air of the moral environment . . ."[45] aligning the legalities of radio technology with moral overtones, as well as the urgency of resistance.

The work of artist Carl Michael von Hausswolff brings forward an appreciation for the ghost in the machine, as spirit transmission with effective and contagious potential. For Hausswolff, the territory of the signal is a site for occupation, a means for disruptive surprise, unconscious energy, and bodily diffusion. The spectral potentiality hovering across the globe lends to the aerial imagination a radical materiality, which Hausswolff readily engages. His ongoing involvement in such phenomena can be glimpsed in many of his audio and visual works, which often seek the mesmerizing, supple, and charged peripheries of perception.

His project on the life and work of Friedrich Jürgenson exemplifies Hausswolff's pursuit of unknown entities. Having discovered the audio archive of Jürgenson while traveling in Sweden, Hausswolff has meticulously sponsored a reappraisal of Jürgenson's work and electronic voice phenomena in general. As an artist and singer, Jürgenson became obsessed with voices heard during tape recordings he produced of his own singing in the late 1950s. As he observed:

> I sat by the table, clearly awake and relaxed. I sensed that soon something was going to happen. Following an inner pleasurable calmness, long sentences in English appeared in my consciousness. I did not perceive these sentences acoustically but they formed themselves as long phonetic sentences and after a closer study I couldn't conceive the words as correct English but in a disfigured almost alphabetical way—completely deformed. I did not hear a voice, a sound nor a whisper. It was all soundless.[46]

Such perceptual phenomena demarcate a zone of slippery signification, a transposition of medial form with the edges of cognition, which technology, and in particular broadcast media, comes to impart. Electromagnetic mechanics unfurl a suggestive interplay between hearing and believing, haunting the auditory with a set of unsteady frequencies that marks every noise with those "disfigured" words Jürgenson came to note.

IMAGE 27 Friedrich Jürgenson, in his archive in Höör, Sweden, early 1980s. Photographer unknown. Courtesy: The Friedrich Jürgenson Foundation.

Continuing his dedication to these "mental messengers," Jürgenson would eventually incorporate a radio receiver into his medial channelling. Connecting a microphone and radio receiver to a tape recorder, Jürgenson held conversations between himself and the perceived voices, producing an extensive archive of tapes. Fixing his ear to the static of transmission, Jürgenson came to chart a material link between the radiophonic and the spirit realm, highlighting a greater legacy of spirit channeling and "imaginative empathy" that itself would find deeper support through the advent of electronic media.

Radio, from its beginning, was immediately drawn into a field of superstition, in which electricity, conduction, and the movements of unseen energies coalesce into images of ghosts, spirits, and telepathic exchange. The very possibility of transmission acts as a proto-reservoir for imaginary projection. As Milutis elaborates, "The ethereal avant-garde—for whom the radio became both a metaphor of modern consciousness and a tool of radiophonic artwork—welcomed the possibility of noise, misprision, and appropriation that would always be in conflict with the standardization of the radio waves."[47]

Hausswolff's concern for spirit transmission and electronic phenomena elaborates this space of imaginary connection, uncovering an ontology of frequency based on Hertzian intensity. The vague terrain of transmission is generative of a radiophonic imaginary, suggesting zones of ethereal animation shadowing and haunting the terrestrial. Hausswolff's focus on the borders of the tangible and intelligible brings into relief such transmitted signals as constituting a set of radical meanings: that the conveyance of messages upon channels of electronic media might give narrative to the other side, and potentially act as subversive, dangerous, and fantastic interventions. Such work can be appreciated through Burroughs' electronic revolution, and the uncanny way in which media can shift upon its own axis of conveyance, distorting the clarity of the signal with occult phenomena.

IMAGE 28 Carl Michael von Hausswolff, 1485.0 kHz radio receiver, 2008. Constructed in Bucharest for the Ars Telephonica exhibition, and also used for the Birdcage project in Stockholm 2009 (edition of 7). Courtesy the artist and Gallery Niklas Belenius, Stockholm. Photo: Anca Benera.

For Hausswolff, the process of audio recording itself, and the playback through various sound systems and home stereos, provides a dynamic platform for channeling and carving out a space for contact. The invasiveness of sounds emitted from a CD into the home for instance performs as a medial channel, and is thereby prone to fluctuation. The audio releases by Hausswolff are steady investigations of the behavior of transmission and the very objects of electrical signaling, forming a significant catalogue of studies into the aerial imagination radically fixed on the ether.

His CD release from 1997, *To Make Things Happen in the Bunker Via the Micro Way*, for example locates the listener within a series of electrical signals, sine wave tones, and minute fluctuations of energy composed into six tracks. As the artist states, "This CD was recorded in my studio/home where I recorded electrical sources such as adapters, fuseboxes, etc, with an induction microphone,"[48] giving audible form to the formless surges enveloping space. The work veers between formal abstraction and occult science, fixing on the ethereal space between signal and listening, home and the aerial. The materiality of the artist's home comes to impart numerous energy waves and electrical oscillations, as an array of ambiguous signifying matter. From humming fuses to electronic currents passing through walls—*what messages hover within the everyday to give influence to who and what we may become?* Yet what extends further from the work is recognition of the means of playback—in listening to the work all the movements of sonic energy seem to incorporate the CD player, the amplifier, and loudspeakers by which the work sounds again, within this room. That is, the electrical energy captured in recording is reanimated as electronic signal and brought back to life upon playback, as an infectious matter to invade and commune with local signals. Electrical signals and related energy take occupation of my listening space to form an unsteady augmentation: I am both within the space of reproduced sound as well as its contaminating effect, as a festering signal seeking occupation, or a new host.

This contaminating infiltration comes to occupy the listening environment, supporting the claim frequency comes to make onto every space by stirring the molecular volume so as to inspire potential transformation. Hausswolff's more recent project for Birdcage (a curatorial project by Daniele Balit) further opens an occult space of audible contagion. Consisting of a customized sound object permanently fixed at 1485.0 kHz (the Jürgenson frequency), the work has been installed within the home of the artist Jan Håfström in Stockholm and can be experienced only upon invitation by Håfström. The work recreates the audible frequency by which Jürgenson had refined much of his "audioscopic" research, recreating the conditions for electronic voice phenomena. The project turns the phenomenon into a domestic appliance, avoiding the static of the radio, the white noise of possible signal, to forge a direct route toward contact. It becomes a material feature of the home. In this way, Hausswolff continues to nurture the emanations and radiations generated by the material world. Following the aerial suggestiveness of the transmitting tower, Hausswolff embraces the hardware of material culture to spark numerous energies that synthesize into possibilities for spectral take-over.

Extending such forms of radiophonic research, and the interlacing of interior states and exterior broadcasting, Upton Sinclair's study of telepathy further exposes frequency as conducting matter. The novelist's fascination with psychology, and the ability to share states of mind, led to a series of experiments with his wife, whose faculty of concentration sparked Sinclair's initial interest. His book *Mental Radio* documents these experiments performed throughout the 1920s, predating McLuhan's electronic age and Orson Welles' *War of the Worlds* broadcast, and figuring through quasi-scientific terms much of the modernist avant-garde fascination around radiophony.

Sinclair's telepathic experiments were conducted mostly through the act of drawing: the author would make a drawing of a simple picture or diagram, such as a house or a tree, insert this drawing into an envelope and then deliver this to his wife, who, lying on a sofa would place the envelope either on her abdomen or nearby on a table. Through a period of deep concentration, his wife would attempt to conjure the image contained within the envelope, and then after some minutes make a drawing herself, which as Sinclair observes, often matched or mirrored the original. This rhythm of correspondences led to a number of observations by Sinclair, and eventually to his proposition that the mind and consciousness contain innumerable possibilities for communication that sidestep the verbal act.

Sinclair's mental radio supplies the aerial imagination with a new form of contact—that of telepathic exchange, which bypasses the hardware of electronic circuit or microphone altogether. The ontology of frequency, in swerving between functional clarity and the potentiality of interference, promises the deliverance of the intended message, while supporting the imaginary fantasy of possible disruption. Media are always prone to invasive contamination and appropriation. To hack the system, steal the signal, and occupy the frequency exists within the technology itself, informing, however unconsciously, visions for possible application or sabotage.

Local and Global

The movements of the aerial imagination shift from immediate physicality to extensive projections of the beyond—from local to global possibilities, which deliver a deep sense for effective involvement. Yet such emanations might be said to diffuse the single physical body into an extensive, networked condition, displacing the corporeal onto an imaginary plane of virtuality. The transmission tower, as I've been proposing here, functions as a proto-object giving material expression to the immaterial, emanating the potentiality of medial reach. The power of transmission continually makes tangible the possibility of immaterial or fugitive presence, coding the propagation of sound with medial energy.

The transmission tower finds its contemporary counterpart in satellite technology. The constructions circulating the globe literally supplement the transmission tower, multiplying the passing and flux of signals as so much heated, infective, and signifying matter. With the satellite comes new forms of aerial figuration—the imagination finds support in the material objects that give suggestion as to possible horizons for projected living. With the satellite, the vocabulary of "emanating" shifts to one of "orbiting," to give way to cosmic figures. The orbiting imagination moves between every point on the globe to the vastness of deep space. Satellite technology thus affords an extremely detailed account of earthly events and mapping through its circulation above, inspiring fantasies of seeing through walls, capturing DNA particles, or projecting avatars.

In addition, the mobile phone has placed sending and receiving in nearly everyone's hands, charging the quotidian with all the generative fevers of transmission while turning it into business. As with the tower, the mobile phone materially suggests connective presence, acting as a mundane coordinate within an always already potentializing network. The mobile phone brings the enormous satellite down into the palm, to embed one within this medial orbit, charging the imagination with the potentiality to circle the globe—*the phone is a node within the flows of so many signals*, aligning calls home with the phantasmic disembodiment of radiophony.

Transmission amplifies this weave of the local and global, the corporeal and its diffuse effective intangibility, pointing toward the sky as a volatile and poignant space full of territorial *and* phantasmic meaning. Whereas radio broadcast defines this relation according to sender and receiver, the air itself is an open channel. With the advent of digital wireless signaling, transmission is relocated onto the conditions of networked connectivity, making every laptop a sender and receiver, each a node in an ever-flexible medial geography. From coffee shops to hotel rooms to bowling alleys, every space may operate as a dramatic medial organ, aligning transmission culture with the quotidian roots of our new sense of place.

Though much has been written on the radical reconfigurations of embodied subjectivity due to the radiophonic—*the disembodied voice* . . .—the built environment, as the condition of the social, as I've been mapping here, has found equal reconfiguration from the dislocative networking of the transmitted. Since the 1950s, as in the work of

Schöffer and cultures of spatial urbanism, the desire and interest to make live, temporal, and transmitted work has significantly developed. As Heidi Grundmann has consistently documented and theorized, media projects since the early 1970s have sought to activate telephone lines, fax machines, videophone, and satellite connections to forge new platforms for collective productions. As seen in the *Wiencouver* projects throughout the 1970s and 1980s, the making of connection is equally the building out of a "communication space." Initially developed in 1979 by Hank Bull, *Wiencouver* was itself an imaginary city bridging Vancouver and Vienna. The project continued to manifest at different times, and in different ways, between 1979 and 1983, involving artists such as Robert Adrian, Bill Bartlett, and Valie Export, among many others, to use varying technological means to connect, transmit, and generate communication between artists, across the globe. Importantly, the technological possibility of reaching around the globe became equally about activating the local, making links between here and there. As Reinhard Braun suggests, "The space created in Wiencouver incorporates the modalities both of the employed technology and of the interpersonal collaboration."[49]

"*Wiencouver* stands for many other cooperations and developments of a radio art beyond the broadcasting paradigm,"[50] as Grundmann states, giving important manifestation to the life of transmission. With the emergence of digital wireless networking, communication space has allowed deeper and more elaborate forms of aerial projection and interpersonal collaboration. The work of Descentro in Brazil gives view to the blending of digital networks, tactical media, and environmental policy indicative of the contemporary mix of local and global perspectives and platforms. The grass-roots issues Descentro has come to engage seek to redress the uneven distribution of digital tools and networking within the country of Brazil. As part of the Cultural Hotspots project of the Brazilian Ministry of Culture, the group, along with others such as Estúdio Livre, has organized workshops, educational platforms, and other tactical media labs to empower mostly rural communities by implementing media centers with free software. Their work participates within a larger network of projects, groups, and activists that currently operate as semi-autonomous collectives looking to support access to digital tools and related knowledge in Brazil and elsewhere.

Whereas Schöffer's multimedia tower machines produced a techno-abstraction onto the plane of local context—with a kinetic phantasmic excess of sound and light hovering over social reality— much of the Descentro work is concerned with the "micro-politics" surrounding new modes of sharing. The production of a network is thus more the development of a means, or the opening of a live channel, for social action. Such work elaborates further on the question of space found in the various histories I've been tracing here, which have at their core the desire to reconstruct architecture as an energetic process. As Luis Fernández-Galiano proposes, the forces of energy that continually circulate as part of buildings, such as thermodynamic expenditure, weathering, the material transubstantiation occurring in construction, and of course sound and light, creates a deep link between architectural forms and animate life.[51] Questions of energy are furthered in the work of architect Kisho Kurokawa, and his theories of Metabolist architecture from the 1960s. For Kurokawa the greater "metabolism" at the core of buildings is "unobstructed by any dualistic division between inside and outside," thereby emphasizing archi- tecture as "a space free from the divisions of walls."[52] Space is understood rather as a temporal and elemental flexing impressed and pressing back, and constituted equally by material texture as well as mediated flows.

In the work of Descentro, along with many other contemporary projects, we find a realization of much of spatial urbanism's models and theories of energetic space. Whereas Friedman's infrastructures and the SI's drifts exist as propositional refiguring of architecture as "participatory," groups such as Descentro recognize that the embed- ded potential of spatial participation is also served according to medial, communication space through which others might build their own transmissions and signaling.

The power of transmission as seen within legacies of radiophonic production, and the aerial figures that come to circulate as psychodynamic embodiments, find their footing within a contemporary landscape where the local is immediately participant within the global. To connect then is to not only send and receive, but to activate an entire field of possibility—the seemingly immaterial radiation, emanation, and orbiting of signals have absolute influence in actualizing concrete reality. The disembodied self found on the radio dial might be said to be finally returning to earth to take up residence once again within the social, lending dynamic input by participating within micro-narratives of interaction. The ghost in the machine is thus the beginning of the construction of an aerial society here on earth. Whether in Wiencouver or New Babylon, such societies are finding firm footing within today's environment, giving productive force to modalities of transmission that are equally recoded into social organization. Such towering visions though, as Ricardo Ruiz of Descentro reminds, have at their core a fundamental desire—that through "believing in [a] micro-politics scenario" we might achieve "more happiness in the world."[53]

Notes

Introduction: Your Sound Is My Sound
Is Your Sound

1   Bruce R. Smith, "Coda: Talking Sound History," in *Hearing History*, ed. Mark M. Smith (Athens and London: University of Georgia Press, 2004), p. 389.

2   Les Back, *The Art of Listening* (Oxford and New York: Berg, 2007), p. 22.

3   Steven Connor, "The Modern Auditory I," in *Rewriting the Self: Histories from the Renaissance to the Present*, ed. Roy Porter (London and New York: Routledge, 1997), p. 211.

4   Ibid., p. 207.

5   See Richard Cullen Rath, *How Early America Sounded* (Ithaca and London: Cornell University Press, 2003).

6   Steven Connor, "The Modern Auditory I", p. 206.

7   Edmund Carpenter and Marshall McLuhan, "Acoustic Space," in *Explorations in Communication*, eds. Edmund Carpenter and Marshall McLuhan (Boston: Beacon Press, 1960), p. 67.

8   Jean-Francois Augoyard and Henry Torgue (eds), *Sonic Experience: A Guide to Everyday Sounds* (Montreal: McGill-Queen's University Press, 2005), p. 130.

9   Ibid., p. 131.

10   This was initially developed from a 1996 Green Paper drafted by the EU, and was followed in 1998 by the creation of a Noise Expert Network which is to provide assistance to the development of European Noise policies.

11   From summary of the ANS found on Mayor of London website: http://www.london.gov.uk/mayor/strategies/noise/index.jsp.

12   For a study on the effects of noise pollution linked to traffic, see *Urban Traffic Problem*, ed. Dietrich Schwela and Olivier Zali (London: E & FN Spon, 1999). Excessive transport is often understood to degrade the urban environment, leading to calls for pedestrian zones, increased quiet areas and green spaces, as witnessed, for example, in Copenhagen's pedestrian movement from the 1960s onward. Of note here is the work of Danish urban planner Jan Gehl, whose influential work on cities and human experience has led to increased demand for open and public space in Copenhagen, as well as other cities, such as Melbourne, where he has also been an urban consultant.

13   From summary of ANS outline found on Mayor of London website.

14   Eric Wilson, "Plagues, Fairs, and Street Cries: Sounding out Society and Space in Early Modern London," *Modern Language Studies*, vol. 25, no. 3 (Summer, 1995): 12.

1 Underground: Busking, Acousmatics, and the Echo

1   Peter Ackroyd, *London: The Biography* (London: Vintage, 2001), pp. 565–6.
2   E. M. Forster, *A Passage to India* (London: Penguin Books, 2000), p. 200.
3   Michel Chion, *Audio-Vision: Sound on Screen* (New York: Columbia University Press, 1994), p. 11.
4   Ibid., p. 13.
5   Ibid., pp. 9–10.
6   Marc Augé, *In the Metro* (Minneapolis: University of Minnesota Press, 2002), p. 30.
7   Peter Mulvey, quoted in "The Subterranean World of Peter Mulvey," in NPR online article, September 22, 2002.
8   "The Subterranean World of Peter Mulvey," in NPR online article, September 22, 2002.
9   Susan Cagle, lyrics to "Stay" from *The Subway Recordings* (New York: Columbia Records, 2006).
10   http://www.myspace.com/susancagle (upon viewing in January 2009).
11   Stuart Dempster, liner notes in *Underground Overlays from the Cistern Chapel* (San Francisco: New Albion Records, 1995).
12   Stuart Dempster, liner notes.
13   See Mladen Dolar, *A Voice and Nothing More* (Cambridge, MA: MIT Press, 2006), p. 61.
14   Emily Cockayne, *Hubbub: Filth, Noise and Stench in England* (New Haven and London: Yale University Press, 2007), p. 122.
15   William Callcott, quoted in David Cohen and Ben Greenwood, *The Buskers: A History of Street Entertainment* (North Pomfert, VT: David and Charles, Inc., 1981), p. 147. The letter appears in a collection that was gathered in 1864 as part of attempts to ban street music altogether.
16   David Cohen and Ben Greenwood, *The Buskers: A History of Street Entertainment* (North Pomfert, VT: David and Charles, Inc., 1981), p. 171.
17   By 1965 Dylan had emerged as a leading figure within the folk music revolution, producing acoustic songs of great power and sentiment. During his appearance at the Newport Folk Festival in 1965 he startled the crowd by "going electric," appearing on stage with electric guitar and accompanied by a band. The crowd subsequently booed Dylan off-stage after a set of songs, leading the organizers into a flurry of distress and rage. This electric presentation was generally heard as a betrayal to the sound and ethos of folk music, based on acoustic integrity.
18   As a curious historical note, the day after the Royal Albert Hall concert, the Beatles played live for the last time together on the rooftop of their Apple studios building. Such a move might be further appreciated through this argument of music's place in the public sphere, and how musicians come to seek routes toward the public outside the mediating structures of commercialism.
19   Upon viewing in January 2009.
20   Jennifer Toth, *The Mole People: Life in the Tunnels beneath New York City* (Chicago: Chicago Review Press, 1993), p. 47.

21   Ibid., p. 46.
22   Ibid., p. 165.
23   Ibid., pp. 165–6.
24   Ibid., p. 168.
25   Mladen Dolar, *A Voice and Nothing More*, p. 64.
26   Michel Chion, *Audio-Vision: Sound on Screen*, p. 72.
27   Mladen Dolar, *A Voice and Nothing More*, p. 67.
28   It has been estimated that between 1915 and 1918 London experienced 118 air raids with 300 tons of bombs being dropped by German bombers. As Peter Ackroyd documents in his encyclopedic biography of London: "It's been estimated that during the First World War, one-third of a million Londoners went underground in February 1918, to shelter in the tube stations which extended below the capital ... This is a constant image in descriptions of the subterranean life. It is *like being dead*, buried alive beneath the great city. The most famous of these caverns under the ground was the 'Tilbury' beneath Commercial Road and Cable Street where thousands of East Enders sheltered from the bombs." Peter Ackroyd, *London: The Biography* (London: Vintage, 2001), pp. 564–5.
29   Quoted in Christian Wolmar, *The Subterranean Railway* (London: Atlantic Books, 2004), p. 211.
30   See Andrew Hyde, "Life in the Shelters," in *The Blitz, Then and Now, Vol. 2*, ed. Winston G. Ramsey (London: Battle of Britain Prints International, 1988), pp. 118–21.
31   Ibid., p. 119.
32   Quoted in Benson Bobrick, *Labyrinths of Iron: A History of the World's Subway* (New York: Newsweek Books, 1982), p. 143.
33   Ibid., p. 157.
34   William Strange, "The Brave and Happy Shelterers," in *London Underground: Poems and Prose about the Tube* (Stuttgart: Reclam, 2003), p. 76.
35   Ibid., p. 80.
36   Alan Seymour, "On a Mortuary Van in the London Blitz," in *The Blitz, Then and Now, Vol. 2*, ed. Winston G. Ramsey, p. 246.
37   Arthur I. Waskow and Stanley L. Newman, *America in Hiding* (New York: Ballantine Books, 1962), p. 10.
38   Ibid., p. 21.
39   Ibid., p. 23.
40   Michel Foucault, "Different Spaces," in *Michel Foucault: Essential Works of Foucault 1954–1984, Volume 2, Aesthetics* (London: Penguin Books, 1998), p. 178.
41   Ivan Jirous, "Report on the Third Czech Musical Revival," in *Primary Documents: A Sourcebook for Eastern and Central European Art since the 1950s*, eds. Laura Hoptman and Tomás Pospiszyl (Cambridge, MA: MIT Press & New York: Museum of Modern Art, 2002), pp. 64–5.
42   Ibid., p. 61.
43   Ladislav Klíma was a Czech philosopher and novelist born in the late nineteenth century whose work fiercely defends individual will over all other social and moral structures. Influenced by Nietzsche and Schopenhauer, Klíma notably put into practice much of his ideas, often rejecting job and money in favor of a highly individualized lifestyle. His philosophical ideas and eccentric practices

would find favorable reception in the 1960s, as questions of individual will and resistance were to take deep hold within the underground cultures.

44   Lyrics to "I Am The Absolute Will (Jsem absolutní vule)," from The Plastic People of the Universe, *Jak bude po smrti* (Prague: Globus Records, 1979/1998).

45   Lazar Kunstmann, "La Mexicaine Le Interview," from greg.org interview, October 10, 2004.

46   Ibid.

47   Michel Chion, "Wasted Words," in *Sound Theory, Sound Practice*, ed. Rick Altman (New York & London: Routledge, 1992), p. 110.

48   For a thoroughly detailed account of the Polish Underground Army, see Marek Ney-Krwawicz, *The Polish Home Army 1939–1945* (London: Polish Underground Movement Study Trust, 2001).

2 Home: Ethical Volumes of Silence and Noise

1   Gaston Bachelard, *The Poetics of Space* (Boston: Beacon Press, 1969), p. 72.

2   David Morley, *Home Territories: Media, Mobility, and Identity* (New York: Routledge, 2008), p. 39.

3   Bachelard writes: "For our house is our corner of the world. As has often been said, it is our first universe, a real cosmos in every sense of the word." Gaston Bachelard, *The Poetics of Space*, p. 4.

4   Charles Rice, *The Emergence of the Interior: Architecture, Modernity, Domesticity* (New York: Routledge, 2007), p. 12.

5   Ibid., p. 16.

6   The theory of the "sonorous envelope" was developed by the psycho-analytic practitioner and theorist Didier Anzieu. Explored in relation to his overall theory of "the skin ego," Anzieu examines the sounding environment of the child as an enveloping sonority, which comes to grant security and warmth, particularly the mother's voice. See Didier Anzieu, *The Skin Ego* (New Haven: Yale University Press, 1989).

7   Karin Bijsterveld, *Mechanical Sound: Technology, Culture, and Public Problems of Noise in the Twentieth Century* (Cambridge, MA: MIT Press, 2008), p. 166.

8   Janet Higgitt, Alan Whitfield, and Rick Groves, "Quiet Homes for London" report, 2004, p. 11.

9   Christopher N. Penn, *Noise Control: The Law and Its Enforcement* (Crayford, UK: Shaw and Sons, 2002), p. 373.

10   Janet Higgitt, Alan Whitfield, and Rick Groves, "Quiet Homes for London" report, p. 11.

11   Georg Simmel, "The Metropolis and Mental Life," in *Classic Essays on the Culture of Cities*, ed. Richard Sennett (Englewood Cliffs, NJ: Prentice-Hall, 1969), p. 48.

12   "Ohio City Passes Ordinance to Target Loud Car Stereos," in *The Dayton Daily News*, July 2, 1997.

13   Edward J. Blakely and Mary Gail Snyder, *Fortress America: Gated Communities in the United States* (Washington, DC: Brookings Institution Press, 1997), p. 8.
14   See Amending Chapter 11.44 of Title 11 "Noise Limits," City of Santa Clarita, California.
15   Dolores Hayden, *Building Suburbia: Green Fields and Urban Growth, 1820–2000* (New York: Vintage Books, 2004), pp. 128–9.
16   Richard Sennett, *The Uses of Disorder: Personal Identity and City Life* (New York: Vintage Books, 1971), p. 72.
17   Richard Sennett, *The Conscience of the Eye: The Design and Social Life of Cities* (London: Faber and Faber, 1990).
18   Richard Sennett, *The Uses of Disorder: Personal Identity and City Life*, p. 43.
19   Michel Serres, *Parasite* (Minneapolis: University of Minnesota Press, 2007), p. 41.
20   Alphonso Lingis, *The Community of Those Who Have Nothing in Common* (Bloomington and Indianapolis: Indiana University Press, 1994), pp. 113–14.
21   Richard Sennett, *The Uses of Disorder: Personal Identity and City Life*, p. 63.
22   Vito Acconci, statement by the artist, provided through an informal correspondence with the author, 2009.
23   Ibid.
24   Michel Foucault, *Discipline and Punish: The Birth of the Prison* (New York: Vintage Books, 1979), pp. 235–6.
25   Norman Johnston, *Forms of Constraint: A History of Prison Architecture* (Urbana and Chicago: University of Illinois Press, 2000), p. 78.
26   Quoted in Orlando F. Lewis, *The Development of American Prisons and Prison Customs 1776 to 1845* (Albany: Prison Association of New York, 1922), p. 81.
27   Jack Henry Abbott, *In the Belly of the Beast: Letters from Prison* (New York: Vintage Books, 1991), pp. 9–10.
28   Orlando F. Lewis, *The Development of American Prisons and Prison Customs 1776 to 1845*, p. 82.
29   Interesting to note, recent architectural projects in Australia are based on forms of communal life among prisoners. The Mobilong Prison in South Australia consists of a series of self-contained duplex units housing five prisoners for each unit. Each prisoner has their own bedroom and is given access to shared living areas, kitchens, bathrooms, and an outdoor area. Such architecture aims to support more humane forms of incarceration, recognizing that, as Elisabeth Grant states, "hard and inflexible environments may result in displays of noncompliant and aggressive behavior among inmates." See Elizabeth Grant's work on prison architecture and communities in Australia, for instance, her article "Mobilong Independent Living Units: New Innovations in Australian Prison Architecture," *Corrections Today*, vol. 68, no. 3: 58–61.
30   Elaine Scarry, *The Body in Pain: The Making and Unmaking of the World* (New York/London: Oxford University Press, 1987), p. 172. Scarry further observes: "World, self, and voice are lost, or nearly lost, through the intense pain

of torture and not through the confession as is wrongly suggested by its connotations of betrayal. The prisoner's confession merely objectifies the fact of their being almost lost, makes their invisible absence, or nearby absence, visible to the torturers. To assent words that through the thick agony of the body can be only dimly heard, or to reach aimlessly for the name of a person or a place that has barely enough cohesion to hold its shape as a word and none to bond it to its worldly referent, is a way of saying, yes, all is almost gone now, there is almost nothing left now, even this voice, the sounds I am making, no longer form my words but the words of another." (See p. 35.)

31   The Miranda law was established in 1966 after a case ruling, *Miranda v. Arizona*. The ruling upheld that information acquired from a defendant was inadmissible in court if the defendant was not informed of the right to have an attorney present and the right to remain silent (the right against self-incrimination) during questioning, and if the defendant had voluntarily waived this right. Subsequently, arresting officers issue a verbal statement of these rights, requesting the suspect understands and voluntarily waives these rights.

32   Adam Jaworski, *The Power of Silence: Social and Pragmatic Perspectives* (London: Sage Publications, 1993), p. 48.

33   Louis Althusser, "Ideology and Ideological State Apparatuses (Notes towards an Investigation)," in *On Ideology* (London: Verso, 2008), p. 56.

34   Edward J. Blakely and Mary Gail Snyder, *Fortress America: Gated Communities in the United States*, p. 3.

35   Ibid., p. 18.

36   William Greer, *A History of Alarm Security* (Bethesda, MD: National Burglar and Fire Alarm Association, 1991), p. 13.

37   Federico Miyara, "Acoustic Violence: A New Name for an Old Social Pain," *Hearing Rehabilitation Quarterly*, vol. 24, no. 1 (1999): 18.

38   Ibid., 21.

39   I am drawing mainly from his book, *Totality and Infinity: An Essay on Exteriority* (Pittsburgh: Duquesne University Press, 1969/1998).

40   Dr. Michael Smith, "Emmanuel Levinas's Ethics of Responsibility," a lecture given at Kennesaw State College, October 7, 2003. Found on the College website. See also Fleurdeliz R. Altez, "Banal and Implied Forms of Violence in Levinas' Phenomenological Ethics," *Kritike*, vol. 1, no. 1 (June 2007): 52–70.

41   Chantal Mouffe, "Artistic Activism and Agonistic Spaces," *Art & Research*, vol. 1, no. 2 (Summer 2007): 2.

42   For more information on the Project, see http://www.positivesoundscapes.org/.

3 Sidewalk: Steps, Gait, and Rhythmic Journey-Forms

1   Jane Jacobs, *The Death and Life of Great American Cities* (London: Penguin Books, 1962), p. 73.

2   Ibid., p. 68.

3   Jean-François Augoyard, *Step By Step: Everyday Walks in a French Urban Housing Project* (Minneapolis: University of Minnesota Press, 2007), p. 128.

4   Ibid., pp. 8–9.

5   Michel de Certeau, *The Practice of Everyday Life* (Berkeley and Los Angeles: University of California Press, 1988), p. 139.

6   Tia DeNora, *Music and Everyday Life* (Cambridge: Cambridge University Press, 2000), pp. 77–8.

7   Ibid., pp. 84–5.

8   Francis Alÿs, quoted in Nicolas Bourriaud, *The Radicant* (New York: Lukas & Sternberg, 2009), p. 96.

9   Michel de Certeau, *The Practice of Everyday Life*, p. 103.

10   See the study by Bill Baranowski, "Pedestrian Crosswalk Signals at Roundabouts: Where are they Applicable?" delivered at the Transportation Research Board's Roundabout Conference, May 2005. Found on the author's related website, www.RoundaboutsUSA.com.

11   Recommended rates are between 30 and 90 pulses per minute for red mode and 60 to 700 pulses for green. Information acquired from technical manuals supplied by Prisma Teknik, 2007. As an interesting note, the DAPS is designed to also deliver up to three voice messages of eight seconds each.

12   Michael Bull, *Sounding Out the City: Personal Stereos and the Management of Everyday Life* (Oxford: Berg, 2000), p. 130.

13   For a thoroughly enlightening consideration of ghosting within the urban, see the important work of Steve Pile, particularly, *Real Cities: Modernity, Space and the Phantasmagorias of City Life* (London: Sage Publications, 2005).

14   Jean-Paul Thibaud, "The Sonic Composition of the City," in *Auditory Culture Reader*, eds. Michael Bull and Les Back (Oxford: Berg, 2003), p. 329.

15   Ibid., p. 338.

16   Steve Pile, *The Body and the City: Psychoanalysis, Space and Subjectivity* (London and New York: Routledge, 1996), p. 229.

17   The project was developed during 2002–2004 by Lalya Gaye, Margot Jacobs, Ramia Mazé, and Daniel Skoglund and was the result of collaborative research between the institutes Future Applications Lab (Viktoria Institute) and PLAY Studio (Interactive Institute), both in Gothenburg, Sweden.

18   Layla Gaye, Lars Erik Holmquist, and Ramia Mazé, "Sonic City: Merging Urban Walkabouts with Electronic Music Making" found on the project's website.

19   Layla Gaye and Lars Erik Holmquist, "In Duet with Everyday Urban Settings: A user study of Sonic City," found on the project's website.

20   Layla Gaye and Ramia Mazé, "Sonic City," found on the project's website.

21   This quote, and following quotes, by Jessica Thompson, from an informal email correspondence with the author, 2009.

22   Andra McCartney, "Soundscape Works, Listening, and the Touch of Sound," in *Aural Cultures*, ed. Jim Drobnick (Toronto: YYZ Books, 2004), p. 179.

23   Henri Lefebvre, *Rhythmanalysis* (London: Continuum, 2004), p. 27.

24   Ibid., p. 15.

25   Nicolas Bourriaud, *The Radicant*, p. 117.

26   Mark M. Smith, "Coda: Talking Sound History," in *Hearing History*, ed. Mark M. Smith (Athens and London: University of Georgia Press, 2004), p. 395.

27   Mitchell Duneier, *Sidewalk* (New York: Farrar, Straus and Giroux, 1999), p. 88.

28   David Fort Godshalk, *Veiled Visions* (Chapel Hill: University of North Carolina Press, 2005), p. 7.

29   Thornwell Jacobs, *The Law of the White Circle* (Athens: The University of Georgia Press, 2006), p. 77.

30   Judith Butler, *Excitable Speech* (New York: Routledge, 1997), p. 11. Later in this book, Butler explores the ramifications of hate speech and its related legislative debates.

31   Clive Bloom, *Violent London* (London: Pan Books, 2003), p. 275.

32   For an engaging overview of Radio Alice, see Mikkel Bolt Rasmussen, "Promises in the Air: Radio Alice and Italian Autonomia," in *Radio Territories*, eds. Erik Granly Jensen and Brandon LaBelle (Los Angeles and Copenhagen: Errant Bodies Press, 2006), pp. 26–47.

33   William H. McNeill, *Keeping Together in Time* (Cambridge, MA: Harvard University Press, 1995), p. 6.

34   Michel Foucault, *Discipline and Punish: The Birth of the Prison* (New York: Vintage Books, 1979), p. 153.

35   John Mowitt, *Percussion: Drumming, Beating, Striking* (Durham: Duke University Press, 2002), p. 92.

36   The rhythmical signaling of the whistle and other timing devices can be found also in early marine armies, such as the Athenian fleet. The team of rowers needed to propel the ship had to unify into an intensely precise mechanism of energy. In order to do so, the ancient crew "pulled their oars in unison by conforming to the beat of a mallet on a special sounding board." See McNeill, *Keeping Together in Time*, p. 117.

37   Jennifer Whitney, "Infernal Noise: The Soundtrack of Insurrection," in *We Are Everywhere: The Irresistible Rise of Global Anticapitalism*, eds. Notes from Nowhere Collective (London: Verso, 2003), p. 224.

38   For an interesting study see George McKay, "A Soundtrack to the insurrection: street music, marching bands and popular protest," *parallax*, vol. 13, no. 42 (2007): 20–31.

4 Street: Auditory Latching, Cars, and the Dynamics of Vibration

1   DJ Funkmaster Flex, quoted in Marco Della Cava in "Flexing Some Muscle," *Automobile*, December 2002.

2   Tia DeNora, *Music and Everyday Life* (Cambridge: Cambridge University Press, 2000), pp. 16–17.

3   Alexander G. Weheliye, *Phonographies: Grooves of Sonic Afro-Modernity* (Durham and London: Duke University Press, 2005), p. 144.

4   John M. Hull, *Touching the Rock: An Experience of Blindness* (London: Arrow Books, 1991), p. 63.

5   Didier Anzieu, *The Skin Ego* (New Haven: Yale University Press, 1989), p. 13.

6   Steven Connor, *Dumbstruck: A Cultural History of Ventriloquism* (Oxford: Oxford University Press, 2000), pp. 9–10.

7   John Shepherd, *Music as Social Text* (Cambridge: Polity Press, 1991), p. 90.

8   Tia DeNora, *Music and Everyday Life*, pp. 85–6.

9   Henri Lefebvre, *Rhythmanalysis* (London: Continuum, 2004), p. 64.

10   John Mowitt, *Percussion: Drumming, Beating, Striking* (Durham, NC: Duke University Press, 2002), pp. 20–21.

11   Steven Connor, *The Book of Skin* (London: Reaktion Books, 2004), p. 39.

12   Ibid., p. 29.

13   John Shepherd, *Music as Social Text*, pp. 90–91.

14   Tia DeNora, *Music and Everyday Life*, Cambridge: Cambridge University Press, 2000, p. 85.

15   The use of personal stereos and iPods by walkers on the street, bus, and train riders, office workers, and bike riders can be read as means through which one comes to "manage" everyday life. It offers ways for negotiating place, of dealing with all that the world presents, and of generating a controllable envelope for oneself, where sound lends greatly to the ability to define contact with place and others. As Michael Bull articulates, personal listening devices impart private structures to latch onto, setting the pace to daily actions and giving personalized structure to the rhythms imposed by existing architectures and social spaces. See Michael Bull, *Sounding Out the City* (Oxford: Berg, 2000) and Michael Bull, "No Dead Air! The iPod and the Culture of Mobile Listening," *Leisure Studies*, vol. 24, no. 4 (2005): 343–55.

16   Michael Bull, "Soundscapes of the Car," in *Car Cultures*, ed. Daniel Miller (Oxford: Berg, 2001), p. 187.

17   Shelley Trower, "Senses of Vibration, 1749–1903," PhD dissertation, Birkbeck College, University of London, 2005.

18   Tia DeNora, *Music and Everyday Life*, p. 86.

19   Barry Blesser and Linda-Ruth Salter, *Spaces Speak, Are You Listening? Experiencing Aural Architecture* (Cambridge, MA: MIT Press, 2007), p. 192.

20   Recent studies in Helsinki by the Department of Transportation were conducted with a view toward improving the conditions of those living in areas with an average noise level of up to 55 decibels. See *Helsingin Sanomat*, January 17, 2008.

21   For an insightful article on this relation see Achim Wollscheid, "Car-radio – Contemporary Music," in *Radio Territories*, eds. Erik Granly Jensen and Brandon LaBelle (Los Angeles & Copenhagen: Errant Bodies Press, 2006).

22   Brenda Jo Bright, "Remapping: Los Angeles Lowrider's," in *Looking High and Low*, eds. B. Bright and L. Bakewell (Tucson: The University of Arizona Press, 1995), p. 96.

23   Lowering cars was finally outlawed in Los Angeles in 1959 as a direct response to lowriding culture (Vehicle Code #24008).

24   The Victoria Police, Melbourne in 1922 developed the first motorized car as well as the first wireless communications system for police vehicles in the world, resulting in two-way communications being established in 1926. In addition, in1939 a specialized radio communications center, D24, was set up at Russell Street Headquarters in Melbourne, facilitating more extensive communications.

25   Such advancements continue in Los Angeles with the recently implemented microphone system throughout South Central Los Angeles, which monitors the streets for gunshots, enabling a more swift response to possible crime scenes.
26   Like car customization, the zoot suit can be read as an appropriation of mainstream fashion. As a style, zoot suits are an exaggerated inflation of white male professional dress, pulling and lifting the suit into baggy pants tapered tightly at the ankles, with a jacket to match, draping down well towards the knees and whose lapels were pulled out towards the shoulders. From a mainstream cultural perspective, the zoot suit was a kind of violation and parody, and in the early 1940s, under concern for material rationing due to the War, zoot suits were outlawed. As Monica Brown proposes, "Their 'drapes' or zoot suits were visible marks of their defiance of norms of mainstream and 'adult' culture." Monica Brown, *Gang Nation* (Minneapolis: University of Minnesota Press, 2002), p. 43.
27   As C. Ondine Chavoya notes, echoing Monica Brown's account of representations of Mexican American culture, mainstream images of lowrider culture are readily equated with gang violence (as seen in the film *Boulevard Nights* (1979)): "A passionate adventure set in explosive East Los Angeles. Here Chicano lowriders parade their exciting customized machines on Whittier Boulevard, 'homeboy' temperaments flare with violence, and cholos—young gang members—brawl and love and meet the challenges of life in the barrio." Quoted in C. Ondine Chavoya, "Customized Hybrids," *The New Centennial Review*, vol. 4, no. 2 (2004): 152.
28   H. L. Myerhoff and B. G. Myerhoff, "Field Observations of Middle Class 'Gangs'," *Social Forces*, vol.42, no. 3 (1964): 328–36.
29   Ted West, quoted in Paige R. Penland, *Lowrider: History, Pride, Culture* (St Paul: Motorbooks International, 2003), p. 33.
30   Public Enemy. 1990. *Fear of a Black Planet*. Def Jam Recordings.
31   Tricia Rose, *Black Noise: Rap Music and Black Culture in Contemporary America* (Hanover and London: Wesleyan University Press, 1994), p. 65.
32   Roach quoted in J. Greenwald, "Hip-Hop Drumming: The Rhyme May Define, but the Groove Makes You Move," *Black Music Research Journal*, vol. 22, no. 2 (2002): 266.
33   Kodwo Eshun, *More Brilliant than the Sun: Adventures in Sonic Fiction* (London: Quartet Books, 1998), pp. 68–70.
34   Daniel Miller, "Driven Societies," in *Car Cultures*, ed. Daniel Miller (Oxford: Berg, 2001), p. 2.
35   J. Bell, *Concept Car Design – Driving the Dream* (Mies, Switzerland: Rotovision, 2003), p. 153.
36   Henri Lefebvre, *Rhythmanalysis*, p. 28

5 Shopping Mall: Muzak, Mishearing, and the Productive Volatility of Feedback

1   Brian Eno, quoted in Mark Prendergast, *Ambient Century* (New York and London: Bloomsbury, 2000), p. 125.
2   Barry Blesser and Linda-Ruth Salter, *Spaces Speak, Are You Listening? Experiencing Aural Architecture* (Cambridge, MA: MIT Press, 2007), p. 156.

3   Christopher N. Penn, *Noise Control: The Law and Its Enforcement* (Crayford, UK: Shaw and Sons, 2002), p. 377.

4   Barry Truax, *Acoustic Communication* (Norwood, NJ: Ablex Publishing, 1994), p. 20.

5   Jonathan Sterne, "Sounds Like the Mall of America: Programmed Music and the Architectonics of Commercial Space," *Ethnomusicology*, vol. 41, no. 1 (Winter 1997): 23.

6   Jerri A. Husch, "Music of the Workplace: A Study of Muzak Culture," PhD dissertation, University of Massachusetts, 1984, p. 5.

7   Ibid., p. 16.

8   Disernes and Fine, quoted in Jerri A. Husch, "Music of the Workplace: A Study of Muzak Culture," p. 52.

9   Jerri A. Husch, "Music of the Workplace: A Study of Muzak Culture," p. 53.

10   Quoted in Joseph Lanza, *Elevator Music: A Surreal History of Muzak, Easy-Listening and Other Moodsong* (London: Quartet Books, 1995), p. 48.

11   Ibid., p. 2.

12   Jonathan Sterne, "Sounds Like the Mall of America: Programmed Music and the Architectonics of Commercial Space," p. 31.

13   Margaret Crawford, "The World in a Shopping Mall," in *Variations on a Theme Park: The New American City and the End of Public Space*, ed. Michael Sorkin (New York: Hill and Wang, 1992), p. 12.

14   Ibid., p. 12.

15   Ibid., p. 13.

16   Phil Kotler, "Atmospherics As a Marketing Tool," *Journal of Retailing*, vol. 49, (1973–4): 48–63.

17   M. Jeffrey Hardwick, *Mall Maker: Victor Gruen, Architect of an American Dream* (Philadelphia: University of Pennsylvania Press, 2004), p. 26.

18   Ibid., p. 39.

19   For instance, for the design of the Ciro shop the floor was made of Monocork (a new material at the time mixing cork and cement), which was extended from within the shop out onto the street, thereby creating a subtle bridge by which to lure the passerby. In addition, transparency became key to attracting customers, allowing them to glimpse the interior of the shop and creating an illusion of unbroken plenitude. Gruen might be said to have perfected, if not created, the experience of "window shopping" by literally making the shop an extensive network of transparency and reflection.

20   M. Jeffrey Hardwick, *Mall Maker: Victor Gruen, Architect of an American Dream*, p. 33.

21   Following the War, Gruen's retail plans grew increasingly interlocked with notions of decentralized planning, coordinating land use with retail expansion. His numerous shopping center designs were made in tandem with developer's visions for a future America, lending a palpable influence to the emergence of geographies of consumerism. Retail shopping centers for Gruen grew out of his recognition of a general malaise of society following the war. Shopping was seen as a remedy, and its architectural equivalent an immediate concrete expression of a society building its own future. See M. Jeffrey Hardwick, *Mall Maker: Victor Gruen, Architect of an American Dream*, p. 90.

22   M. Jeffrey Hardwick, *Mall Maker: Victor Gruen, Architect of an American Dream*, p. 115.

23   Margaret Crawford, "The World in a Shopping Mall," pp. 13–14.

24   See Adrian C. North and David J. Hargreaves, "Music an Consumer Behavior," in *The Social Psychology of Music*, eds. Adrian C. North and David J. Hargreaves (Oxford: Oxford University Press, 1997), pp. 274–5.

25   Barry Truax, *Acoustic Communication*, p. 121.

26   Ibid.

27   Paul Carter, "Ambiguous Traces, Mishearing, and Auditory Space," in *Hearing Cultures: Essays on Sound, Listening and Modernity*, ed. Veit Erlmann (Oxford: Berg, 2004), p. 44.

28   Ibid., p. 45.

29   Bing Chen and Jian Kang, "Acoustic Comfort in Shopping Mall Atrium Spaces – A Case Study in Sheffield Meadowhall," *Architectural Science Review*, vol. 47 (2004): 107–15.

30   Jeffrey Hopkins, "Orchestrating an Indoor City: Ambient Noise Inside a Mega-Mall," *Environment and Behavior*, vol. 26 (1994): 786.

31   Ibid., 792.

32   Paul Carter, "Ambiguous Traces, Mishearing, and Auditory Space," p. 61.

33   Don Ihde, *Listening and Voice: Phenomenologies of Sound* (Albany: State University of New York Press, 2007), p. 151.

34   Ibid., p. 149.

35   Ibid., p. 147.

36   Ray Conniff, a composer and arranger regularly featured on the Muzak network, released numerous records built upon fictitious locational specificity, with titles such as the Hawaiian Album, Laughter in the Rain, or The Happy Beat, that, like the plethora of other releases in the 1950s and 1960s of easy listening records aim to riff on the joyful or melancholy of certain moods and their related contexts. "Theme music" was not only for the movies, but could lend to the shape and experience of everyday life.

37   Ray Conniff, quoted in Joseph Lanza, *Elevator Music: A Surreal History of Muzak, Easy-Listening and other Moodsong* (London: Quartet Books, 1995), pp. 104–5.

38   Howard Stapleton, quoted in Richard Alleyne, "Plagued by Teenagers? You'll like the sound of this," in *Telegraph*, February 16, 2006.

39   Steve Goodman, "Audio Virology: On the Sonic Mnemonics of Pre-emptive Power," in *Sonic Mediations: Body, Sound, Technology*, ed. C. Birdsall (Cambridge: Cambridge Scholars, 2009), p. 30.

40   Ligna, "Transient Radio Laboratory in Liverpool," notes supplied by the group, 2009.

41   Ibid.

42   Marc Augé, *Non-Places: Introduction to an Anthropology of Supermodernity* (London: Verso, 2000), p. 103.

43   Arjun Appadurai, *Modernity at Large: Cultural Dimensions of Globalization* (Minneapolis: University of Minnesota Press, 1996), p. 4.

44   See Michael Taussig, *The Magic of the State* (New York and London: Routledge, 1997).

45   Thanks to Asbjørn Tiller, a researcher at the Norwegian University of Science and Technology, for drawing my attention to Nordheim's installation projects, and for providing great insight into the projects.

46   Peter Zumthor, *Thinking Architecture* (Zürich: Lars Muller Publishers, 1998), p. 37.

47   Jean-Paul Thibaud, "The Three Dynamics of Urban Ambiances," in *Site of Sound: of architecture and the ear*, eds. Brandon LaBelle and Claudia Martinho, forthcoming.

48   In *The Soundscape*, R. Murray Schafer blasts against the "sound wall of paradise" found in Muzak, which he terms "Moozak," casting it as a player within the overall surge of consumerism and industrial packaging within modern society. See R. Murray Schafer, *The Soundscape: Our Sonic Environment and the Tuning of the World* (Rochester, VT: Destiny Books, 1977/1994).

6 Sky: Radio, Spatial Urbanism, and Cultures of Transmission

1   Ken Ehrlich, "Transmission's History and the Leotard Conundrum," in *Trepan* 1, eds. Jawad Ali and Ken Ehrlich (Valencia, CA: California Institute of the Arts, 1999), pp. 59–61.

2   Steven Connor, "Next to Nothing: The Arts of Air", a talk given at *Art Basel*, June 13, 2007: p. 2. Found on author's website.

3   Joe Milutis, *Ether: The Nothing That Connects Everything* (Minneapolis: University of Minnesota Press, 2006), p. 85.

4   Richard Cullen Rath, *How Early America Sounded* (Ithaca and London: Cornell University Press, 2003), p. 31.

5   The event was decided upon at the International Conference on Time held in 1912, establishing the need to "rationalize public time." See Stephen Kern, *The Cultures of Time and Space, 1880–1918* (Cambridge, MA: Harvard University Press, 1983/2003).

6   Sigfried Giedion, *Space, Time, and Architecture* (Cambridge, MA: Harvard University Press, 1997), p. 281.

7   Science and technology were integrated into an overarching project of the imagination, turning the extravagances of artistic expression into forms of idiosyncratic engineering: from the synaesthetic to the occult to the pataphysical, modernity is replete with instances of weaving rational thought with more occult or sensational cultural productions. In Kandinsky's publication *Concerning the Spiritual in Art* and *Point and Line to Plane* the artist theorizes the relation of sensation and abstraction to questions of inner experience, devising synaesthetic correspondences, for instance, yellow corresponding to the sound of Middle-C on the piano. See *Kandinsky: Complete Writings on Art*, eds. Kenneth C. Lindsay and Peter Vergo (New York: Da Capo Press,1994).

8   The Eiffel Tower also served as an experimental TV transmitter in 1935, broadcasting on shortwave, marking the beginning of European television broadcasting.

9   Wilhelm E. Schrage, "German Television," in *Radio News*, July 1935.

10   The Tower is soon to be made obsolete with the development of the new Tokyo Tower to be completed in 2011, which will stand as the tallest structure in the world measuring 610 m.

11   One might add the promise in acting as a tourist attraction, which both the Eiffel Tower and the Tokyo Tower have served radically, with each receiving well over a million visitors each year.

12   Sigfried Giedion, *Space, Time, and Architecture*, p. 284.

13   Originally standing in its place was the Royal Palace, which was initially damaged during the war and demolished in 1952.

14   Concrete transmitting towers, initially appearing throughout Europe beginning in 1953 (with the South German Radio Stuttgart Television Tower), allow not only aesthetic benefits but structural ones as well, for concrete is ultimately more resistant to wind change, reducing the level of transmission interference by minimizing the vacillation of its antennae at such heights. In addition, concrete profoundly reduces the amount of vibration through muffling, which steel frames are particularly susceptible to. By the 1980s, there were roughly 180 transmission towers spanning the West German countryside. See Erwin Heinle and Fritz Leonhardt, *Towers: A Historical Survey* (London: Butterworth Architecture, 1989), p. 227. Steel frame towers appear more widely along highways, local broadcasting stations, and as the carrier of electrical and telephone cabling, cutting through the landscape, as connecting and relaying towers and less now as architectural and governmental symbols than concrete towers.

15   Larry Busbea, *Topologies: The Urban Utopia in France, 1960–1970* (Cambridge, MA: MIT Press, 2007), p. 37.

16   Ibid., p. 26.

17   See Beatriz Colomina, "Introduction," in *Cold War Hothouses: Inventing Postwar Culture from Cockpit to Playboy*, eds. Beatriz Colomina, Annmarie Brennan, and Jeannie Kim (Princeton: Princeton Architectural Press, 2003).

18   Buckminster Fuller, *Your Private Sky: R. Buckminster Fuller* (Baden: Lars Müller Publishers, 1999), p. 106.

19   Simon Sadler, *The Situationist City* (Cambridge, MA: The MIT Press, 1998), p. 94.

20   Georg Simmel, "The Metropolis and Mental Life", in *Classic Essays on the Culture of Cities*, ed. Richard Sennett (Englewood Cliffs, NJ: Prentice-Hall, 1969), p. 56.

21   Gernot Böhme, "Acoustic Atmospheres," *Soundscape Journal*, vol. 1, no. 1 (spring 2000): 15.

22   See Yona Friedman, *Towards a Scientific Architecture* (Cambridge, MA: The MIT Press, 1975).

23   Mark Wigley, *Constant's New Babylon: The Hyper-Architecture of Desire* (Rotterdam: Witte de With/010 Publishers, 1998), p. 18.

24   Libero Andreotti, "Architecture and Play," in *Guy Debord and the Situationist International*, ed. Tm McDonough (Cambridge, MA: The MIT Press, 2004), p. 226. A related text in the Internationale Situationiste #4 from January 1960 gives further elaboration on how the exhibition was meant to function. "The operational dérive around Amsterdam must be related to the micro-dérive organized in this concentrated labyrinth. Two groups, each containing three situationists, would dérive for three days, on foot or eventually by boat (sleeping in hotels along the way) without leaving the center of Amsterdam. By means of the walkie-talkies with which they would be equipped, these groups would remain in contact, with each other, if possible and in any case with the radio truck of the cartographic team, from where the director of the dérive—in this case Constant—

moving around so as to maintain contact, would define their routes and some-times give instructions (it was also the director of the dérive's responsibility to prepare experiments at certain locations and secretly arranged events)." Found at Situationist International online, "Die Welt als Labyrinth."

25   Michele Bertomen, *Transmission Towers: On the Long Island Expressway – A Study of The Language of Form* (New York: Princeton Architectural Press, 1991), p. 9.

26   Ibid., p. 52.

27   Ibid., p. 60.

28   Ibid., p. 61.

29   Nicolas Schöffer, "Definition of Spatiodynamism." in *Nicolas Schöffer* (Neuchatel, Swiss: Editions du Griffon, 1963), p. 20.

30   Guy Habasque, "From Space to Time," in *Nicolas Schöffer* (Neuchatel, Swiss: Editions du Griffon, 1963), p. 12. It is worth noting that Schöffer also envisioned practical uses for the Tower, significantly radio transmission and radar. Later, Schöffer would ultimately build the first cybernetic sculpture, *CYSP 1* (1956), which in addition to being animated through the movements of mirror plates and sound would come to move in space according to input from the environment. This was premiered at the Sarah-Bernhardt Theater in Paris along with dancers, and later on top of Le Corbusier's Unite d'Habitation in Marseilles, as part of the avant-garde art festival, 1956.

31   See Henri Lefebvre, *The Production of Space* (Oxford: Blackwell, 2000).

32   Ibid.

33   Steen Eiler Rasmussen, *Experiencing Architecture* (Cambridge, MA: The MIT Press, 1980), p. 33.

34   Vincent Kauffman, "Angels of Purity," in *Guy Debord and the Situationist International*, ed. Tm McDonough (Cambridge, MA: The MIT Press, 2004), p. 293.

35   Ibid., p. 306.

36   Editorial Note (original *Internationale situationiste* 7 (1962)), trans. Tom McDonough in *Guy Debord and the Situationist International*, p. 129.

37   Doctor Jacques Ménétrier, in *Nicolas Schöffer* (Neuchatel, Swiss: Editions du Griffon, 1963), p. 91.

38   Constant, "A Different City for a Different Life," in *Guy Debord and the Situationist International*, ed. Tm McDonough (Cambridge, MA: The MIT Press, 2004), p. 101.

39   Editorial Note (original *Internationale situationiste* 7 (1962), trans. Tom McDonough, in *Guy Debord and the Situationist International*, p. 130.

40   Buckminster Fuller, *Your Private Sky: R. Buckminster Fuller*, p. 106.

41   Ibid., p. 111.

42   For an engaging study of pirate radio, see Matthew Fuller, *Media Ecologies: Materialist Energies in Art and Technoculture* (Cambridge, MA: MIT press, 2005).

43   See Ralph C. Humphries, *Radio Caroline: The Pirate Years* (Mon., UK: The Oakwood Press, 2003), p. 21.

44   William S. Burroughs, *Electronic Revolution* (Bonn: Expanded Media Editions, 2001), p. 21.

45   Allan Conrad Christensen, *Nineteenth-Century Narratives of Contagion* (London: Routledge, 2005), p. 6.

46   Friedrich Jürgenson, liner notes to *Friedrich Jürgenson – from the Studio for Audioscopic Research*, CD release, London: Ash International, 2000.

47   Joe Milutis, *Ether: The Nothing That Connects Everything*, p. 80.

48   Carl Michael von Hausswolff, from an informal communication with the author, 2009.

49   Reinhard Braun, "Radio Amidst Technological Ideologies," in *Re-Inventing Radio: Aspects of Radio as Art*, eds. Heidi Grundmann, Elisabeth Zimmermann, Reinhard Braun, Dieter Daniels, Andreas Hirsch, and Anne Thurmann-Jajes (Frankfurt: Revolver, 2008), p. 239.

50   Heidi Grundmann, "Beyond Broadcasting: The Wiencouver Series," in *Radio Territories*, eds. Erik Granly Jensen and Brandon LaBelle (Los Angeles and Copenhagen: Errant Bodies Press, 2007), p. 201.

51   Luis Fernández-Galiano, *Fire and Memory: On Architecture and Energy* (Cambridge, MA: MIT Press, 2000).

52   Kisho Kurokawa, *The Philosophy of Symbiosis* (London: Academy Editions, 1994), p. 156.

53   Ricardo Ruiz, Descentro, Brazil, at http://www.interviewingthecrisis.org/?p=51.

Bibliography

Abbott, Jack Henry. *In the Belly of the Beast: Letters from Prison.* New York: Vintage Books, 1991.

Ackroyd, Peter. *London: The Biography.* London: Vintage, 2001.

Alleyne, Richard. "Plagued by Teenagers? You'll like the sound of this." In *Telegraph*, February 16, 2006.

Altez, Fleurdeliz R. "Banal and Implied Forms of Violence in Levinas' Phenomenological Ethics." In *Kritike*, vol. 1, no. 1 (June 2007): 52–70.

Althusser, Louis. "Ideology and Ideological State Apparatuses (Notes towards an Investigation)." In *On Ideology*. London: Verso, 2008. 1–60.

Andreotti, Libero. "Architecture and Play." In *Guy Debord and the Situationist International*, ed. Tm McDonough. Cambridge, MA: The MIT Press, 2004. 213–40.

Anzieu, Didier. *The Skin Ego.* New Haven: Yale University Press, 1989.

Appadurai, Arjun. *Modernity at Large: Cultural Dimensions of Globalization.* Minneapolis: University of Minnesota Press, 1996.

Augé, Marc. *Non-Places: Introduction to an Anthropology of Supermodernity.* London: Verso, 2000.

———. *In the Metro.* Minneapolis: University of Minnesota Press, 2002.

Augoyard, Jean-François. *Step By Step: Everyday Walks in a French Urban Housing Project.* Minneapolis: University of Minnesota Press, 2007.

Augoyard, Jean-François and Torgue, Henry (eds). *Sonic Experience: A Guide to Everyday Sounds.* Montreal: McGill-Queen's University Press, 2005.

Bachelard, Gaston. *The Poetics of Space.* Boston: Beacon Press, 1969.

Back, Les. *The Art of Listening.* Oxford and New York: Berg, 2007.

Baranowski, Bill. "Pedestrian Crosswalk Signals at Roundabouts: Where Are They Applicable?" Delivered at the Transportation Research Board's Roundabout Conference, May 2005. Found on the author's related website, www.RoundaboutsUSA.com.

Bell, J. *Concept Car Design – Driving the Dream.* Mies, Switzerland: Rotovision, 2003.

Bertomen, Michele. *Transmission Towers: On the Long Island Expressway – A Study of the Language of Form.* New York: Princeton Architectural Press, 1991.

Bijsterveld, Karin. *Mechanical Sound: Technology, Culture, and Public Problems of Noise in the Twentieth Century.* Cambridge, MA: The MIT Press, 2008.

Blakely, Edward J. and Snyder, Mary Gail. *Fortress America: Gated Communities in the United States.* Washington, DC: Brookings Institution Press, 1997.

259

Blesser, Barry and Salter, Linda-Ruth. *Spaces Speak, Are You Listening? Experiencing Aural Architecture*. Cambridge, MA: The MIT Press, 2007.

Bloom, Clive. *Violent London*. London: Pan Books, 2003.

Bobrick, Benson. *Labyrinths of Iron: A History of the World's Subway*. New York: Newsweek Books, 1982.

Böhme, Gernot. "Acoustic Atmospheres." In *Soundscape Journal*, vol. 1, no. 1 (Spring 2000). 14–18.

Bourriaud, Nicolas. *The Radicant*. New York: Lukas & Sternberg, 2009.

Braun, Reinhard. "Radio Amidst Technological Ideologies." In *Re-Inventing Radio: Aspects of Radio as Art*, eds. Heidi Grundmann, Elisabeth Zimmermann, Reinhard Braun, Dieter Daniels, Andreas Hirsch, and Anne Thurmann-Jajes. Frankfurt: Revolver, 2008. 233–46.

Bright, Brenda Jo. "Remappings: Los Angeles Lowrider's." In *Looking High and Low,* eds. Brenda Jo Bright and Liza Bakewell. Tucson: The University of Arizona Press, 1995. 89–123.

Brown, Monica. *Gang Nation*. Minneapolis: University of Minnesota Press, 2002.

Bull, Michael. *Sounding Out the City: Personal Stereos and the Management of Everyday Life*. Oxford: Berg, 2000.

— — —. "No Dead Air! The iPod and the Culture of Mobile Listening." In *Leisure Studies*, vol. 24, no. 4 (2005): 343–55.

— — —. "Soundscapes of the Car." In *Car Cultures*, ed. Daniel Miller. Oxford: Berg, 2001. 185–202.

Burroughs, William S. *Electronic Revolution*. Bonn: Expanded Media Editions, 2001.

Busbea, Larry. *Topologies: The Urban Utopia in France, 1960–1970*. Cambridge, MA: The MIT Press, 2007.

Butler, Judith. *Excitable Speech*. New York: Routledge, 1997.

Cagle, Susan. "Stay" from *The Subway Recordings*. New York: Columbia Records, 2006.

Carpenter, Edmund and McLuhan, Marshall. "Acoustic Space." In *Explorations in Communication*, eds. Edmund Carpenter and Marshall McLuhan. Boston: Beacon Press, 1960. 65–70.

Carter, Paul. "Ambiguous Traces, Mishearing, and Auditory Space." In *Hearing Cultures: Essays on Sound, Listening and Modernity*, ed. Veit Erlmann. Oxford: Berg, 2004. 43–64.

Cava, Marco Della. "DJ Funkmaster Flex: Flexing Some Muscle." *Automobile* (Dec. 2002).

Certeau, Michel de. *The Practice of Everyday Life*. Berkeley and Los Angeles: University of California Press, 1988.

Chavoya, C. Ondine. "Customized Hybrids." In *The New Centennial Review*, vol. 4, no. 2 (2004): 141–84.

Chen, Bing and Kang, Jian. "Acoustic Comfort in Shopping Mall Atrium Spaces – A Case Study in Sheffield Meadowhall." In *Architectural Science Review*, vol. 47 (2004).

Chion, Michel. *Audio-Vision: Sound on Screen*. New York: Columbia University Press, 1994.

Chion, Michel. "Wasted Words." In *Sound Theory, Sound Practice*, ed. Rick Altman. New York and London: Routledge, 1992. 104–12.

Christensen, Allan Conrad. *Nineteenth-Century Narratives of Contagion*. London: Routledge, 2005.

Cockayne, Emily. *Hubbub: Filth, Noise and Stench in England*. New Haven and London: Yale University Press, 2007.

Cohen, David and Greenwood, Ben. *The Buskers: A History of Street Entertainment*. North Pomfert, VT: David and Charles, Inc., 1981.

Colomina, Beatriz. "Introduction." In *Cold War Hothouses: Inventing Postwar Culture from Cockpit to Playboy*, eds. Beatriz Colomina, Annmarie Brennan, and Jeannie Kim. Princeton: Princeton Architectural Press, 2003. 10–21.

Constant. "A Different City for a Different Life." In *Guy Debord and the Situationist International*, ed. Tm McDonough. Cambridge, MA: The MIT Press, 2004. 101.

Connor, Steven. "The Modern Auditory I." In *Rewriting the Self: Histories from the Renaissance to the Present*, ed. Roy Porter. London and New York: Routledge, 1997. 203–23.

———. *The Book of Skin*. London: Reaktion Books, 2004.

———. *Dumbstruck: A Cultural History of Ventriloquism*. Oxford: Oxford University Press, 2000.

———. "Next to Nothing: The Arts of Air." Talk given at *Art Basel*, June 13, 2007. Found on author's website, http://www.bbk.ac.uk/english/skc/.

Crawford, Margaret. "The World in a Shopping Mall." In *Variations on a Theme Park: The New American City and the End of Public Space*, ed. Michael Sorkin. New York: Hill and Wang, 1992. 3–30.

Dempster, Stuart. Liner notes in *Underground Overlays from the Cistern Chapel*. San Francisco: New Albion Records, 1995.

DeNora, Tia. *Music and Everyday Life*. Cambridge: Cambridge University Press, 2000.

Dolar, Mladen. *A Voice and Nothing More*. Cambridge, MA: The MIT Press, 2006.

Duneier, Mitchell. *Sidewalk*. New York: Farrar, Straus and Giroux, 1999.

Ehrlich, Ken. "Transmission's History and the Leotard Conundrum." In *Trepan 1*, eds. Jawad Ali and Ken Ehrlich. Valencia, CA: California Institute of the Arts, 1999.

Eshun, Kodwo. *More Brilliant than the Sun: Adventures in Sonic Fiction*. London: Quartet Books, 1998.

Fernández-Galiano, Luis. *Fire and Memory: On Architecture and Energy*. Cambridge, MA: The MIT Press, 2000.

Forster, E. M. *A Passage to India*. London: Penguin Books, 2000.

Foucault, Michel. *Discipline and Punish: The Birth of the Prison*. New York: Vintage Books, 1979.

———. "Different Spaces." In *Michel Foucault: Essential Works of Foucault 1954–1984, Volume 2, Aesthetics*. London: Penguin Books, 1998. 175–86.

Friedman, Yona. *Towards a Scientific Architecture*. Cambridge, MA: The MIT Press, 1975.

Fuller, Buckminster. *Your Private Sky: R. Buckminster Fuller*. Baden: Lars Müller Publishers, 1999.

Fuller, Matthew. *Media Ecologies: Materialist Energies in Art and Technoculture*. Cambridge, MA: The MIT press, 2005.

Gaye, Layla and Holmquist, Lars Erik. "In Duet with Everyday Urban Settings: A User Study of Sonic City." Found on the project's website, http://www.tii.se/reform/projects/pps/soniccity/index.html.

Gaye, Layla, Holmquist, Lars Erik, and Mazé, Ramia. "Sonic City: Merging Urban Walkabouts with Electronic Music Making." Found on the project's website, http://www.tii.se/reform/projects/pps/soniccity/index.html.

Gaye, Layla and Mazé, Ramia. "Sonic City." Found on the project's website, http://www.tii.se/reform/projects/pps/soniccity/index.html.

Giedion, Sigfried. *Space, Time, and Architecture*. Cambridge, MA: Harvard University Press, 1997.

Godshalk, David Fort. *Veiled Visions*. Chapel Hill: University of North Carolina Press, 2005.

Goodman, Steve. "Audio Virology: On the Sonic Mnemonics of Pre-emptive Power." In *Sonic Mediations: Body, Sound, Technology*, ed. Carolyn Birdsall. Cambridge: Cambridge Scholars, 2009. 27–42.

Grant, Elizabeth. "Mobilong Independent Living Units: New Innovations in Australian Prison Architecture." *Corrections Today*, vol. 68, no. 3 (2006): 58–61.

Greenwald, J. "Hip-Hop Drumming: The Rhyme May Define, but the Groove Makes You Move." In *Black Music Research Journal*, vol. 22, no. 2 (2002): 259–71.

Greer, William. *A History of Alarm Security*. Bethesda, MD: National Burglar and Fire Alarm Association, 1991.

Grundmann, Heidi. "Beyond Broadcasting: The Wiencouver Series." In *Radio Territories*, eds. Erik Granly Jensen and Brandon LaBelle. Los Angeles and Copenhagen: Errant Bodies Press, 2007. 200–17.

Habasque, Guy. "From Space to Time." In *Nicolas Schöffer*. Neuchatel, Switzerland: Editions du Griffon, 1963. 10–17.

Hardwick, M. Jeffrey. *Mall Maker: Victor Gruen, Architect of an American Dream*. Philadelphia: University of Pennsylvania Press, 2004.

Hayden, Dolores. *Building Suburbia: Green Fields and Urban Growth, 1820–2000*. New York: Vintage Books, 2004.

Heinle, Erwin and Leonhardt, Fritz. *Towers: A Historical Survey*. London: Butterworth Architecture, 1989.

Higgitt, Janet, Whitfield, Alan, and Groves, Rick. "Quiet Homes for London" report, 2004. Commissioned as part of the Ambient Noise Strategy, London. Found at http://www.london.gov.uk/mayor/strategies/noise/index.jsp.

Hopkins, Jeffrey. "Orchestrating an Indoor City: Ambient Noise inside a Mega-Mall." In *Environment and Behavior*, vol. 26, no. 6 (1994): 785–812.

Hull, John M. *Touching the Rock: An Experience of Blindness*. London: Arrow Books, 1991.

Humphries, Ralph C. *Radio Caroline: The Pirate Years*. Mon., UK: The Oakwood Press, 2003.

Husch, Jerri A. "Music of the Workplace: A Study of Muzak Culture." PhD dissertation, University of Massachusetts, 1984.

Hyde, Andrew. In *The Blitz, Then and Now, Vol. 2*, ed. Winston G. Ramsey. London: Battle of Britain Prints International, 1988.

Ihde, Don. *Listening and Voice: Phenomenologies of Sound*. Albany: State University of New York Press, 2007.

Jacobs, Jane. *The Death and Life of Great American Cities*. London: Penguin Books, 1962.

Jacobs, Thornwell. *The Law of the White Circle*. Athens: The University of Georgia Press, 2006.

Jaworski, Adam. *The Power of Silence: Social and Pragmatic Perspectives*. London: Sage Publications, 1993.

Jirous, Ivan. "Report on the Third Czech Musical Revival." In *Primary Documents: A Sourcebook for Eastern and Central European Art since the 1950s*, eds. Laura Hoptman and Tomás Pospiszyl. Cambridge, MA: The MIT Press and New York: Museum of Modern Art, 2002. 56–65.

Johnston, Norman. *Forms of Constraint: A History of Prison Architecture*. Urbana and Chicago: University of Illinois Press, 2000.

Jürgenson, Friedrich. Liner notes to *Friedrich Jürgenson – from the Studio for Audioscopic Research*, CD release, London: Ash International, 2000.

Kandinsky: Complete Writings on Art, eds. Kenneth C. Lindsay and Peter Vergo. New York: Da Capo Press, 1994.

Kauffman, Vincent. "Angels of Purity." In *Guy Debord and the Situationist International*, ed. Tm McDonough. Cambridge, MA: The MIT Press, 2004. 285–312.

Kern, Stephen. *The Cultures of Time and Space, 1880–1918*. Cambridge, MA: Harvard University Press, 1983/2003.

Kotler, Phil. "Atmospherics as a Marketing Tool." In *Journal of Retailing*, vol. 49 (1973–4): 48–63.

Kunstmann, Lazar. "La Mexicaine Le Interview." From an interview found at greg. org, October 10, 2004.

Kurokawa, Kisho. *The Philosophy of Symbiosis*. London: Academy Editions, 1994.

Lanza, Joseph. *Elevator Music: A Surreal History of Muzak, Easy-Listening and other Moodsong*. London: Quartet Books, 1995.

Lefebvre, Henri. *Rhythmanalysis*. London: Continuum, 2004.

— — —. *The Production of Space*. Oxford: Blackwell, 2000.

Levinas, Emmanuel. *Totality and Infinity: An Essay on Exteriority*. Pittsburgh: Duquesne University Press, 1969/1998.

Lewis, Orlando F. *The Development of American Prisons and Prison Customs 1776 to 1845*. Albany: Prison Association of New York, 1922.

Ligna, "Transient Radio Laboratory in Liverpool." Notes supplied by the group, 2009.

Lingis, Alphonso. *The Community of Those Who Have Nothing in Common*. Bloomington and Indianapolis: Indiana University Press, 1994.

McCartney, Andra. "Soundscape Works, Listening, and the Touch of Sound." In *Aural Cultures*, ed. Jim Drobnick. Toronto: YYZ Books, 2004. 179–85.

McKay, George. "A Soundtrack to the Insurrection: Street Music, Marching Bands and Popular Protest." In *parallax*, vol. 13, no. 42 (2007): 20–31.

McNeill, William H. *Keeping Together in Time*. Cambridge, MA: Harvard University Press, 1995.

Ménétrier, Dr. Jacques. in *Nicolas Schöffer*. Neuchatel, Switzerland: Editions du Griffon, 1963.

Miller, Daniel. "Driven Societies." In *Car Cultures*, ed. Daniel Miller. Oxford: Berg, 2001. 1–34.

Milutis, Joe. *Ether: The Nothing that Connects Everything*. Minneapolis: University of Minnesota Press, 2006.

Miyara, Federico. "Acoustic Violence: A New Name for an Old Social Pain."In *Hearing Rehabilitation Quarterly*, vol. 24, no. 1 (1999): 18–21.

Morley, David. *Home Territories: Media, Mobility, and Identity.* New York: Routledge, 2008.

Mouffe, Chantal. "Artistic Activism and Agonistic Spaces." In *Art & Research*, vol. 1, no. 2 (Summer 2007).

Mowitt, John. *Percussion: Drumming, Beating, Striking.* Durham: Duke University Press, 2002.

Mulvey, Peter. In "The Subterranean World of Peter Mulvey." NPR online article, Sept. 22, 2002.

Myerhoff, Howard L. and Myerhoff, Barbara G. "Field Observations of Middle Class 'Gangs'." In *Social Forces*, vol. 42, no. 3 (1964): 328–36.

Ney-Krwawicz, Marek. *The Polish Home Army 1939–1945.* London: Polish Underground Movement Study Trust, 2001.

North, Adrian C. and Hargreaves, David J. "Music and Consumer Behavior." In *The Social Psychology of Music*, eds. Adrian C. North and David J. Hargreaves. Oxford: Oxford University Press, 1997. 268–87.

Penland, Paige R. *Lowrider: History, Pride, Culture.* St Paul: Motorbooks International, 2003.

Penn, Christopher N. *Noise Control: The Law and Its Enforcement.* Crayford, UK: Shaw and Sons, 2002.

Pile, Steve. *Real Cities: Modernity, Space and the Phantasmagorias of City Life.* London: Sage Publications, 2005.

— — —. *The Body and the City: Psychoanalysis, Space and Subjectivity.* London and New York: Routledge, 1996.

The Plastic People of the Universe, *Jak bude po smrti.* Prague: Globus Records, 1979/1998.

Prendergast, Mark. *Ambient Century.* New York and London: Bloomsbury, 2000.

Public Enemy. *Fear of a Black Planet.* Def Jam Recordings, 1990.

Rasmussen, Mikkel Bolt. "Promises in the Air: Radio Alice and Italian Autonomia." In *Radio Territories*, eds. Erik Granly Jensen and Brandon LaBelle. Los Angeles and Copenhagen: Errant Bodies Press, 2006. 26–47.

Rasmussen, Steen Eiler. *Experiencing Architecture.* Cambridge, MA: The MIT Press, 1980.

Rath, Richard Cullen. *How Early America Sounded.* Ithaca and London: Cornell University Press, 2003.

Rice, Charles. *The Emergence of the Interior: Architecture, Modernity, Domesticity.* New York: Routledge, 2007.

Rose, Tricia. *Black Noise: Rap Music and Black Culture in Contemporary America.* Hanover and London: Wesleyan University Press, 1994.

Sadler, Simon. *The Situationist City.* Cambridge, MA: The MIT Press, 1998.

Scarry, Elaine. *The Body in Pain: The Making and Unmaking of the World.* New York and London: Oxford University Press, 1987.

Schafer, R. Murray. *The Soundscape: Our Sonic Environment and the Tuning of the World.* Rochester, VT: Destiny Books, 1977/1994.

Schrage, Wilhelm E. "German Television." In *Radio News*, July 1935.

Schöffer, Nicolas. "Definition of Spatiodynamism." In *Nicolas Schöffer.* Neuchatel, Switzerland: Editions du Griffon, 1963. 20–21.

Schwela, Dietrich and Zali, Olivier (eds). *Urban Traffic Problem*. London: E & FN Spon, 1999.

Sennett, Richard. *The Uses of Disorder: Personal Identity and City Life*. New York: Vintage Books, 1971.

———. *The Conscience of the Eye: The Design and Social Life of Cities*. London: Faber and Faber, 1990.

Serres, Michel. *Parasite*. Minneapolis: University of Minnesota Press, 2007.

Seymour, Alan. "On a Mortuary Van in the London Blitz." In *The Blitz, Then and Now, Vol. 2*, ed. Winston G. Ramsey. London: Battle of Britain Prints International, 1988.

Shepherd, John. *Music as Social Text*. Cambridge: Polity Press, 1991.

Simmel, Georg. "The Metropolis and Mental Life." In *Classic Essays on the Culture of Cities*, ed. Richard Sennett. Englewood Cliffs, NJ: Prentice-Hall, 1969. 47–60.

Smith, Mark M. "Coda: Talking Sound History." In *Hearing History*, ed. Mark M. Smith. Athens and London: University of Georgia Press, 2004. 365–404.

Smith, Dr. Michael. "Emmanuel Levinas's Ethics of Responsibility," a lecture given at Kennesaw State College, October 7, 2003. Found at http://www.kennesaw.edu.

Sterne, Jonathan. *The Audible Past*. Durham: Duke University Press, 2002.

———. "Sounds Like the Mall of America: Programmed Music and the Architectonics of Commercial Space." In *Ethnomusicology*, vol. 41, no. 1 (winter 1997): 22–47.

Strange, William. "The Brave and Happy Shelterers." In *London Underground: Poems and Prose about the Tube*. Stuttgart: Reclam, 2003. 73–81.

Taussig, Michael. *The Magic of the State*. New York and London: Routledge, 1997.

Thibaud, Jean-Paul. "The Sonic Composition of the City." In *Auditory Culture Reader*, eds. Michael Bull and Les Back. Oxford: Berg, 2003. 329–42.

———. "The Three Dynamics of Urban Ambiances." In *Site of Sound: Of Architecture and the Ear, Vol. II*, eds. Brandon LaBelle and Claudia Martinho. Berlin and Los Angeles: Errant Bodies Press, forthcoming.

Toth, Jennifer. *The Mole People: Life in the Tunnels beneath New York City*. Chicago: Chicago Review Press, 1993.

Trower, Shelley. "Senses of Vibration, 1749–1903." PhD dissertation, Birkbeck College, University of London, 2005.

Truax, Barry. *Acoustic Communication*. Norwood, NJ: Ablex Publishing, 1994.

Waskow, Arthur I. and Newman, Stanley L. *America in Hiding*. New York: Ballantine Books, 1962.

Weheliye, Alexander G. *Phonographies: Grooves of Sonic Afro-Modernity*. Durham and London: Duke University Press, 2005.

Whitney, Jennifer. "Infernal Noise: The Soundtrack of Insurrection." In *We Are Everywhere: The Irresistible Rise of Global Anticapitalism*, eds. Notes from Nowhere Collective. London: Verso, 2003. 216–27.

Wigley, Mark. *Constant's New Babylon: The Hyper-Architecture of Desire*. Rotterdam: Witte de With/010 Publishers, 1998.

Wilson, Eric. "Plagues, Fairs, and Street Cries: Sounding out Society and Space in Early Modern London." In *Modern Language Studies*, vol. 25, no. 3. (summer, 1995): 1–42.

Wollscheid, Achim. "Car-radio – Contemporary Music." In *Radio Territories*, eds. Erik Granly Jensen and Brandon LaBelle. Los Angeles and Copenhagen: Errant Bodies Press, 2006. 180–93.

Wolmar, Christian. *The Subterranean Railway*. London: Atlantic Books, 2004.

Zumthor, Peter. *Thinking Architecture*. Zürich: Lars Muller Publishers, 1998.

Index

NOTE: Page references in *italics* refer to illustrations.